Presented by
NICO

No Matter How I Look at It, It's You Guys' Fault I'm Not Popular!

5

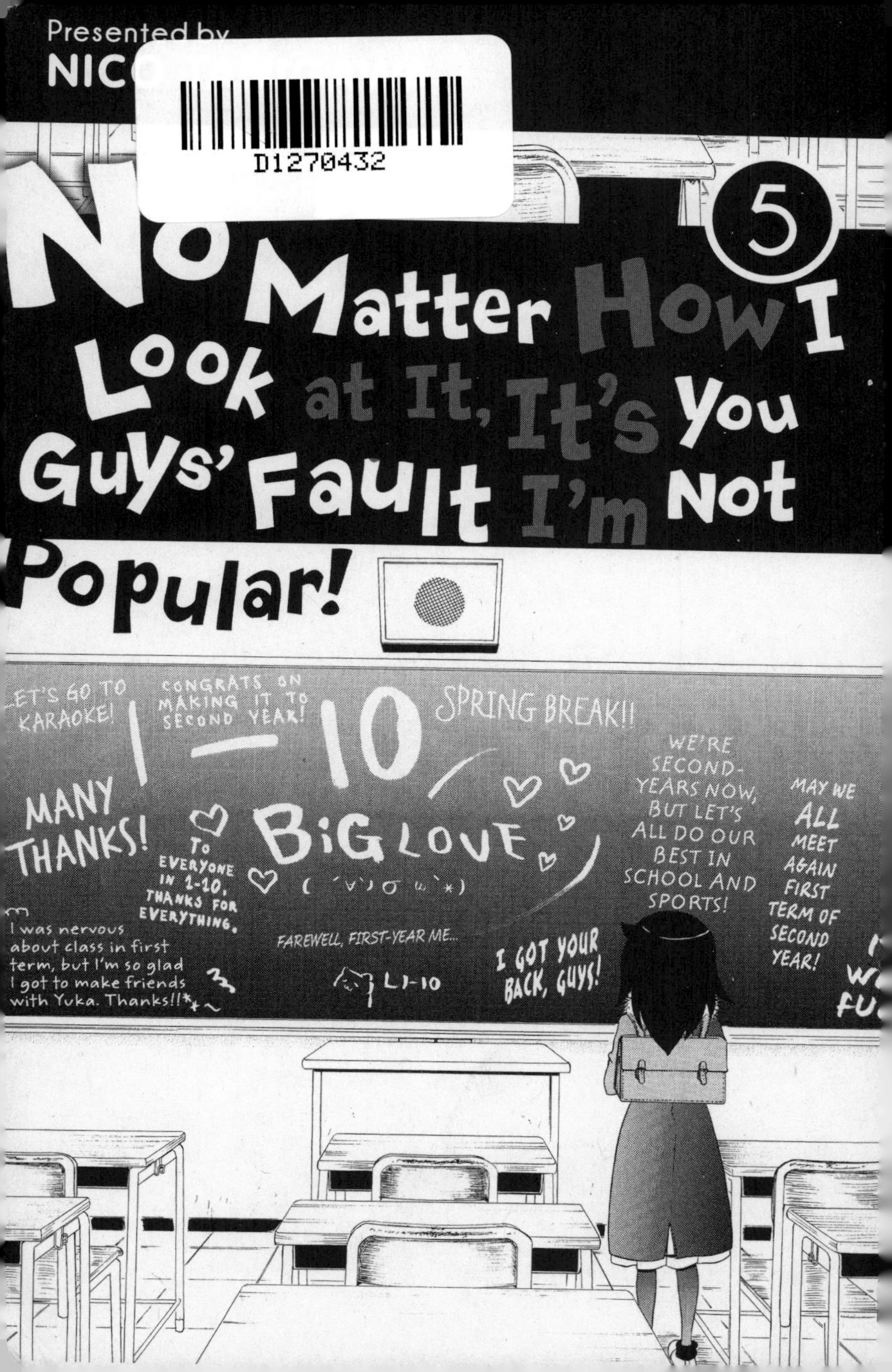

LET'S GO TO KARAOKE!
CONGRATS ON MAKING IT TO SECOND YEAR!
1—10
SPRING BREAK!!
MANY THANKS!
BIG LOVE
TO EVERYONE IN 1-10, THANKS FOR EVERYTHING.
WE'RE SECOND-YEARS NOW, BUT LET'S ALL DO OUR BEST IN SCHOOL AND SPORTS!
MAY WE ALL MEET AGAIN FIRST TERM OF SECOND YEAR!
I was nervous about class in first term, but I'm so glad I got to make friends with Yuka. Thanks!!
FAREWELL, FIRST-YEAR ME...
L1-10
I GOT YOUR BACK, GUYS!

...AWW, IF I'D BEEN A WORM, I WOULD'VE HAD A MAN FROM THE GET-GO AND DEFINITELY HAVE HAD S●X, NOT TO MENTION KIDS...

FAIL 37: I'M NOT POPULAR, SO I'LL ATTEND GRADUATION.

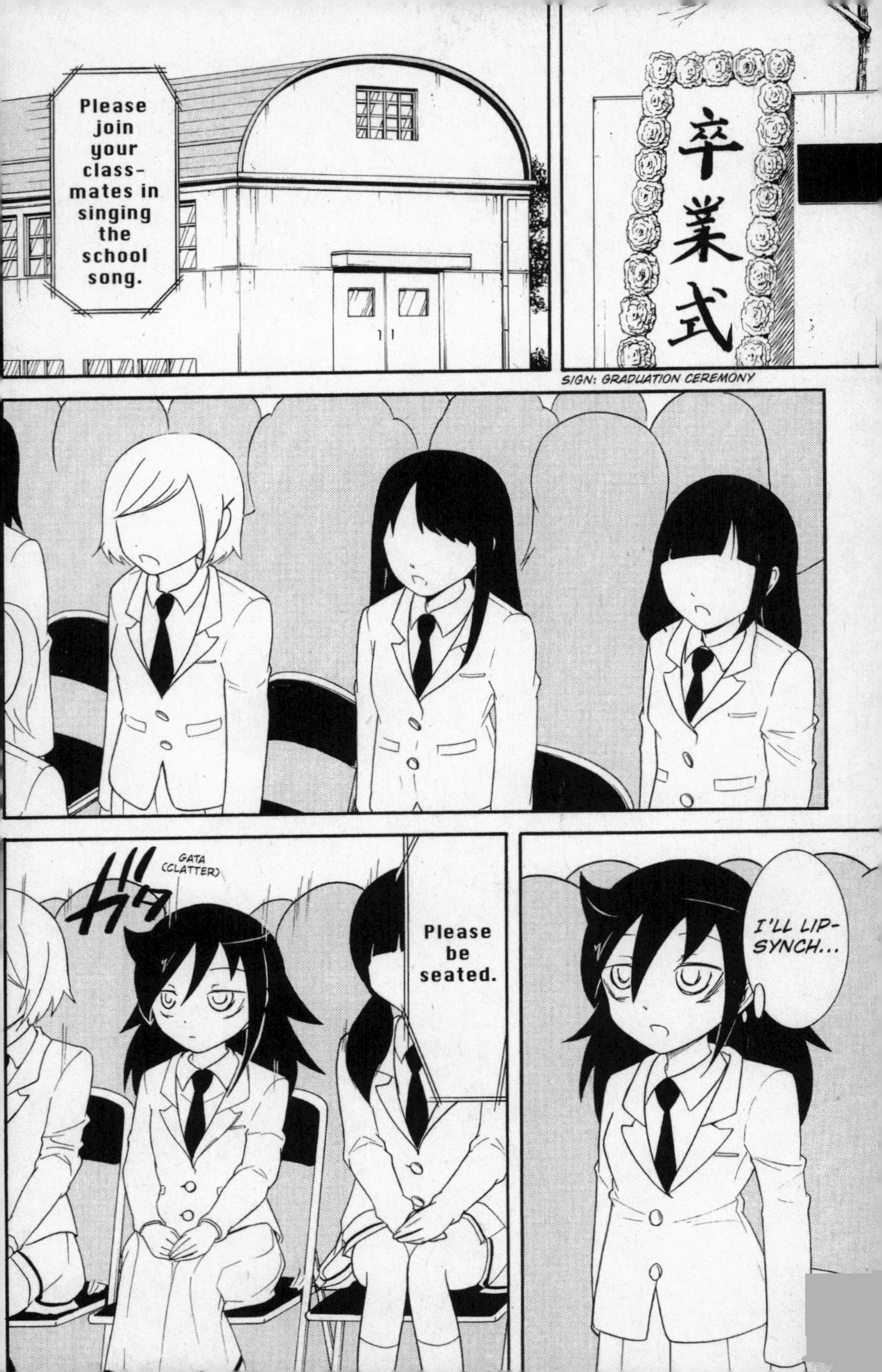
卒業式
SIGN: GRADUATION CEREMONY
Please join your classmates in singing the school song.
I'LL LIP-SYNCH...
Please be seated.
ガタ
GATA (CLATTER)

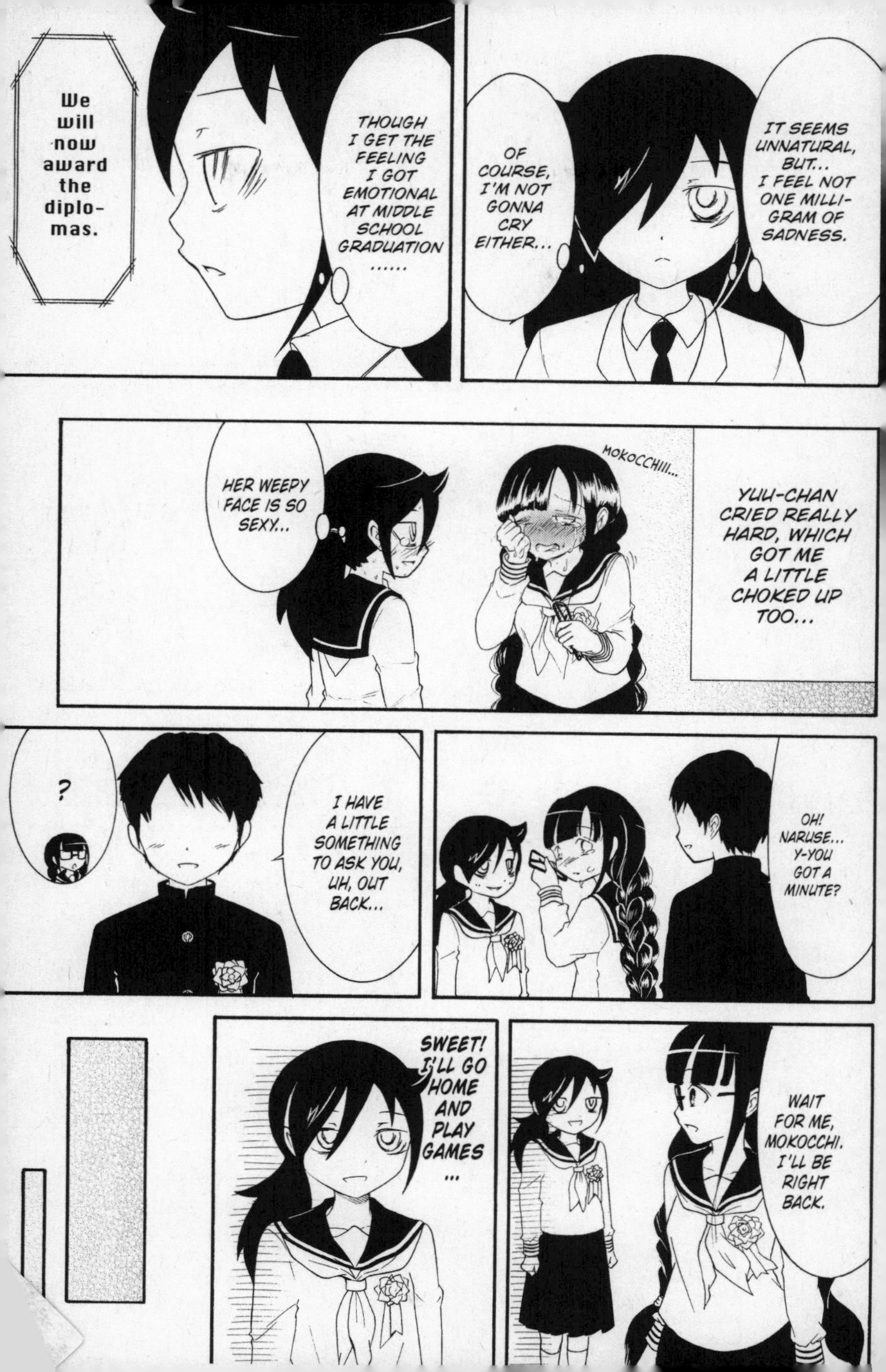
IT SEEMS UNNATURAL, BUT... I FEEL NOT ONE MILLIGRAM OF SADNESS.
OF COURSE, I'M NOT GONNA CRY EITHER...
THOUGH I GET THE FEELING I GOT EMOTIONAL AT MIDDLE SCHOOL GRADUATION ......
We will now award the diplomas.
YUU-CHAN CRIED REALLY HARD, WHICH GOT ME A LITTLE CHOKED UP TOO...
MOKOCCHIII...
HER WEEPY FACE IS SO SEXY...
OH! NARUSE... Y-YOU GOT A MINUTE?
I HAVE A LITTLE SOMETHING TO ASK YOU, UH, OUT BACK...
?
WAIT FOR ME, MOKOCCHI. I'LL BE RIGHT BACK.
SWEET! I'LL GO HOME AND PLAY GAMES ...

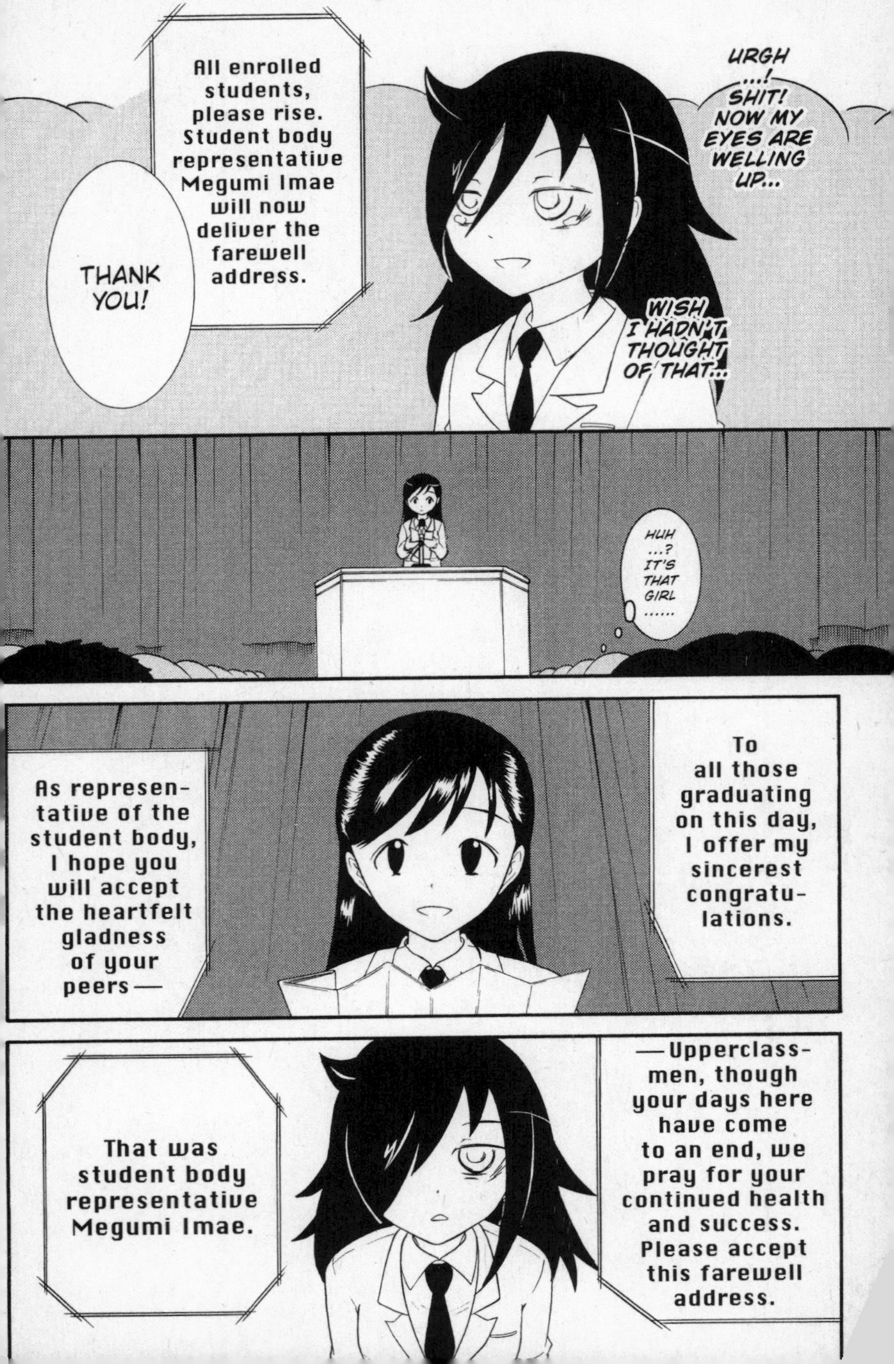
URGH ...! SHIT! NOW MY EYES ARE WELLING UP...
WISH I HADN'T THOUGHT OF THAT...
All enrolled students, please rise. Student body representative Megumi Imae will now deliver the farewell address.
THANK YOU!
HUH ...? IT'S THAT GIRL ......
To all those graduating on this day, I offer my sincerest congratulations.
As representative of the student body, I hope you will accept the heartfelt gladness of your peers—
—Upperclassmen, though your days here have come to an end, we pray for your continued health and success. Please accept this farewell address.
That was student body representative Megumi Imae.

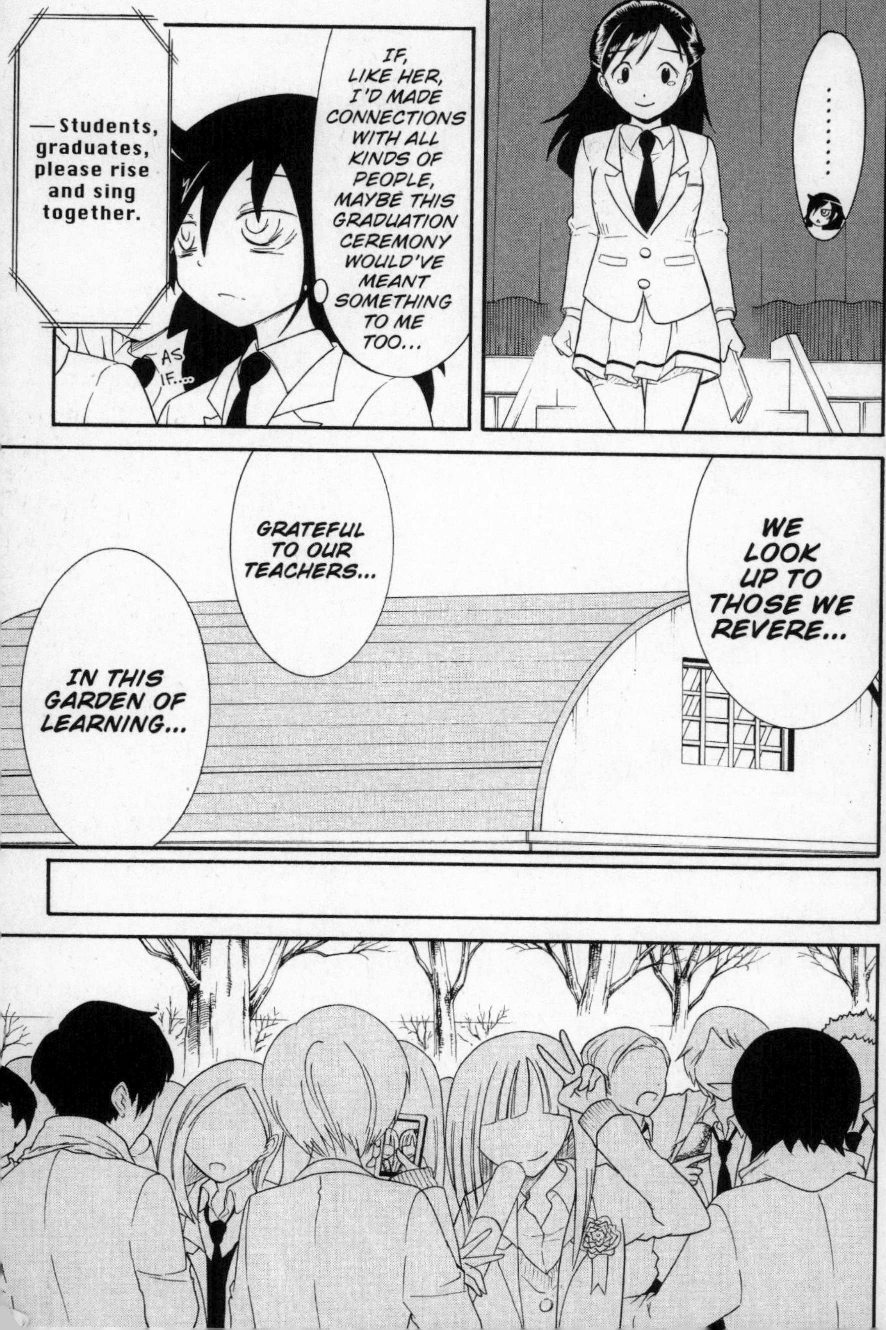
....
IF, LIKE HER, I'D MADE CONNECTIONS WITH ALL KINDS OF PEOPLE, MAYBE THIS GRADUATION CEREMONY WOULD'VE MEANT SOMETHING TO ME TOO...
AS IF...
— Students, graduates, please rise and sing together.
WE LOOK UP TO THOSE WE REVERE...
GRATEFUL TO OUR TEACHERS...
IN THIS GARDEN OF LEARNING...

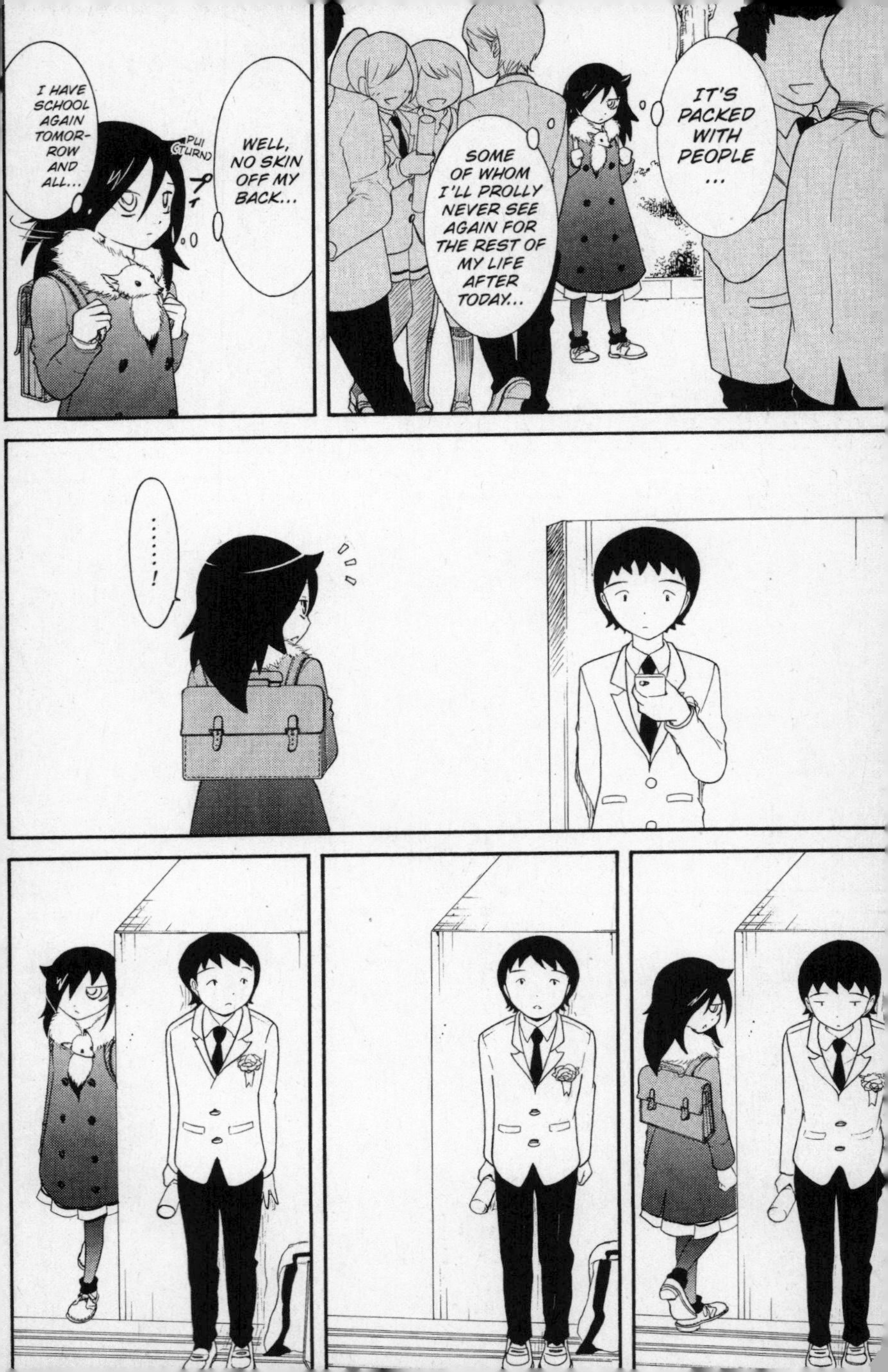
IT'S PACKED WITH PEOPLE...
SOME OF WHOM I'LL PROLLY NEVER SEE AGAIN FOR THE REST OF MY LIFE AFTER TODAY...
WELL, NO SKIN OFF MY BACK...
PUI (TURN)
I HAVE SCHOOL AGAIN TOMORROW AND ALL...
......!

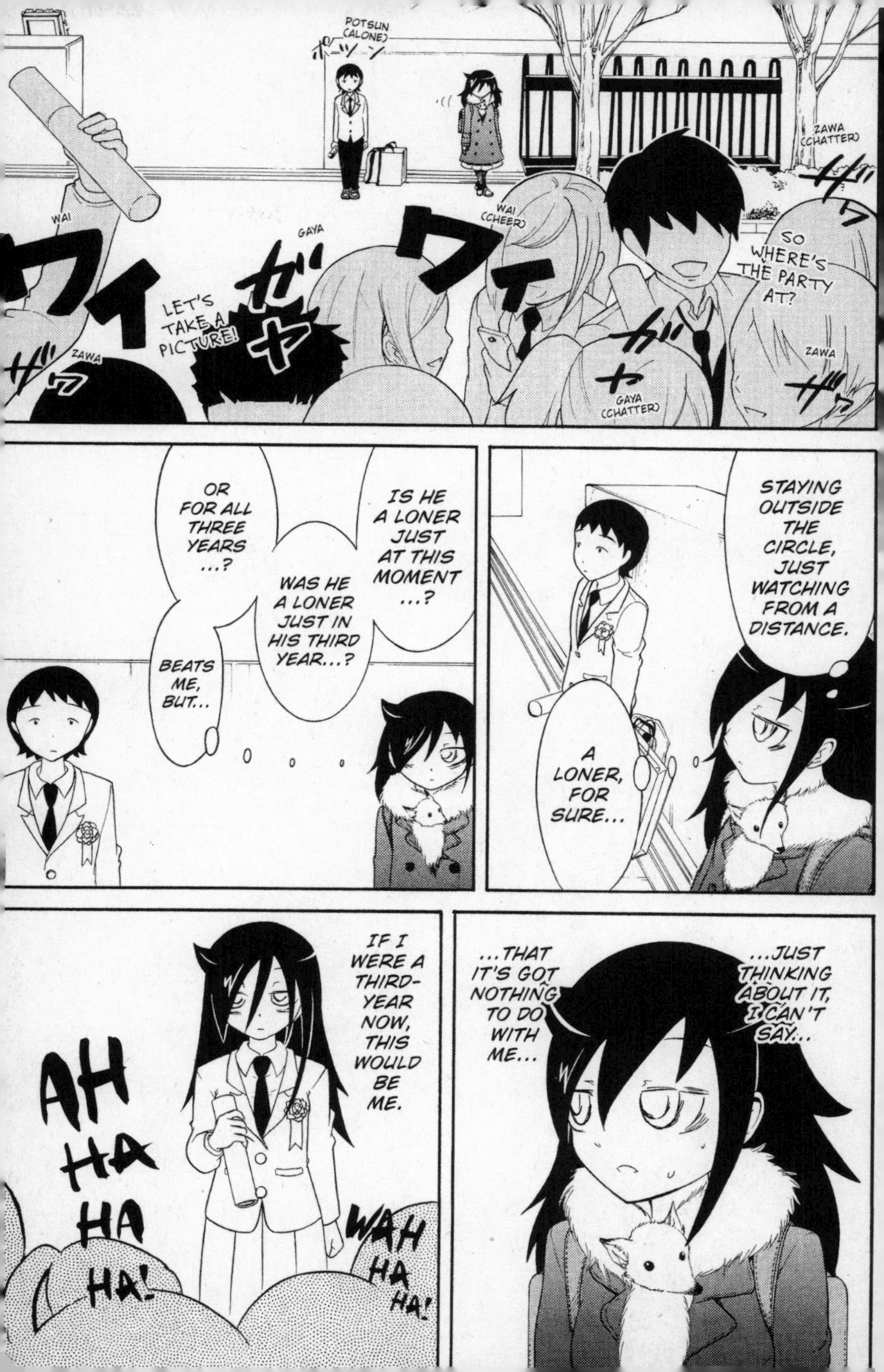
ZAWA (CHATTER)
SO WHERE'S THE PARTY AT?
POTSUN (ALONE)
WAI (CHEER)
ZAWA
GAYA (CHATTER)
GAYA
LET'S TAKE A PICTURE!
WAI
ZAWA
STAYING OUTSIDE THE CIRCLE, JUST WATCHING FROM A DISTANCE.
A LONER, FOR SURE...
IS HE A LONER JUST AT THIS MOMENT...?
WAS HE A LONER JUST IN HIS THIRD YEAR...?
OR FOR ALL THREE YEARS...?
BEATS ME, BUT...
...JUST THINKING ABOUT IT, I CAN'T SAY...
...THAT IT'S GOT NOTHING TO DO WITH ME...
IF I WERE A THIRD-YEAR NOW, THIS WOULD BE ME.
WAH HA HA HA!
AH HA HA HA!

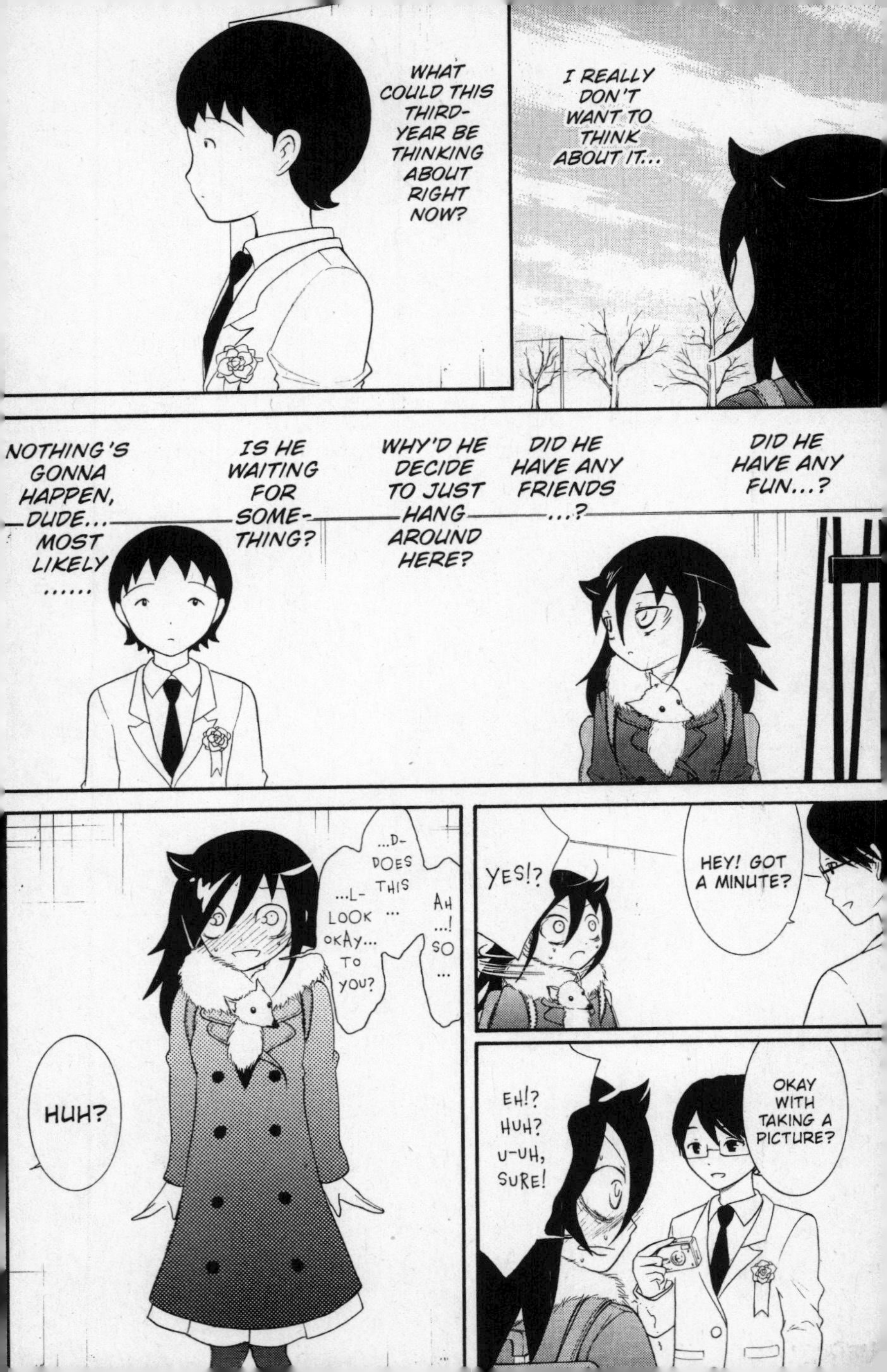
I REALLY DON'T WANT TO THINK ABOUT IT...
WHAT COULD THIS THIRD-YEAR BE THINKING ABOUT RIGHT NOW?
DID HE HAVE ANY FUN...?
DID HE HAVE ANY FRIENDS...?
WHY'D HE DECIDE TO JUST HANG AROUND HERE?
IS HE WAITING FOR SOME-THING?
NOTHING'S GONNA HAPPEN, DUDE... MOST LIKELY ......
HEY! GOT A MINUTE?
YES!?
OKAY WITH TAKING A PICTURE?
EH!? HUH? U-UH, SURE!
AH ...! SO ...
...D-DOES THIS ... ...L-LOOK OKAY... TO YOU?
HUH?

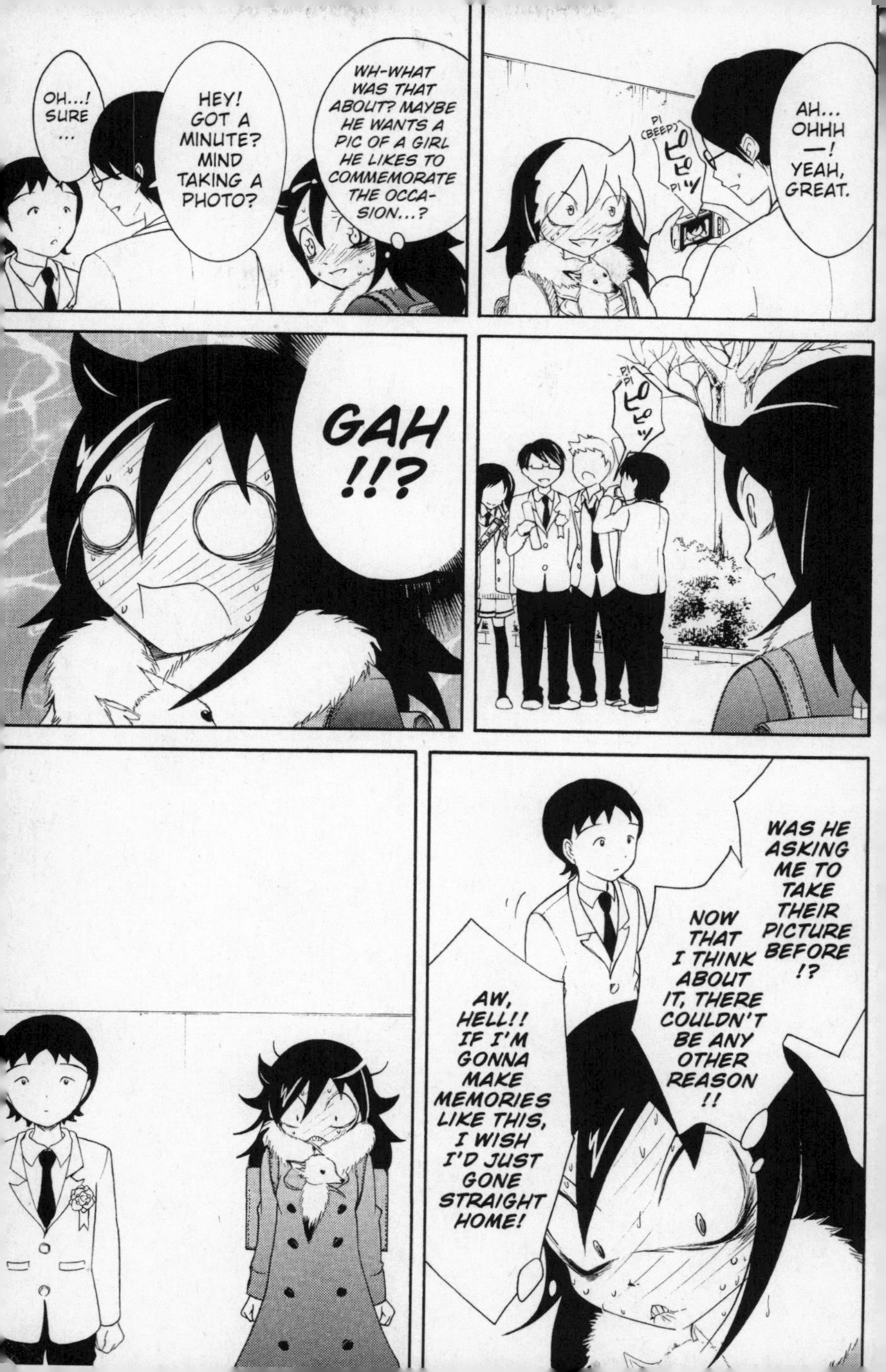
AH... OHHH—! YEAH, GREAT.
PI (BEEP) PI
WH-WHAT WAS THAT ABOUT? MAYBE HE WANTS A PIC OF A GIRL HE LIKES TO COMMEMORATE THE OCCA-SION...?
HEY! GOT A MINUTE? MIND TAKING A PHOTO?
OH...! SURE...
PI PI
GAH !!?
WAS HE ASKING ME TO TAKE THEIR PICTURE BEFORE !?
NOW THAT I THINK ABOUT IT, THERE COULDN'T BE ANY OTHER REASON !!
AW, HELL!! IF I'M GONNA MAKE MEMORIES LIKE THIS, I WISH I'D JUST GONE STRAIGHT HOME!

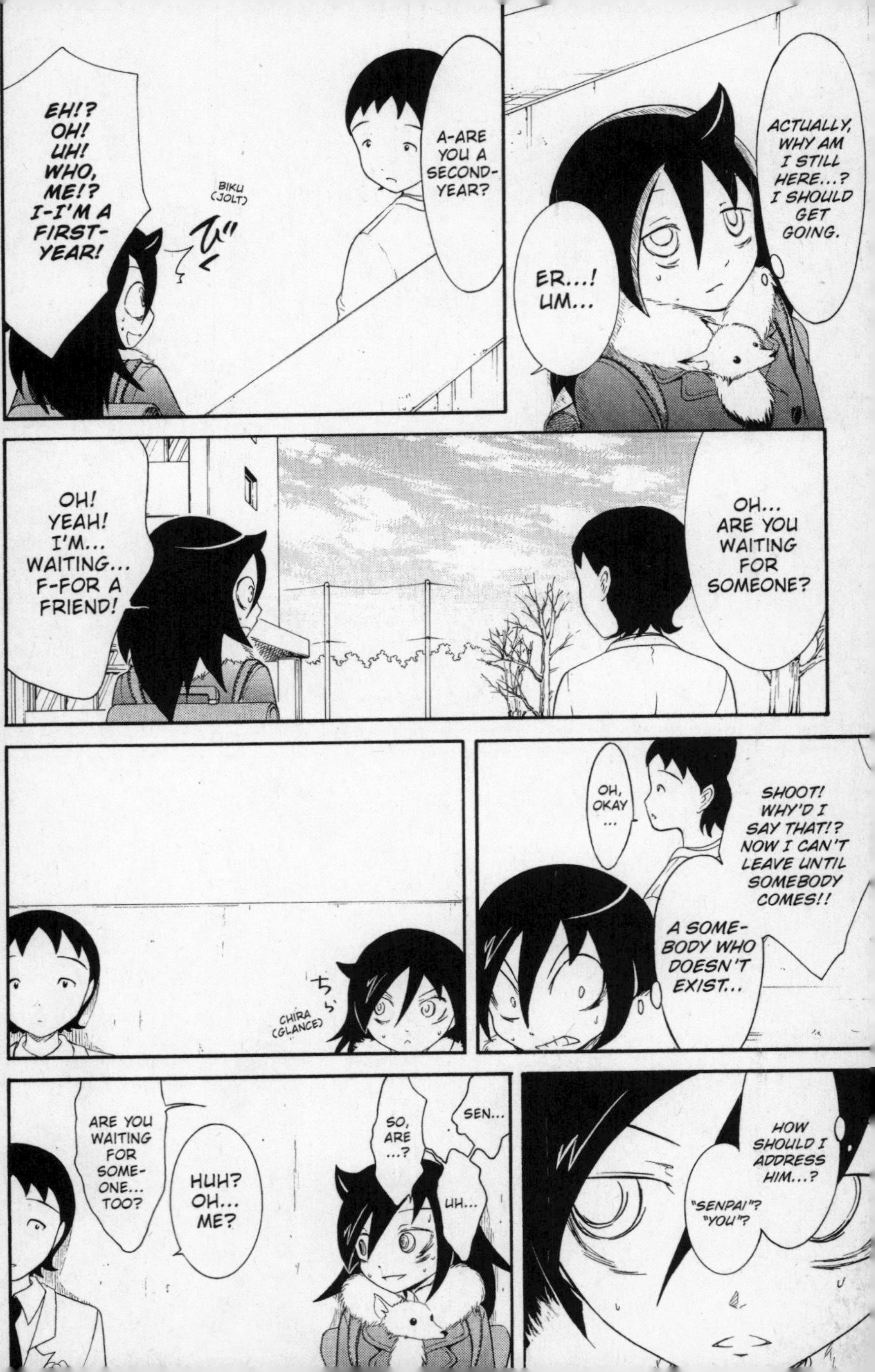

ACTUALLY, WHY AM I STILL HERE...? I SHOULD GET GOING.
ER...! UM...
A-ARE YOU A SECOND-YEAR?
BIKU (JOLT)
EH!? OH! UH! WHO, ME!? I-I'M A FIRST-YEAR!
OH... ARE YOU WAITING FOR SOMEONE?
OH! YEAH! I'M... WAITING... F-FOR A FRIEND!
SHOOT! WHY'D I SAY THAT!? NOW I CAN'T LEAVE UNTIL SOMEBODY COMES!!
OH, OKAY...
A SOMEBODY WHO DOESN'T EXIST...
CHIRA (GLANCE)
HOW SHOULD I ADDRESS HIM...?
"SENPAI"? "YOU"?
SEN...
UH...
SO, ARE ...?
ARE YOU WAITING FOR SOME-ONE... TOO?
HUH? OH... ME?

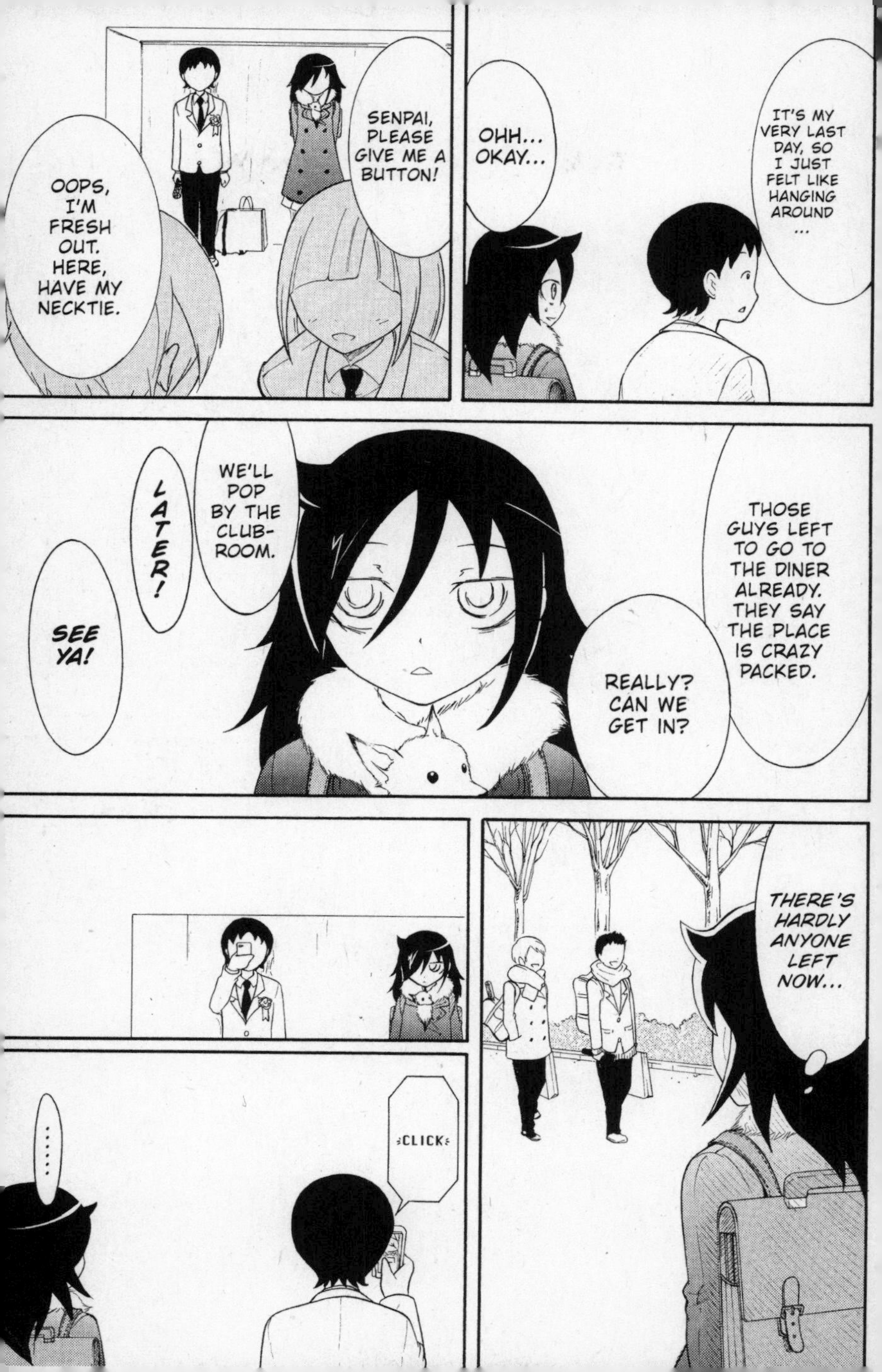
IT'S MY VERY LAST DAY, SO I JUST FELT LIKE HANGING AROUND ...
OHH... OKAY...
SENPAI, PLEASE GIVE ME A BUTTON!
OOPS, I'M FRESH OUT. HERE, HAVE MY NECKTIE.
THOSE GUYS LEFT TO GO TO THE DINER ALREADY. THEY SAY THE PLACE IS CRAZY PACKED.
REALLY? CAN WE GET IN?
WE'LL POP BY THE CLUB-ROOM.
LATER!
SEE YA!
THERE'S HARDLY ANYONE LEFT NOW...
CLICK
......

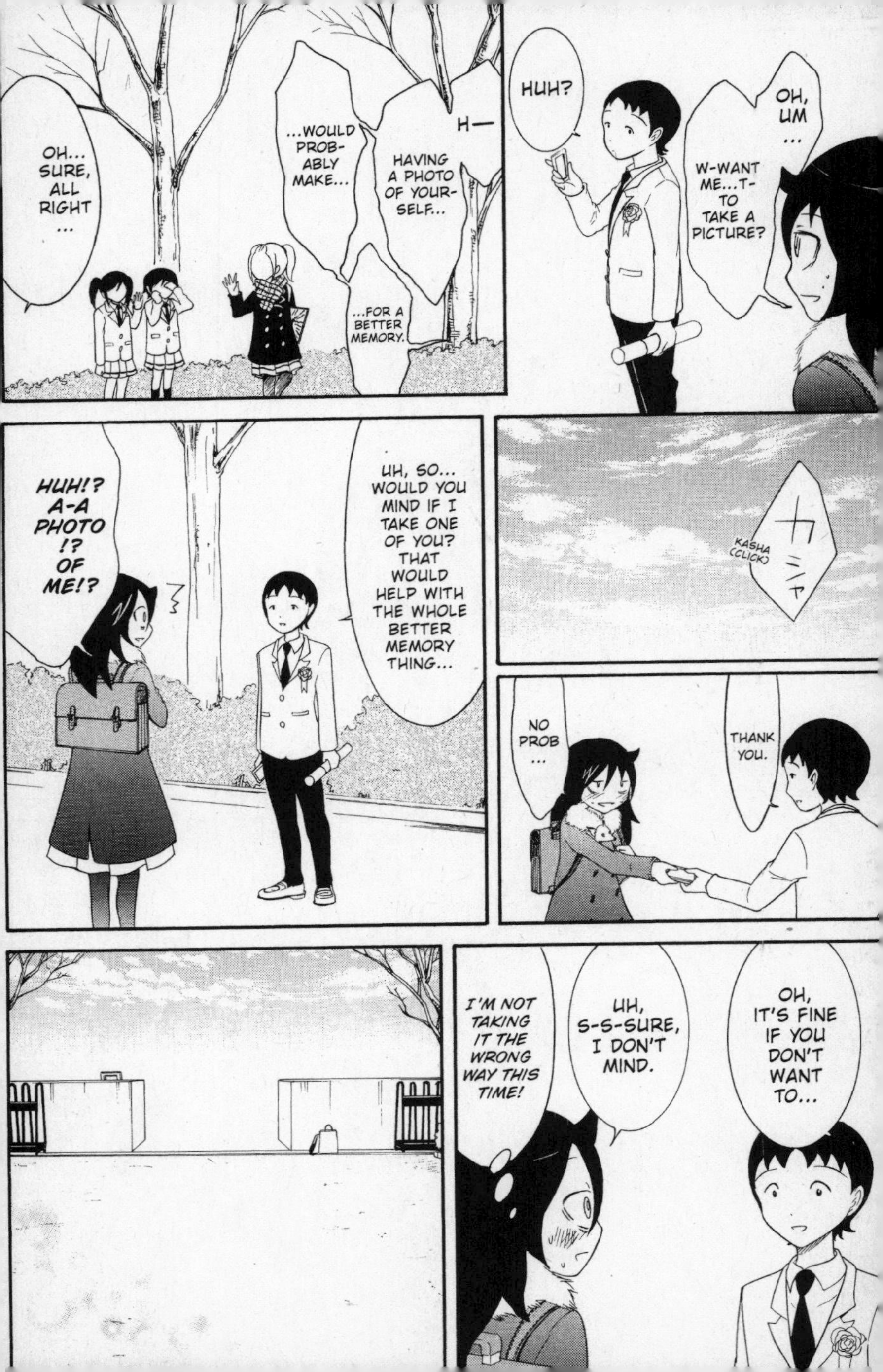
HUH?
OH, UM...
W-WANT ME...T-TO TAKE A PICTURE?
H—
HAVING A PHOTO OF YOUR-SELF...
...WOULD PROBABLY MAKE...
...FOR A BETTER MEMORY.
OH... SURE, ALL RIGHT...
KASHA (CLICK)
THANK YOU.
NO PROB...
UH, SO... WOULD YOU MIND IF I TAKE ONE OF YOU? THAT WOULD HELP WITH THE WHOLE BETTER MEMORY THING...
HUH!? A-A PHOTO!? OF ME!?
OH, IT'S FINE IF YOU DON'T WANT TO...
UH, S-S-SURE, I DON'T MIND.
I'M NOT TAKING IT THE WRONG WAY THIS TIME!

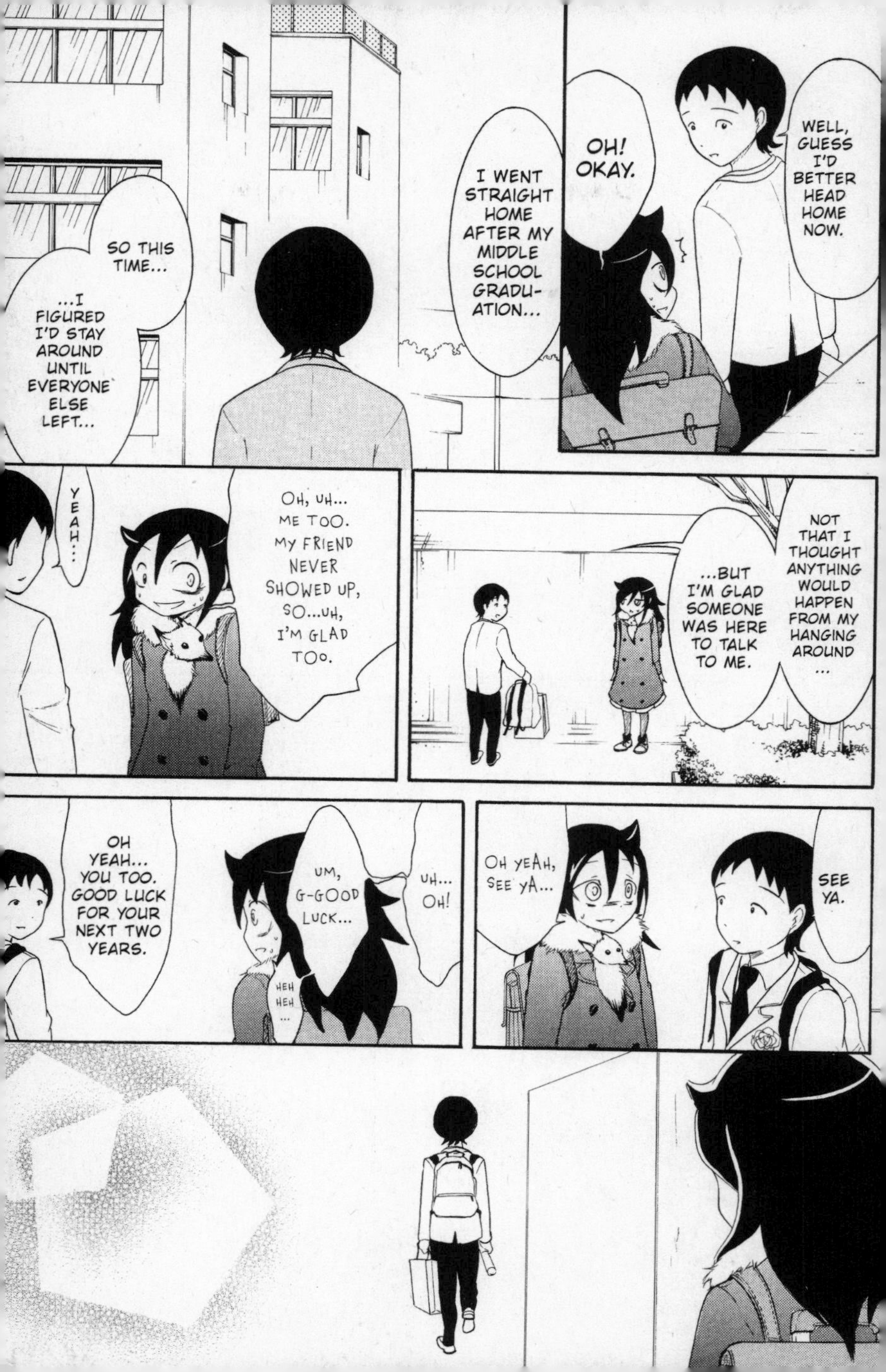
WELL, GUESS I'D BETTER HEAD HOME NOW.
OH! OKAY.
I WENT STRAIGHT HOME AFTER MY MIDDLE SCHOOL GRADUATION...
SO THIS TIME...
...I FIGURED I'D STAY AROUND UNTIL EVERYONE ELSE LEFT...
NOT THAT I THOUGHT ANYTHING WOULD HAPPEN FROM MY HANGING AROUND...
...BUT I'M GLAD SOMEONE WAS HERE TO TALK TO ME.
OH, UH... ME TOO. MY FRIEND NEVER SHOWED UP, SO...UH, I'M GLAD TOO.
YEAH...
SEE YA.
OH YEAH, SEE YA...
UH... OH!
UM, G-GOOD LUCK...
HEH HEH...
OH YEAH... YOU TOO. GOOD LUCK FOR YOUR NEXT TWO YEARS.

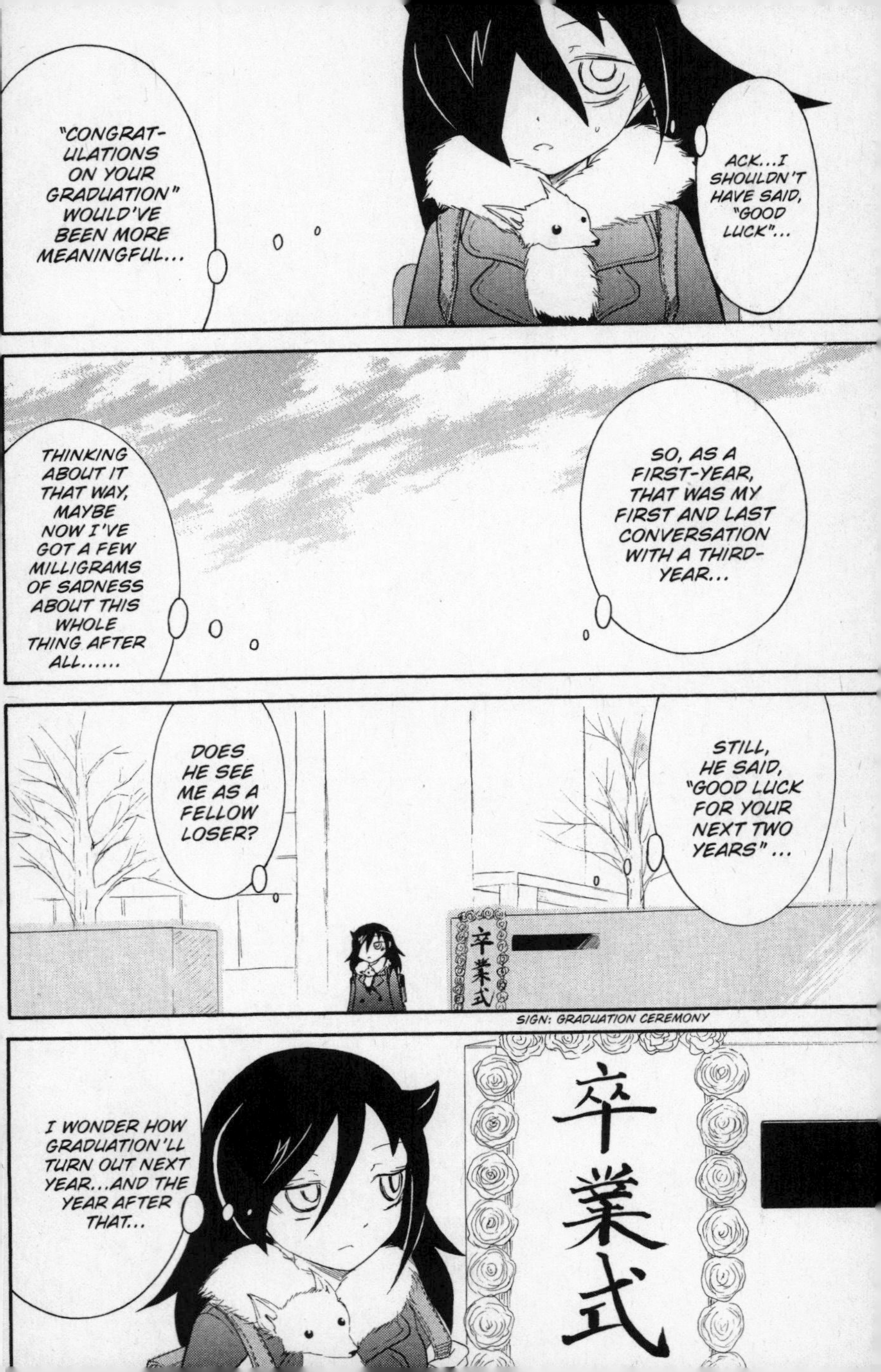
ACK...I SHOULDN'T HAVE SAID, "GOOD LUCK"...
"CONGRATULATIONS ON YOUR GRADUATION" WOULD'VE BEEN MORE MEANINGFUL...
SO, AS A FIRST-YEAR, THAT WAS MY FIRST AND LAST CONVERSATION WITH A THIRD-YEAR...
THINKING ABOUT IT THAT WAY, MAYBE NOW I'VE GOT A FEW MILLIGRAMS OF SADNESS ABOUT THIS WHOLE THING AFTER ALL......
STILL, HE SAID, "GOOD LUCK FOR YOUR NEXT TWO YEARS" ...
DOES HE SEE ME AS A FELLOW LOSER?
卒業式
SIGN: GRADUATION CEREMONY
卒業式
I WONDER HOW GRADUATION'LL TURN OUT NEXT YEAR...AND THE YEAR AFTER THAT...

No Matter How I Look at It, It's You Guys' Fault I'm Not Popular!

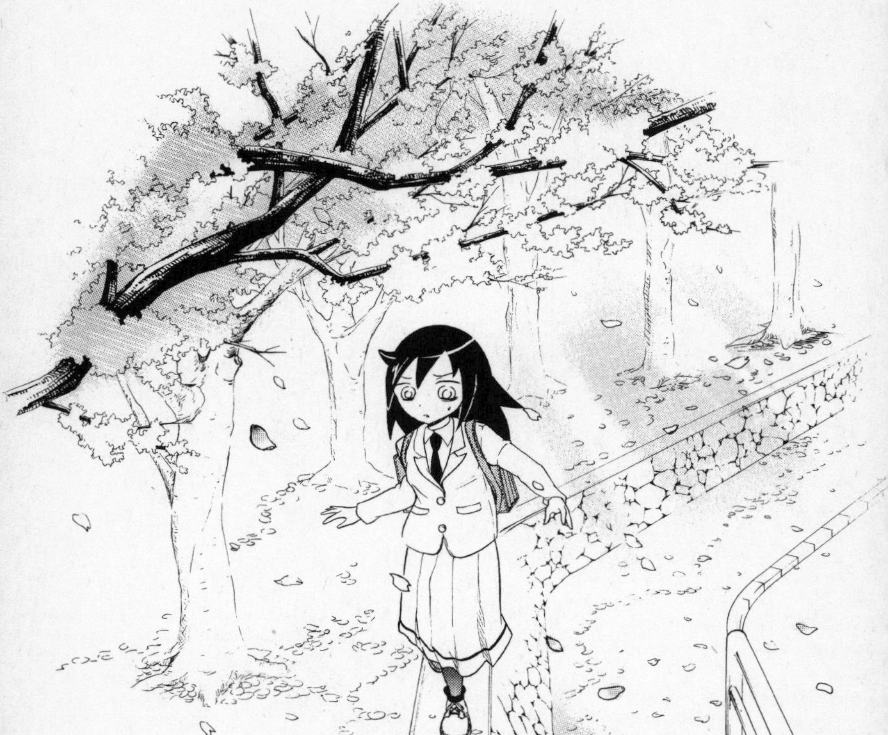

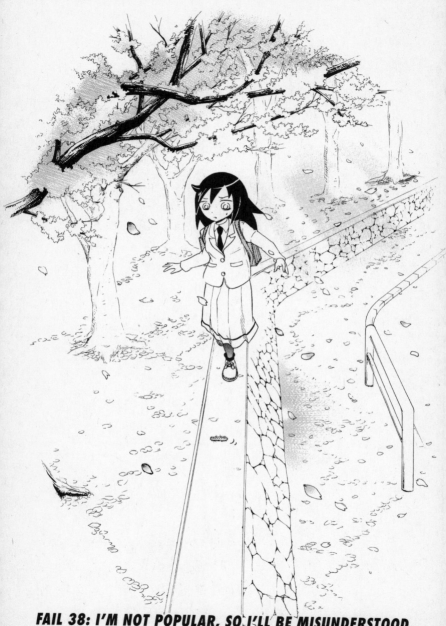

FAIL 38: I'M NOT POPULAR, SO I'LL BE MISUNDERSTOOD.

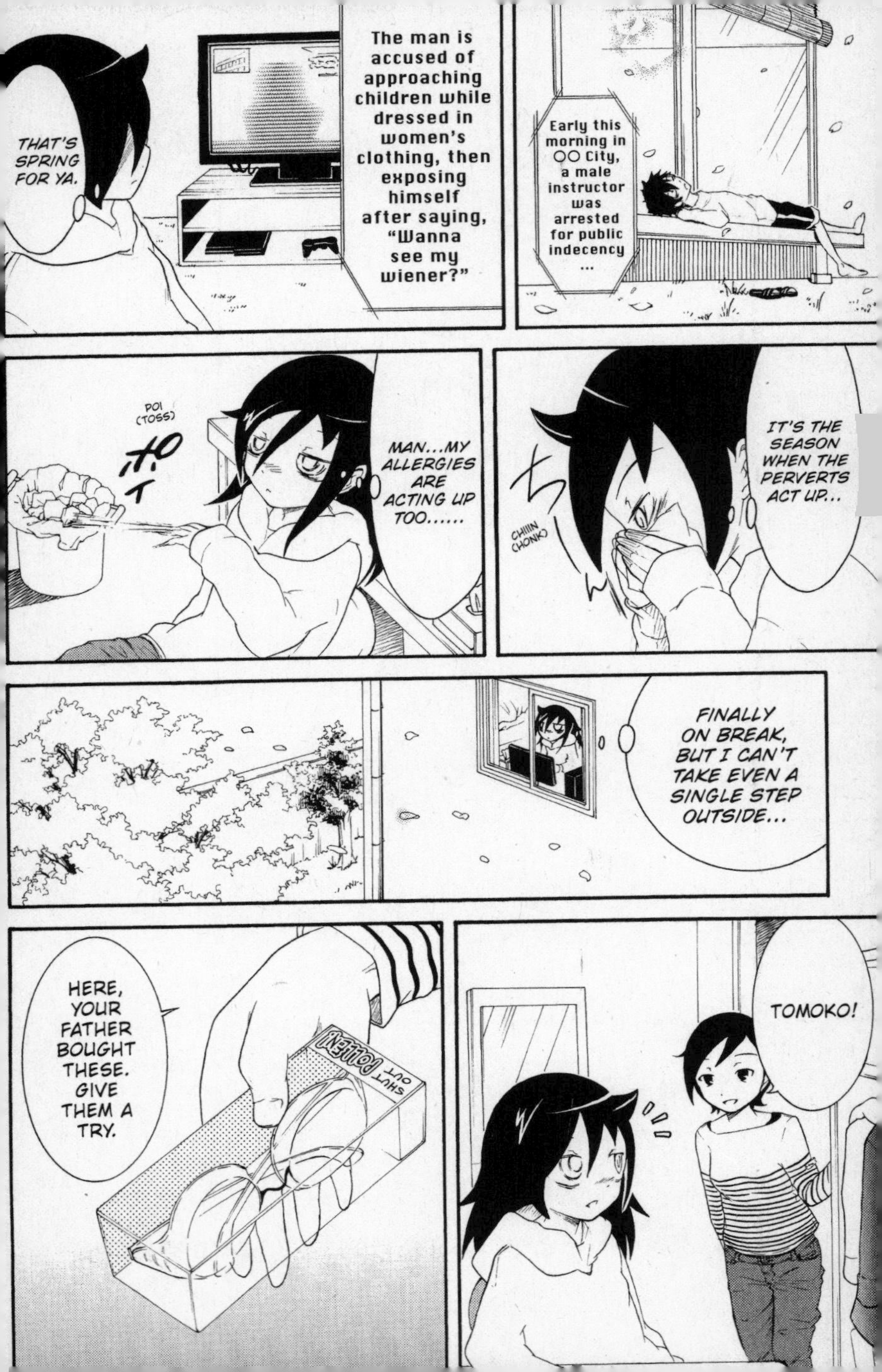
Early this morning in 〇〇 City, a male instructor was arrested for public indecency ...
The man is accused of approaching children while dressed in women's clothing, then exposing himself after saying, "Wanna see my wiener?"
THAT'S SPRING FOR YA.
IT'S THE SEASON WHEN THE PERVERTS ACT UP...
CHIIIN (HONK)
MAN...MY ALLERGIES ARE ACTING UP TOO......
POI (TOSS)
FINALLY ON BREAK, BUT I CAN'T TAKE EVEN A SINGLE STEP OUTSIDE...
TOMOKO!
HERE, YOUR FATHER BOUGHT THESE. GIVE THEM A TRY.
SHUT OUT POLLEN!

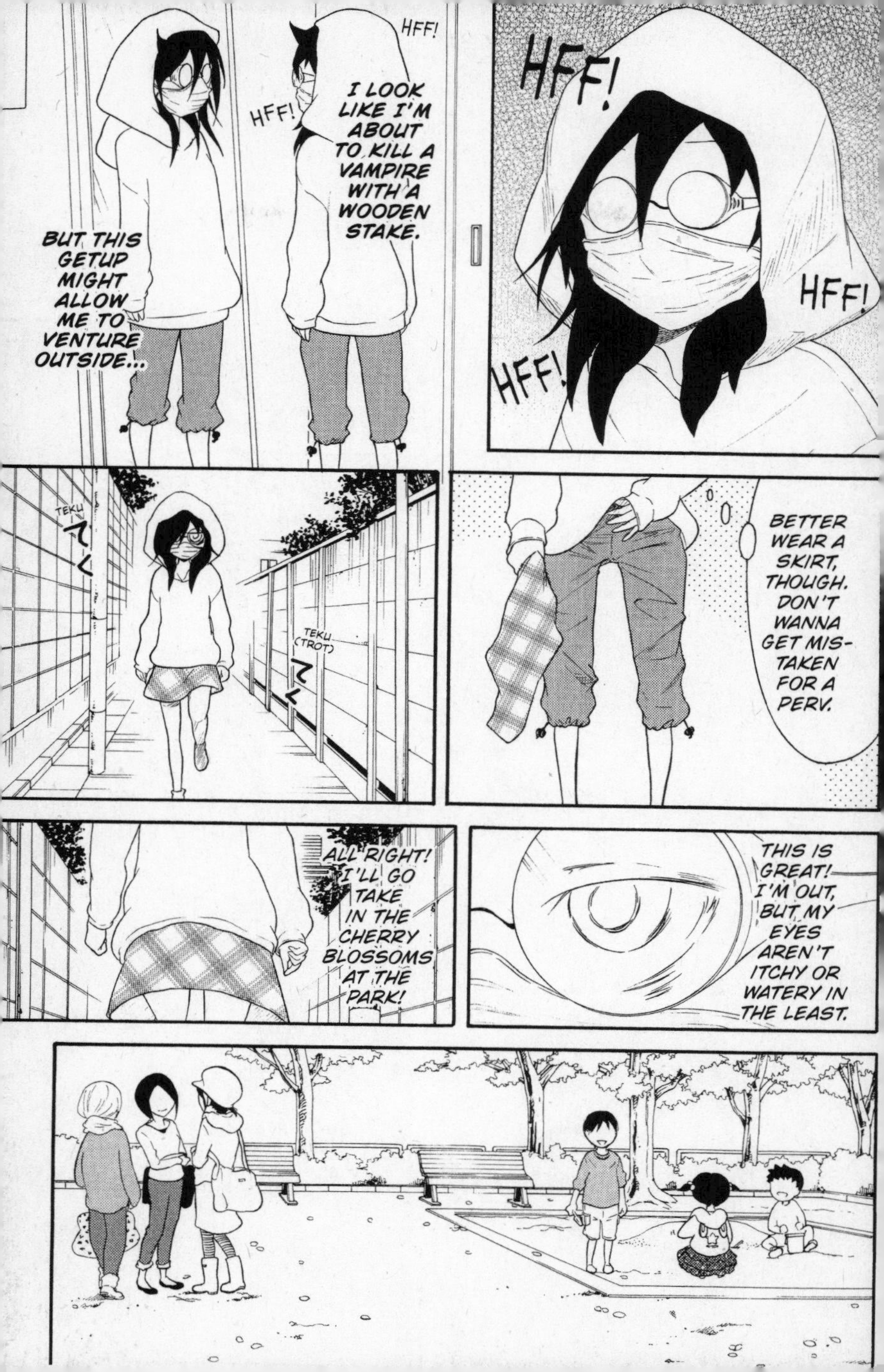
HFF!
HFF!
HFF!
HFF!
I LOOK LIKE I'M ABOUT TO KILL A VAMPIRE WITH A WOODEN STAKE.
HFF!
BUT THIS GETUP MIGHT ALLOW ME TO VENTURE OUTSIDE...
BETTER WEAR A SKIRT, THOUGH. DON'T WANNA GET MIS-TAKEN FOR A PERV.
TEKU (TROT)
TEKU
THIS IS GREAT! I'M OUT, BUT MY EYES AREN'T ITCHY OR WATERY IN THE LEAST.
ALL RIGHT! I'LL GO TAKE IN THE CHERRY BLOSSOMS AT THE PARK!

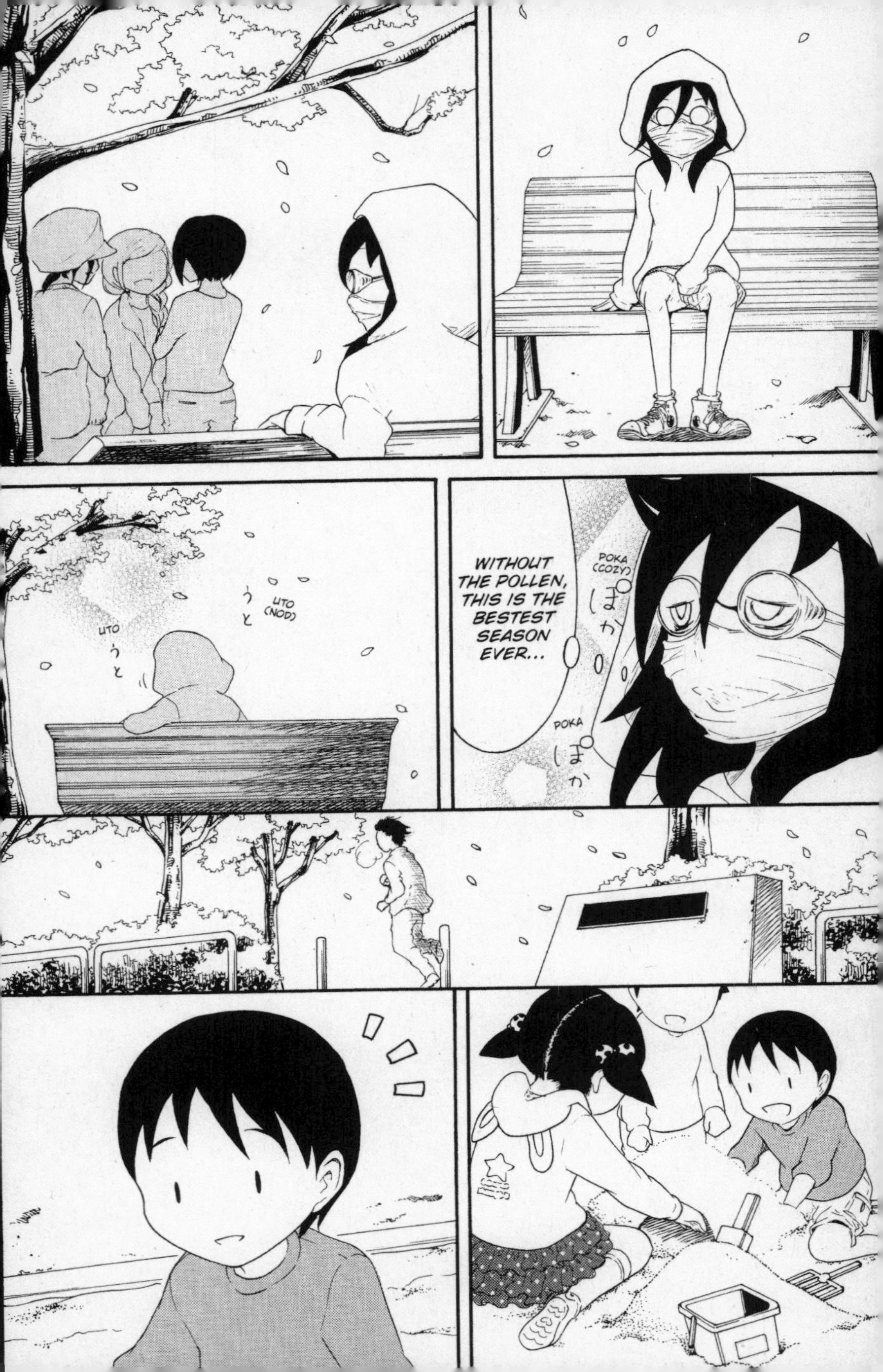
WITHOUT THE POLLEN, THIS IS THE BESTEST SEASON EVER...
POKA (COZY)
ぽか
POKA
ぽか
UTO (NOD)
うと
UTO
うと

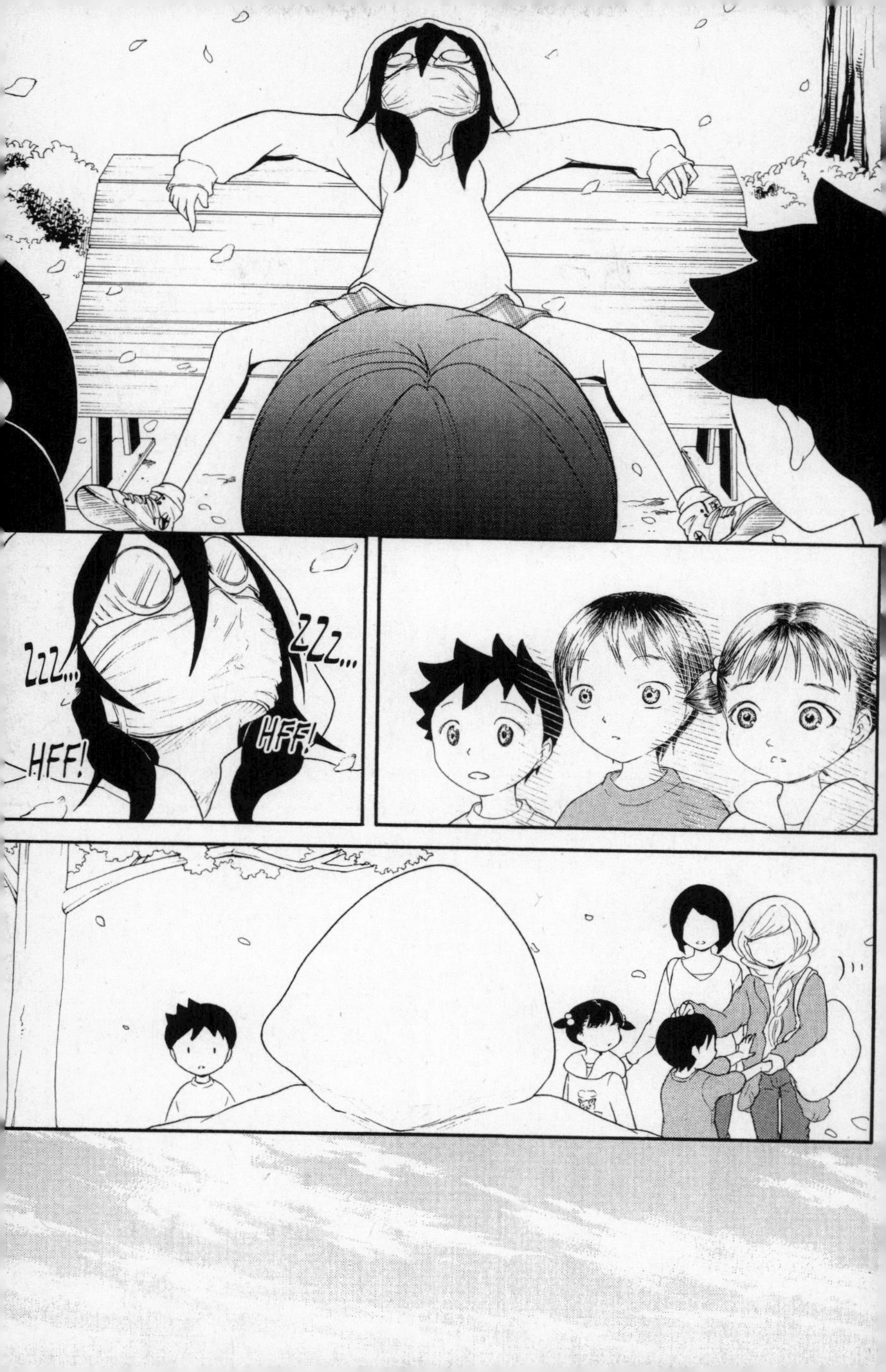
ZZZ...
Zzz...
HFF!
HFF!

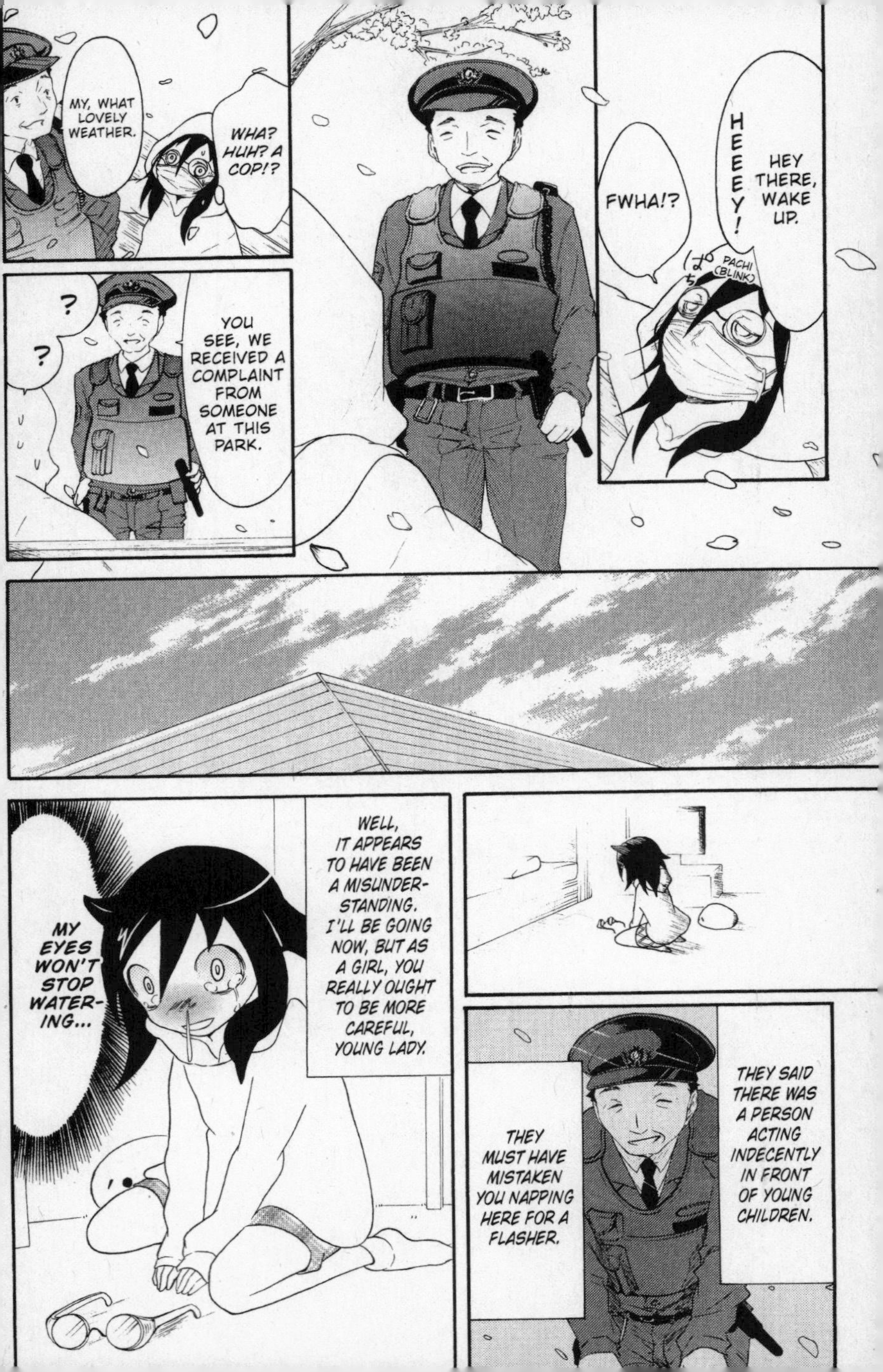
HEY THERE, WAKE UP.
HEEEY!
FWHA!?
ぱち
PACHI (BLINK)
MY, WHAT LOVELY WEATHER.
WHA? HUH? A COP!?
YOU SEE, WE RECEIVED A COMPLAINT FROM SOMEONE AT THIS PARK.
?
?
THEY SAID THERE WAS A PERSON ACTING INDECENTLY IN FRONT OF YOUNG CHILDREN.
THEY MUST HAVE MISTAKEN YOU NAPPING HERE FOR A FLASHER.
WELL, IT APPEARS TO HAVE BEEN A MISUNDERSTANDING. I'LL BE GOING NOW, BUT AS A GIRL, YOU REALLY OUGHT TO BE MORE CAREFUL, YOUNG LADY.
MY EYES WON'T STOP WATERING...

No Matter How I Look at It, It's You Guys' Fault I'm Not Popular!

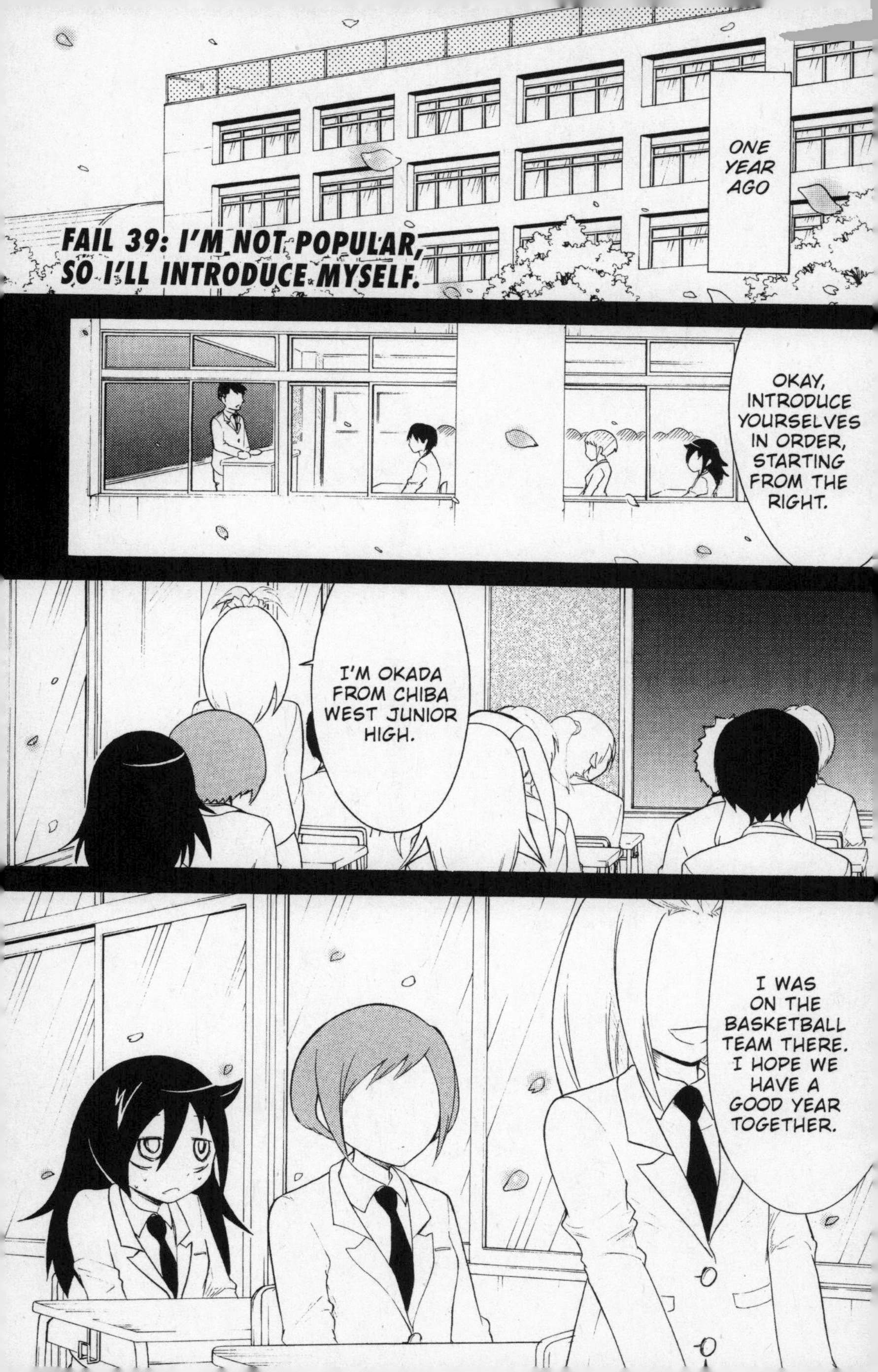
ONE YEAR AGO
FAIL 39: I'M NOT POPULAR, SO I'LL INTRODUCE MYSELF.
OKAY, INTRODUCE YOURSELVES IN ORDER, STARTING FROM THE RIGHT.
I'M OKADA FROM CHIBA WEST JUNIOR HIGH.
I WAS ON THE BASKETBALL TEAM THERE. I HOPE WE HAVE A GOOD YEAR TOGETHER.

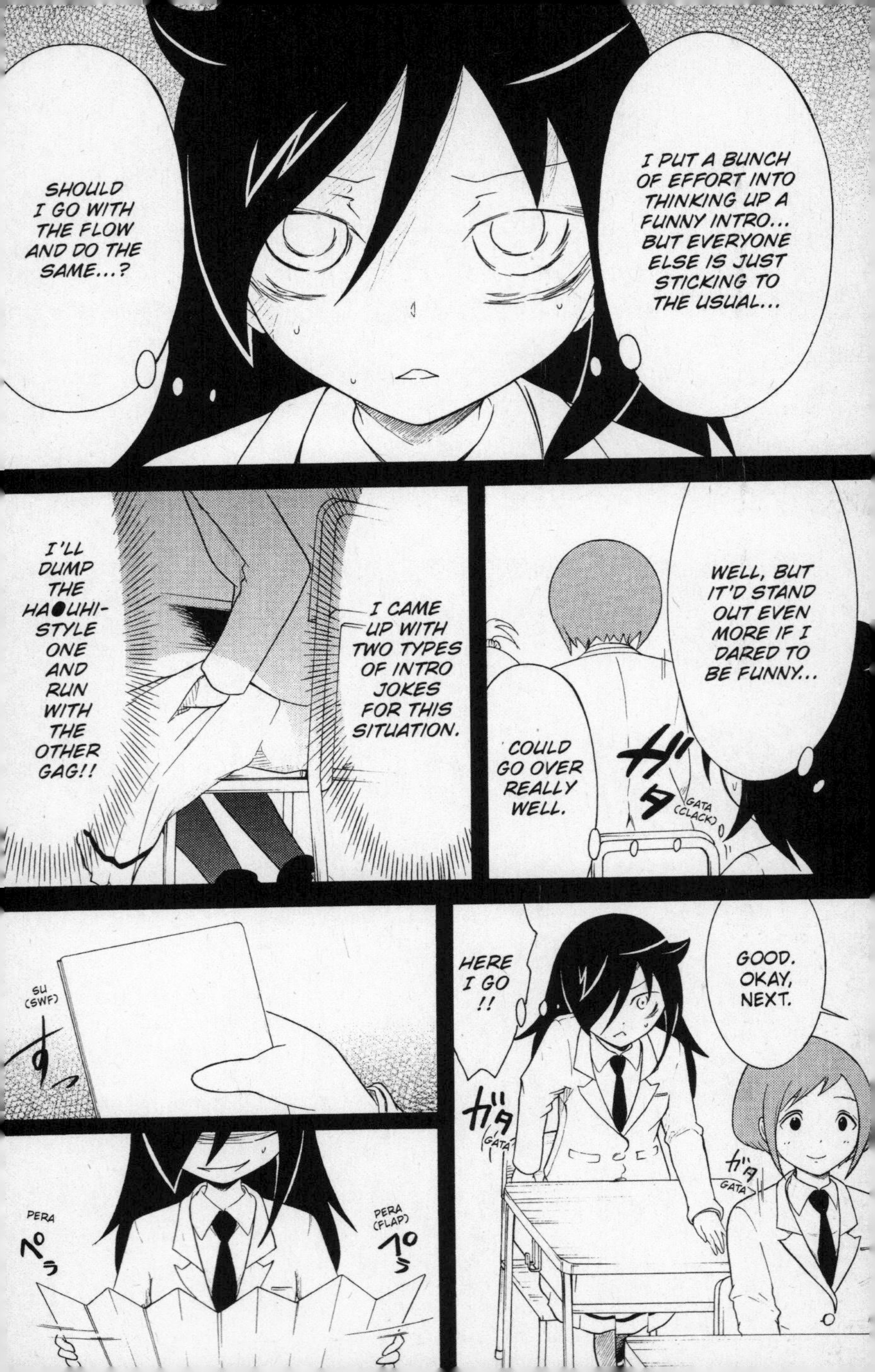
I PUT A BUNCH OF EFFORT INTO THINKING UP A FUNNY INTRO... BUT EVERYONE ELSE IS JUST STICKING TO THE USUAL...
SHOULD I GO WITH THE FLOW AND DO THE SAME...?
WELL, BUT IT'D STAND OUT EVEN MORE IF I DARED TO BE FUNNY...
COULD GO OVER REALLY WELL.
GATA (CLACK)
I CAME UP WITH TWO TYPES OF INTRO JOKES FOR THIS SITUATION.
I'LL DUMP THE HA●UHI-STYLE ONE AND RUN WITH THE OTHER GAG!!
GOOD. OKAY, NEXT.
GATA
HERE I GO !!
GATA
SU (SWF)
PERA (FLAP)
PERA

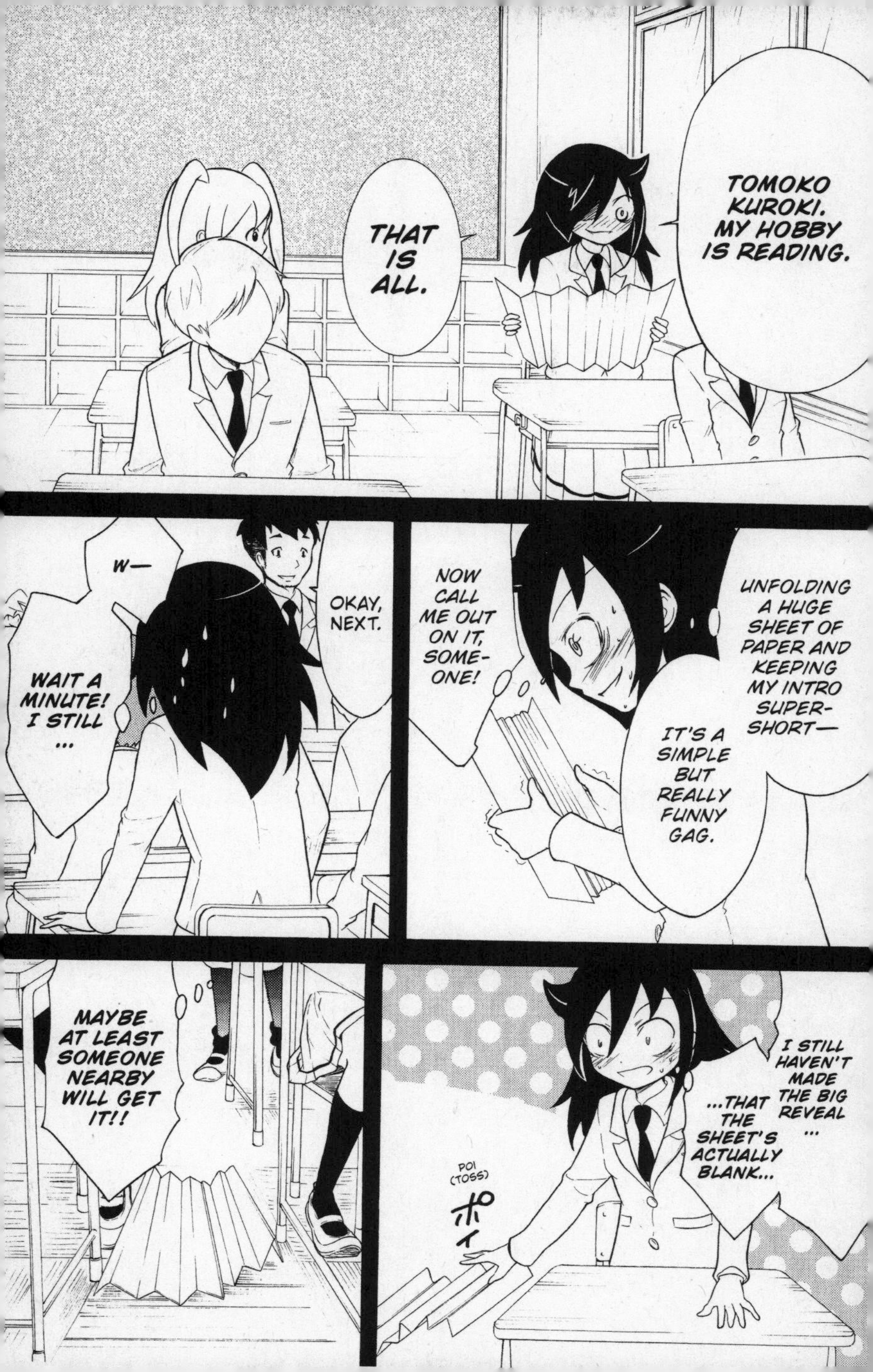
TOMOKO KUROKI. MY HOBBY IS READING.
THAT IS ALL.
UNFOLDING A HUGE SHEET OF PAPER AND KEEPING MY INTRO SUPER-SHORT—
IT'S A SIMPLE BUT REALLY FUNNY GAG.
NOW CALL ME OUT ON IT, SOMEONE!
OKAY, NEXT.
W—
WAIT A MINUTE! I STILL ...
I STILL HAVEN'T MADE THE BIG REVEAL ...
...THAT THE SHEET'S ACTUALLY BLANK...
POI (TOSS)
ポイ
MAYBE AT LEAST SOMEONE NEARBY WILL GET IT!!

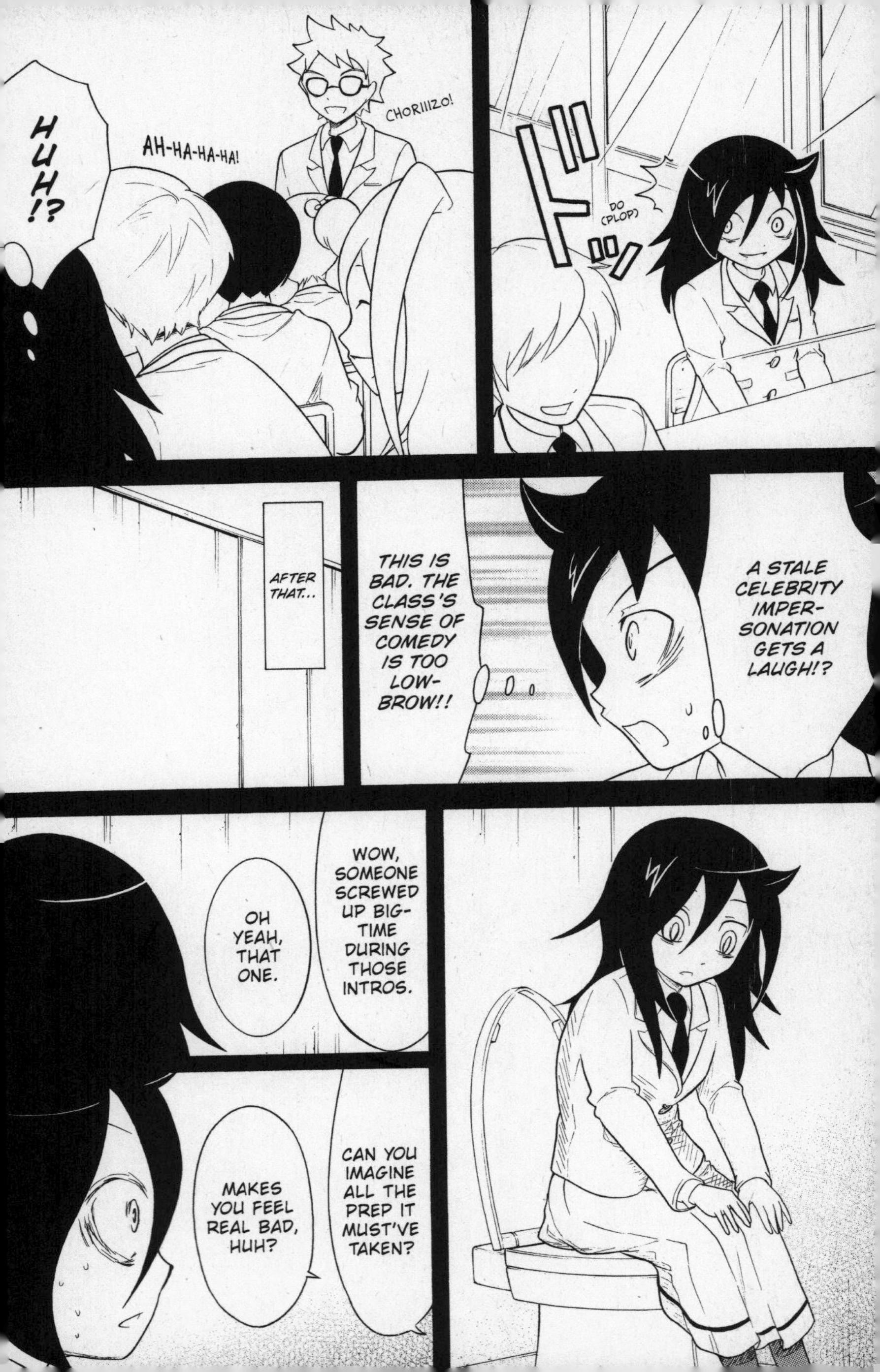
DO (PLOP)
CHORIIIZO!
AH-HA-HA-HA!
HUH!?
A STALE CELEBRITY IMPERSONATION GETS A LAUGH!?
THIS IS BAD. THE CLASS'S SENSE OF COMEDY IS TOO LOW-BROW!!
AFTER THAT...
WOW, SOMEONE SCREWED UP BIG-TIME DURING THOSE INTROS.
OH YEAH, THAT ONE.
CAN YOU IMAGINE ALL THE PREP IT MUST'VE TAKEN?
MAKES YOU FEEL REAL BAD, HUH?

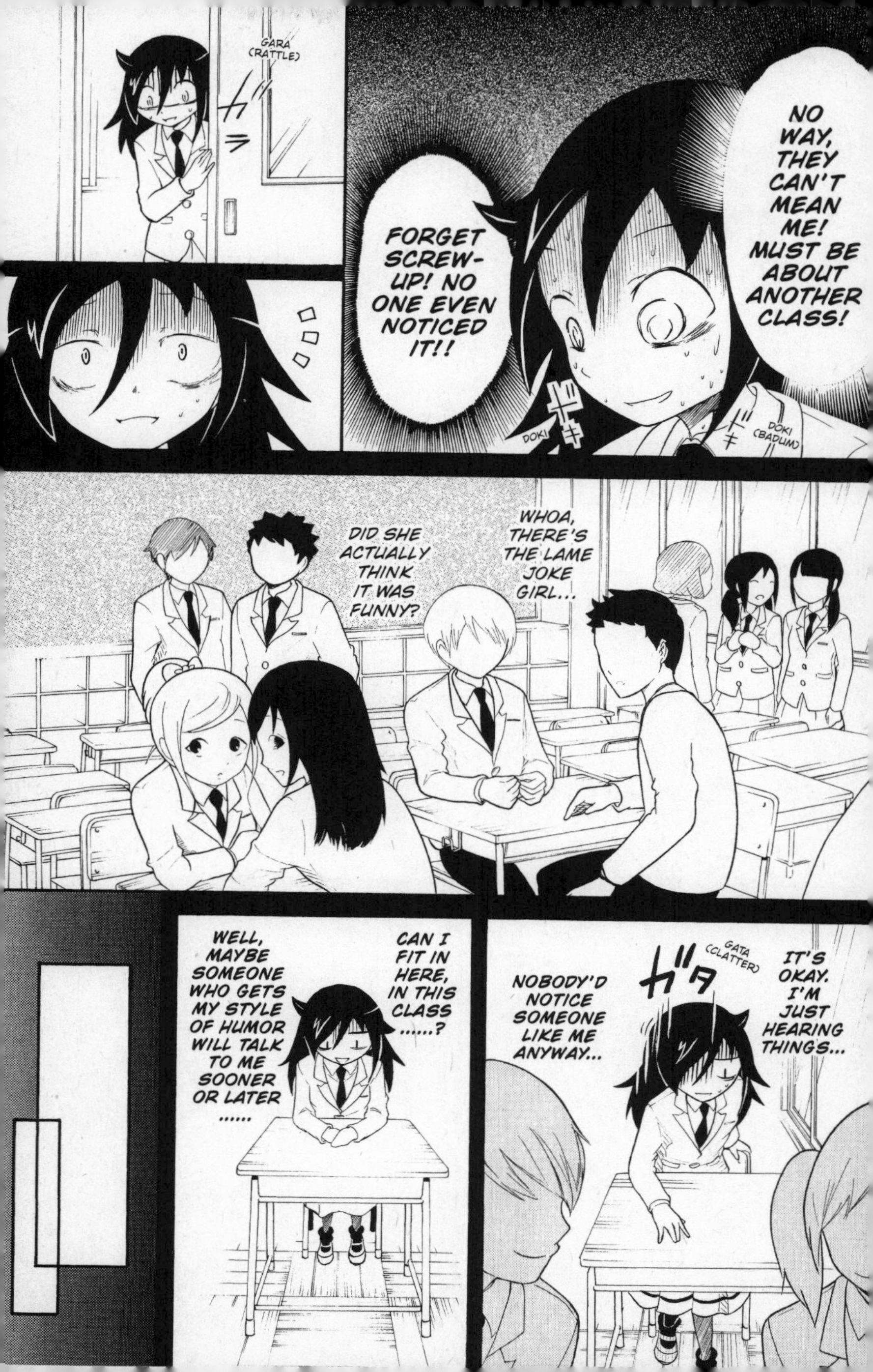
NO WAY, THEY CAN'T MEAN ME! MUST BE ABOUT ANOTHER CLASS!
FORGET SCREW-UP! NO ONE EVEN NOTICED IT!!
DOKI (BADUM)
DOKI
GARA (RATTLE)
WHOA, THERE'S THE LAME JOKE GIRL...
DID SHE ACTUALLY THINK IT WAS FUNNY?
IT'S OKAY. I'M JUST HEARING THINGS...
GATA (CLATTER)
NOBODY'D NOTICE SOMEONE LIKE ME ANYWAY...
CAN I FIT IN HERE, IN THIS CLASS ......?
WELL, MAYBE SOMEONE WHO GETS MY STYLE OF HUMOR WILL TALK TO ME SOONER OR LATER ......

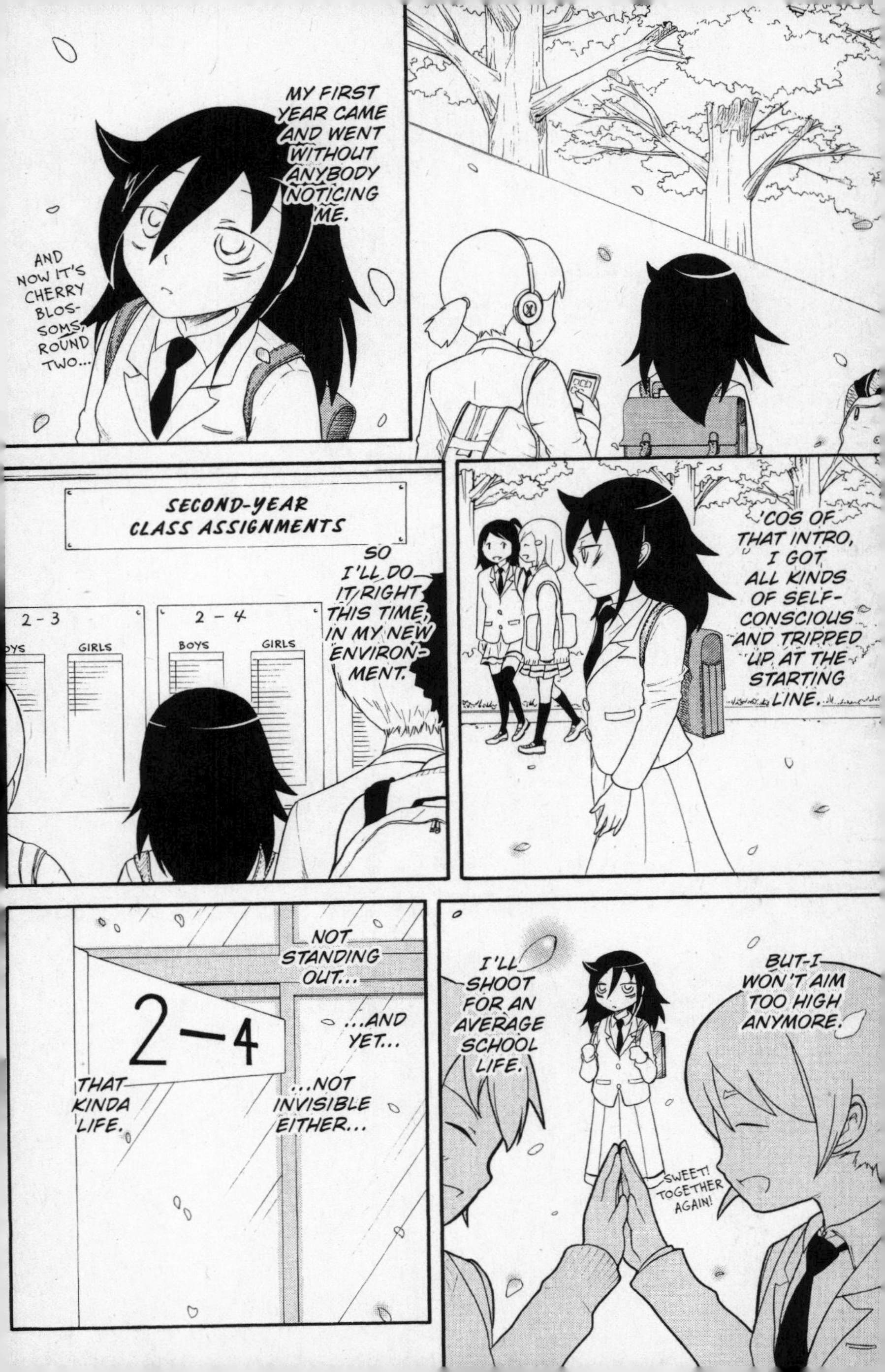
MY FIRST YEAR CAME AND WENT WITHOUT ANYBODY NOTICING ME.
AND NOW IT'S CHERRY BLOSSOMS, ROUND TWO...
'COS OF THAT INTRO, I GOT ALL KINDS OF SELF-CONSCIOUS AND TRIPPED UP AT THE STARTING LINE.
SO I'LL DO IT RIGHT THIS TIME, IN MY NEW ENVIRONMENT.
SECOND-YEAR CLASS ASSIGNMENTS
2-3
GIRLS
2-4
BOYS
GIRLS
BUT I WON'T AIM TOO HIGH ANYMORE.
I'LL SHOOT FOR AN AVERAGE SCHOOL LIFE.
SWEET! TOGETHER AGAIN!
NOT STANDING OUT...
...AND YET...
...NOT INVISIBLE EITHER...
2-4
THAT KINDA LIFE.

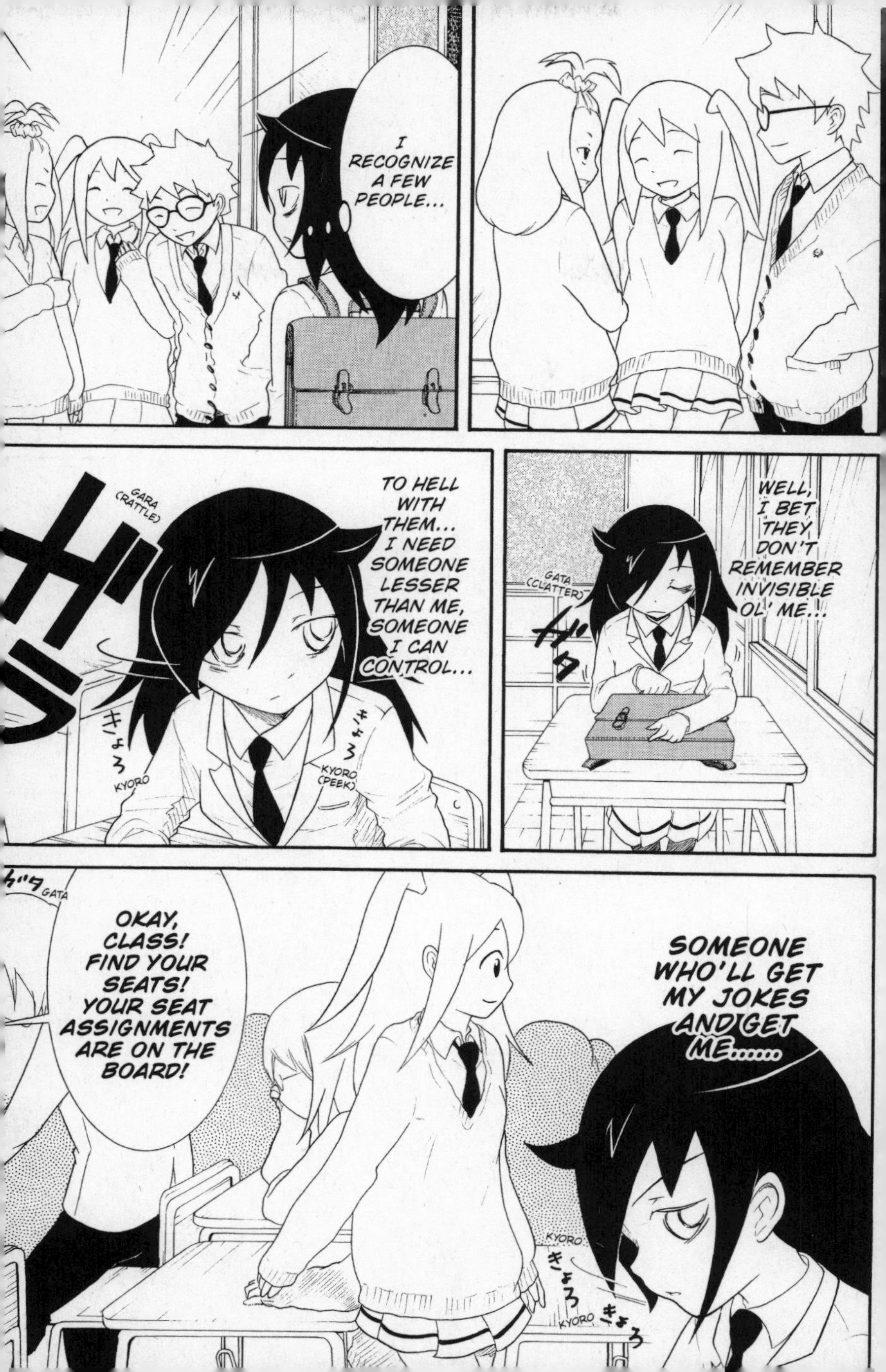

I RECOGNIZE A FEW PEOPLE...
WELL, I BET THEY DON'T REMEMBER INVISIBLE OL' ME...
ガタ
GATA (CLATTER)
TO HELL WITH THEM... I NEED SOMEONE LESSER THAN ME, SOMEONE I CAN CONTROL...
ガラ
GARA (RATTLE)
きょろ
KYORO (PEEK)
きょろ
KYORO
SOMEONE WHO'LL GET MY JOKES AND GET ME......
きょろ
KYORO
きょろ
KYORO
OKAY, CLASS! FIND YOUR SEATS! YOUR SEAT ASSIGNMENTS ARE ON THE BOARD!
ガタ
GATA

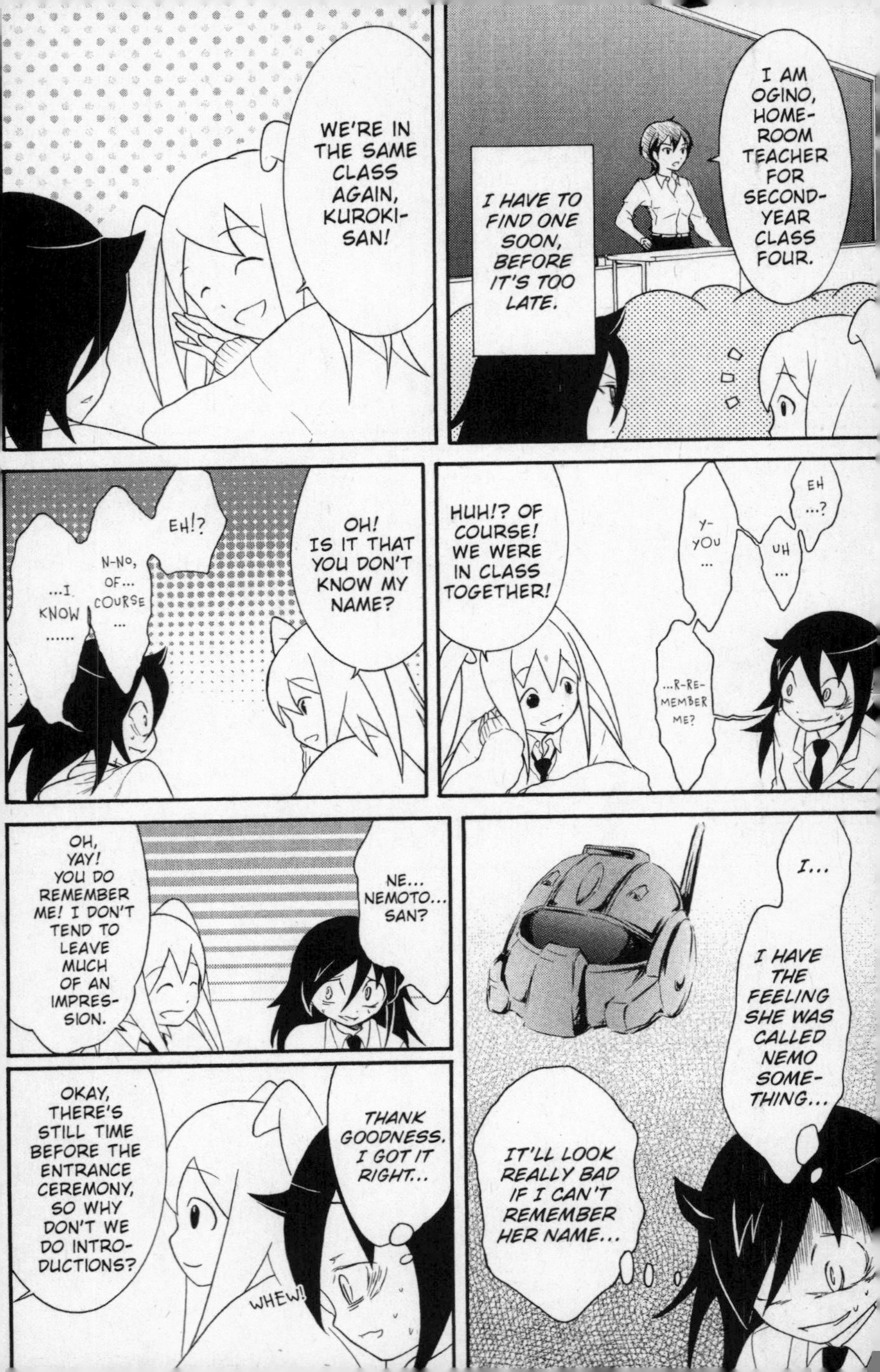
I AM OGINO, HOME-ROOM TEACHER FOR SECOND-YEAR CLASS FOUR.
I HAVE TO FIND ONE SOON, BEFORE IT'S TOO LATE.
WE'RE IN THE SAME CLASS AGAIN, KUROKI-SAN!
EH ...?
UH ...
Y-YOU ...
...R-REMEMBER ME?
HUH!? OF COURSE! WE WERE IN CLASS TOGETHER!
OH! IS IT THAT YOU DON'T KNOW MY NAME?
EH!?
N-NO, OF... COURSE ...
...I KNOW ......
I...
I HAVE THE FEELING SHE WAS CALLED NEMO SOME-THING...
IT'LL LOOK REALLY BAD IF I CAN'T REMEMBER HER NAME...
NE... NEMOTO... SAN?
OH, YAY! YOU DO REMEMBER ME! I DON'T TEND TO LEAVE MUCH OF AN IMPRES-SION.
THANK GOODNESS. I GOT IT RIGHT...
WHEW!
OKAY, THERE'S STILL TIME BEFORE THE ENTRANCE CEREMONY, SO WHY DON'T WE DO INTRO-DUCTIONS?

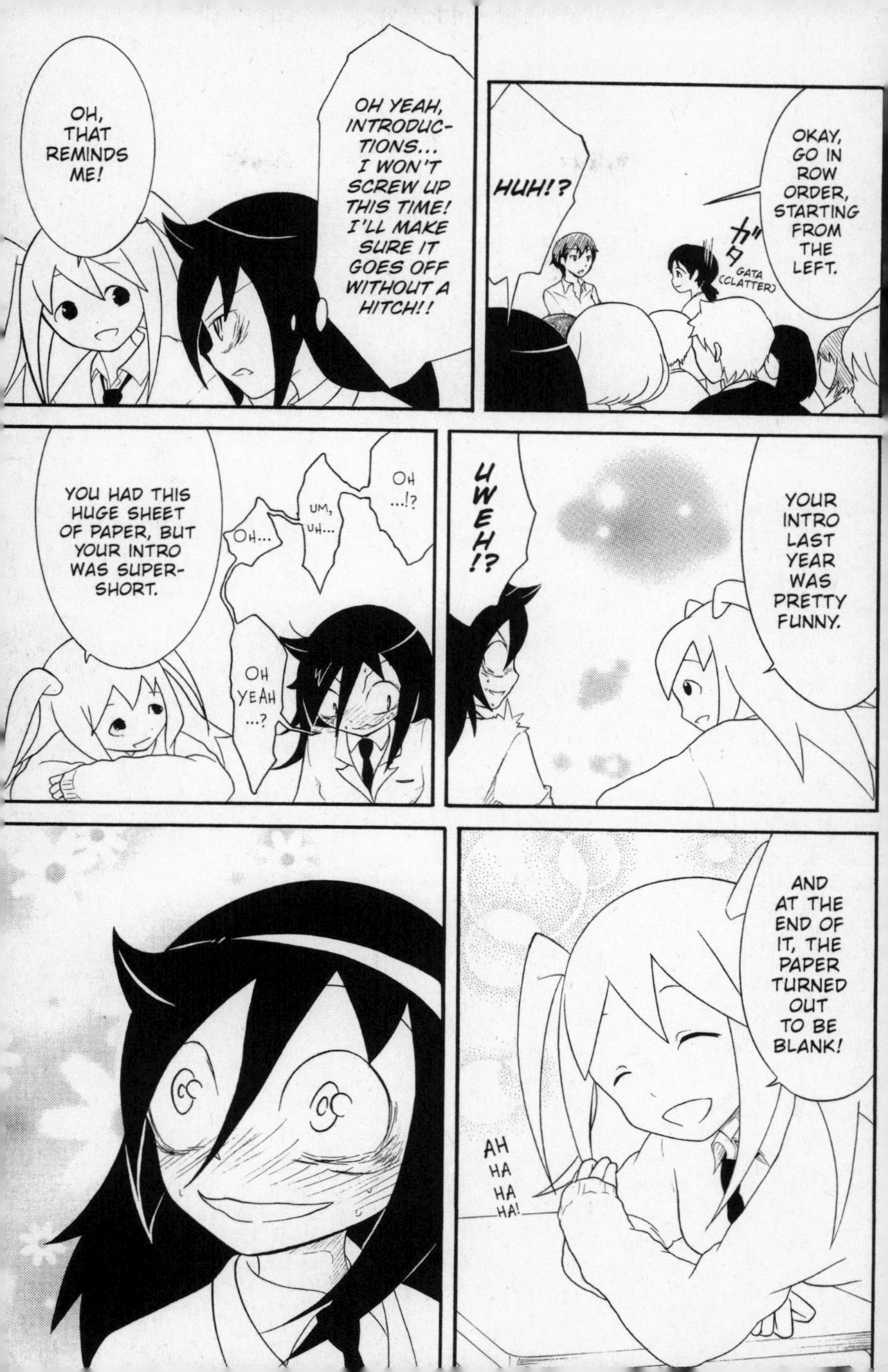
OKAY, GO IN ROW ORDER, STARTING FROM THE LEFT.
ガタ
GATA (CLATTER)
HUH!?
OH YEAH, INTRODUCTIONS... I WON'T SCREW UP THIS TIME! I'LL MAKE SURE IT GOES OFF WITHOUT A HITCH!!
OH, THAT REMINDS ME!
YOUR INTRO LAST YEAR WAS PRETTY FUNNY.
UWEH!?
OH ...!?
UM, UH...
OH...
YOU HAD THIS HUGE SHEET OF PAPER, BUT YOUR INTRO WAS SUPER-SHORT.
OH YEAH ...?
AND AT THE END OF IT, THE PAPER TURNED OUT TO BE BLANK!
AH HA HA HA!

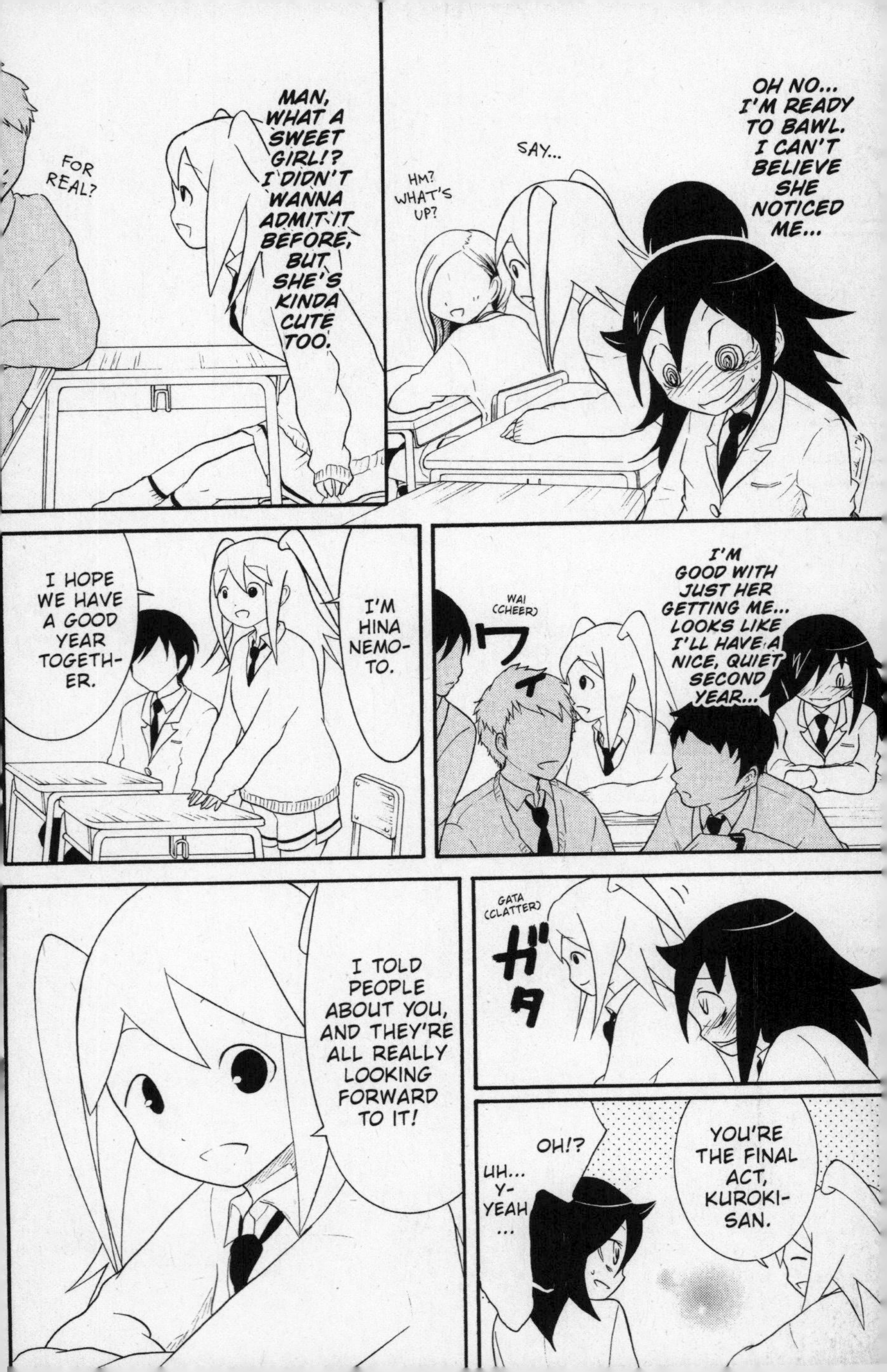
OH NO... I'M READY TO BAWL. I CAN'T BELIEVE SHE NOTICED ME...
SAY...
HM? WHAT'S UP?
MAN, WHAT A SWEET GIRL!? I DIDN'T WANNA ADMIT IT BEFORE, BUT SHE'S KINDA CUTE TOO.
FOR REAL?
I'M GOOD WITH JUST HER GETTING ME... LOOKS LIKE I'LL HAVE A NICE, QUIET SECOND YEAR...
WAI (CHEER)
ワイ
I'M HINA NEMOTO.
I HOPE WE HAVE A GOOD YEAR TOGETHER.
GATA (CLATTER)
ガタ
YOU'RE THE FINAL ACT, KUROKI-SAN.
OH!?
UH... Y-YEAH...
I TOLD PEOPLE ABOUT YOU, AND THEY'RE ALL REALLY LOOKING FORWARD TO IT!

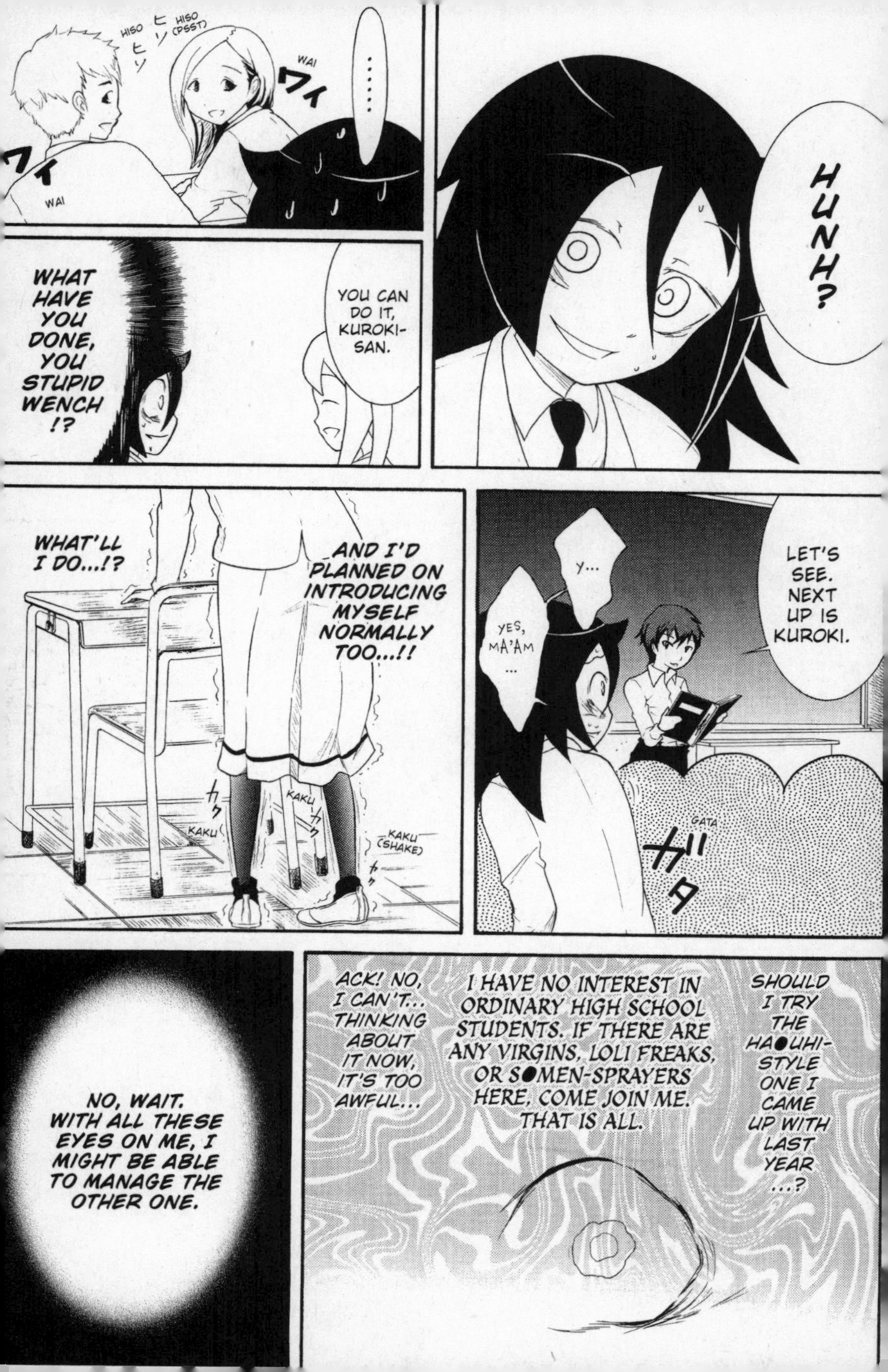

HUNH?
......
WAI
ワイ
HISO ヒソ HISO ヒソ (PSST)
ワイ
WAI
YOU CAN DO IT, KUROKI-SAN.
WHAT HAVE YOU DONE, YOU STUPID WENCH!?
LET'S SEE. NEXT UP IS KUROKI.
Y...
YES, MA'AM...
GATA
ガタ
AND I'D PLANNED ON INTRODUCING MYSELF NORMALLY TOO...!!
WHAT'LL I DO...!?
KAKU
KAKU
KAKU (SHAKE)
SHOULD I TRY THE HA●UHI-STYLE ONE I CAME UP WITH LAST YEAR...?
I HAVE NO INTEREST IN ORDINARY HIGH SCHOOL STUDENTS. IF THERE ARE ANY VIRGINS, LOLI FREAKS, OR S●MEN-SPRAYERS HERE, COME JOIN ME. THAT IS ALL.
ACK! NO, I CAN'T... THINKING ABOUT IT NOW, IT'S TOO AWFUL...
NO, WAIT. WITH ALL THESE EYES ON ME, I MIGHT BE ABLE TO MANAGE THE OTHER ONE.

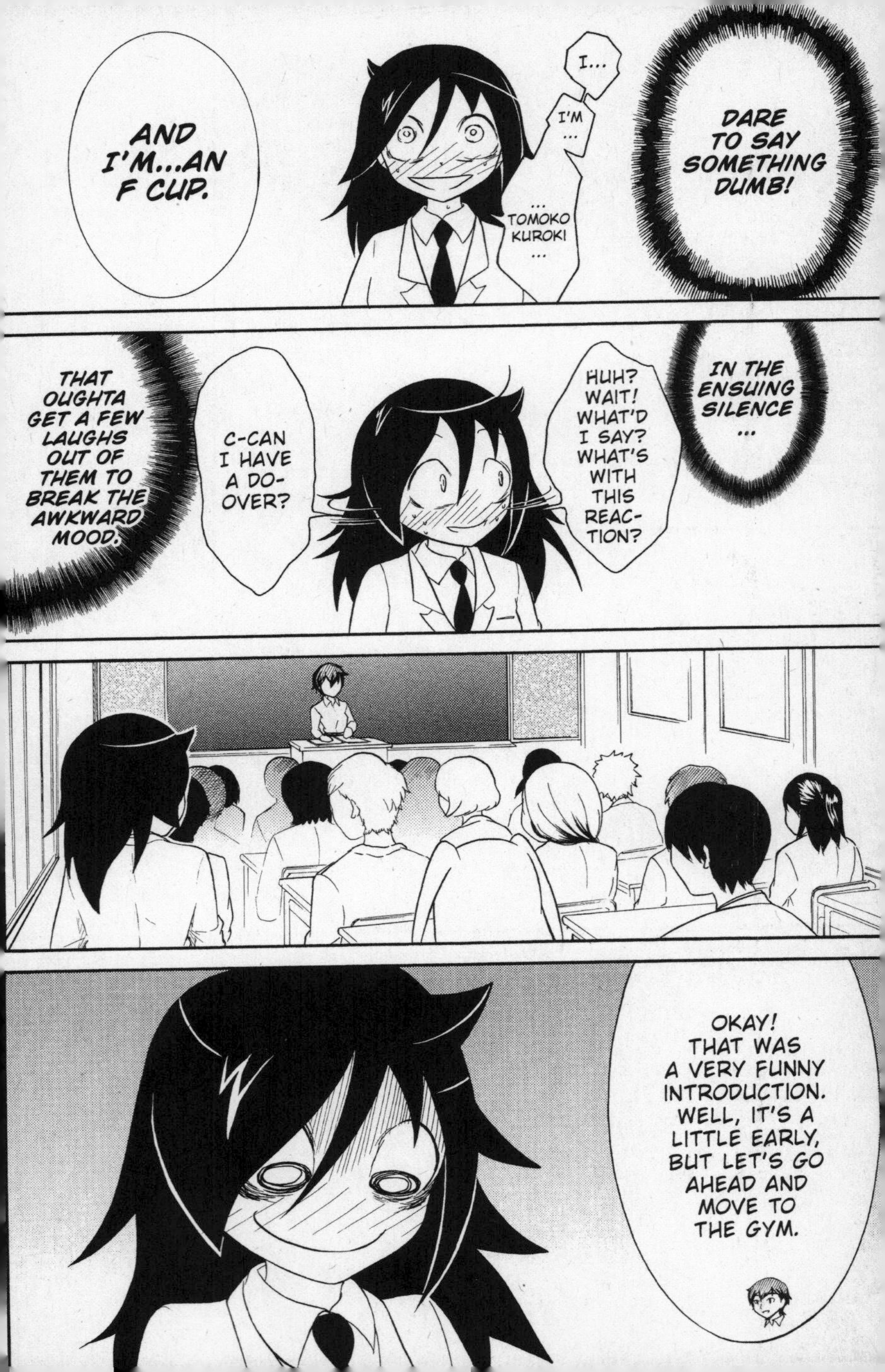
DARE TO SAY SOMETHING DUMB!
I...
I'M ...
...TOMOKO KUROKI ...
AND I'M...AN F CUP.
IN THE ENSUING SILENCE ...
HUH? WAIT! WHAT'D I SAY? WHAT'S WITH THIS REACTION?
C-CAN I HAVE A DO-OVER?
THAT OUGHTA GET A FEW LAUGHS OUT OF THEM TO BREAK THE AWKWARD MOOD.
OKAY! THAT WAS A VERY FUNNY INTRODUCTION. WELL, IT'S A LITTLE EARLY, BUT LET'S GO AHEAD AND MOVE TO THE GYM.

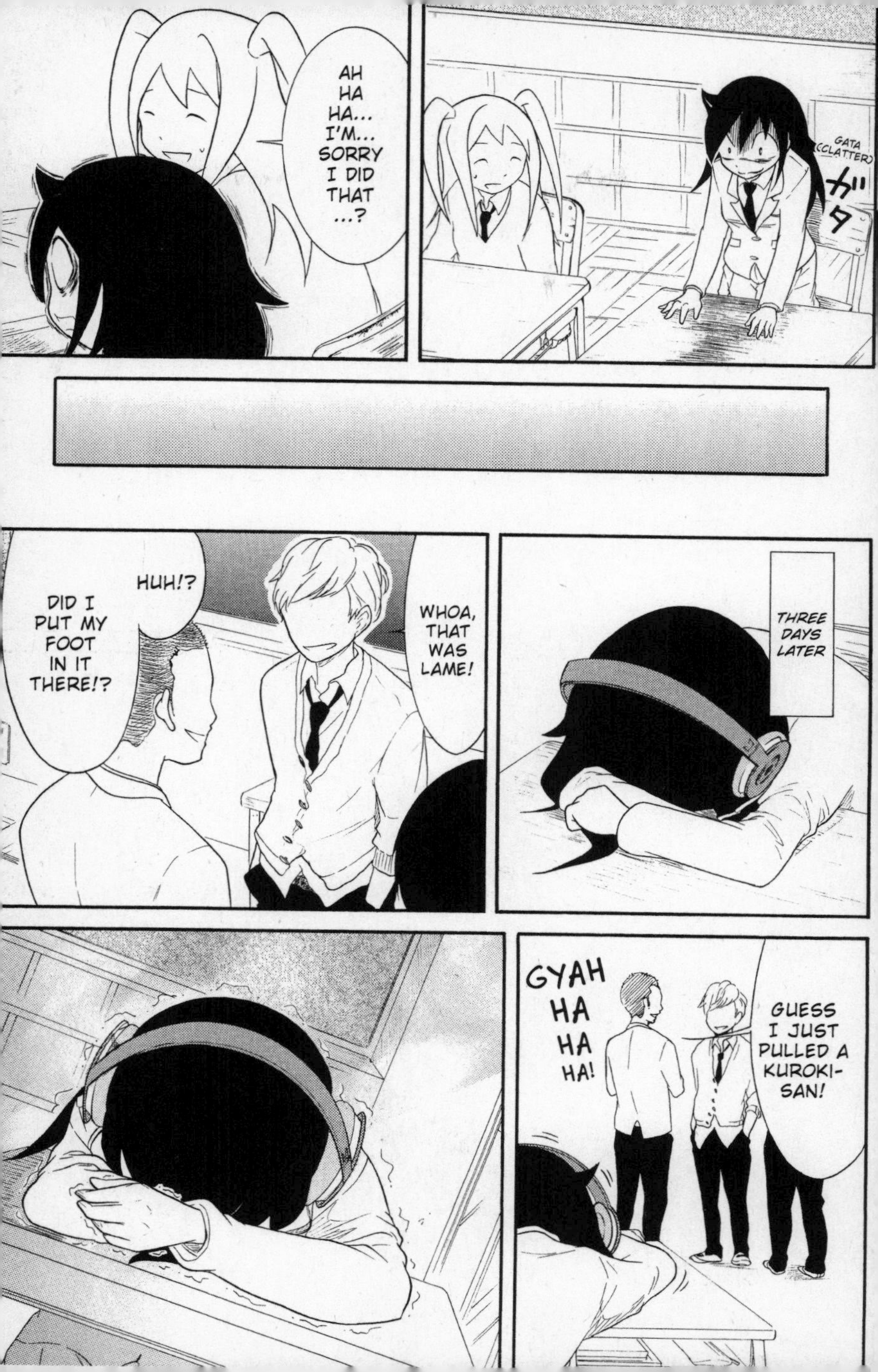
GATA (CLATTER)
ガタ
AH HA HA... I'M... SORRY I DID THAT ...?
THREE DAYS LATER
WHOA, THAT WAS LAME!
HUH!?
DID I PUT MY FOOT IN IT THERE!?
GUESS I JUST PULLED A KUROKI-SAN!
GYAH HA HA HA!

No Matter How I Look at It, It's You Guys' Fault I'm Not Popular!

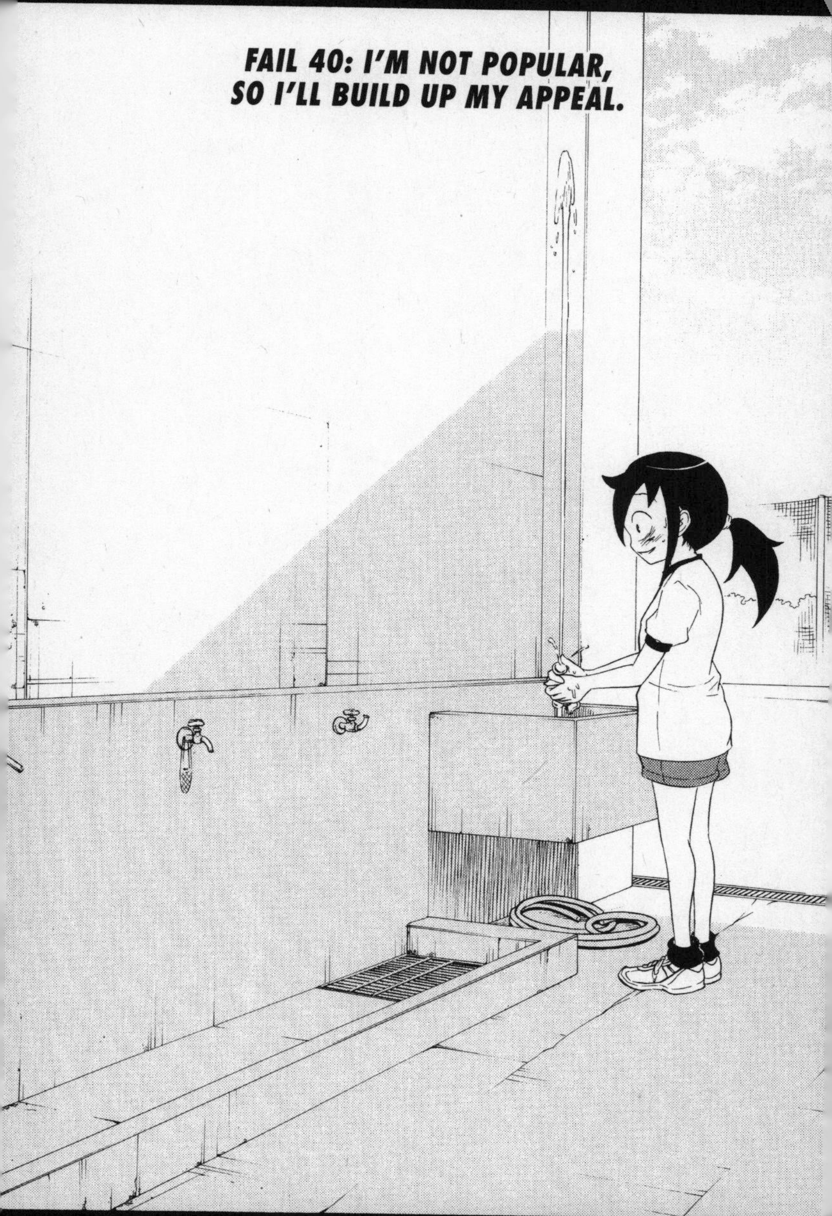
FAIL 40: I'M NOT POPULAR,
SO I'LL BUILD UP MY APPEAL.

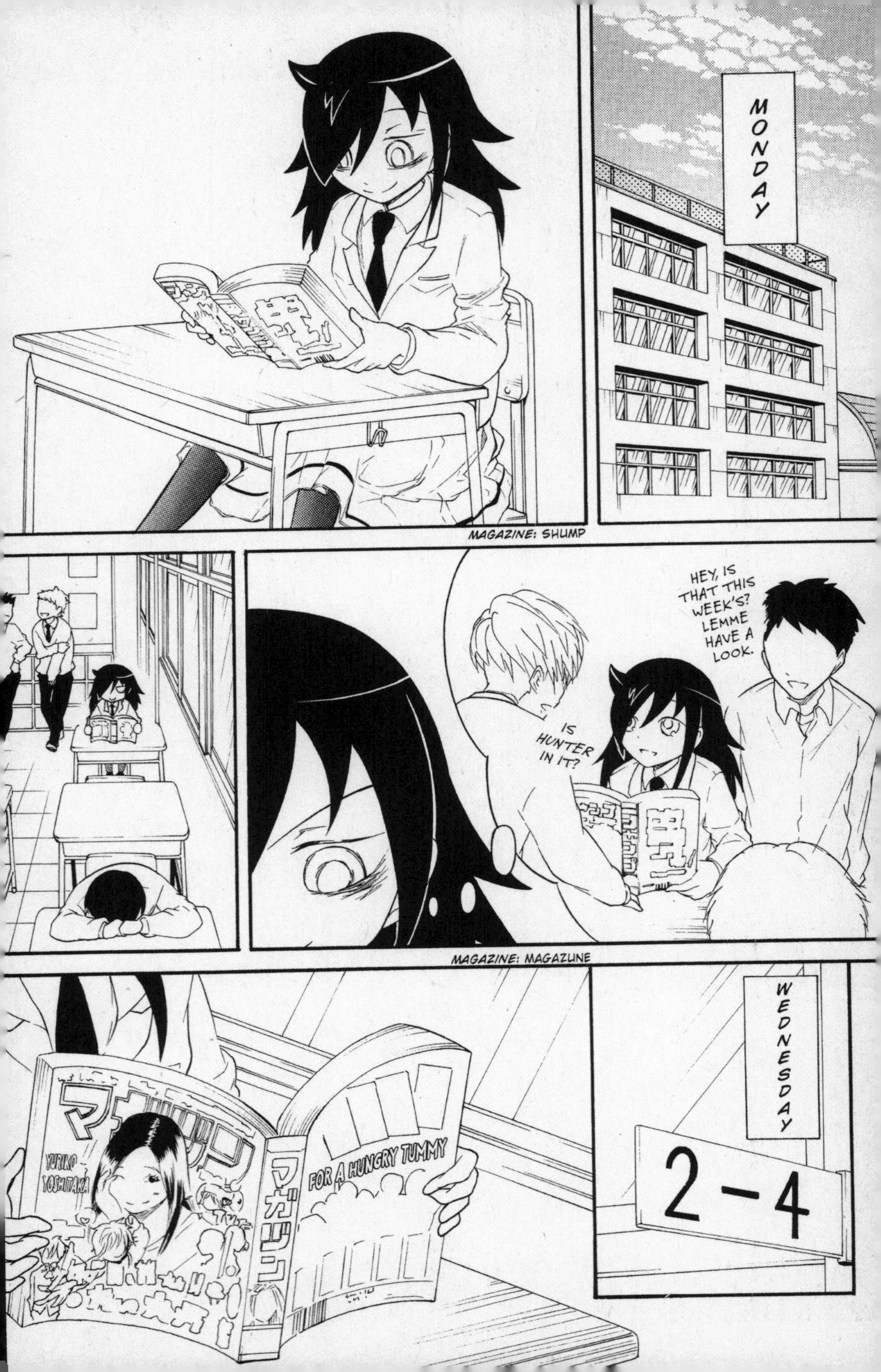
MONDAY
MAGAZINE: SHUMP
HEY, IS THAT THIS WEEK'S? LEMME HAVE A LOOK.
IS HUNTER IN IT?
MAGAZINE: MAGAZUNE
WEDNESDAY
2-4
YURIKO YOSHITAKA
FOR A HUNGRY TUMMY

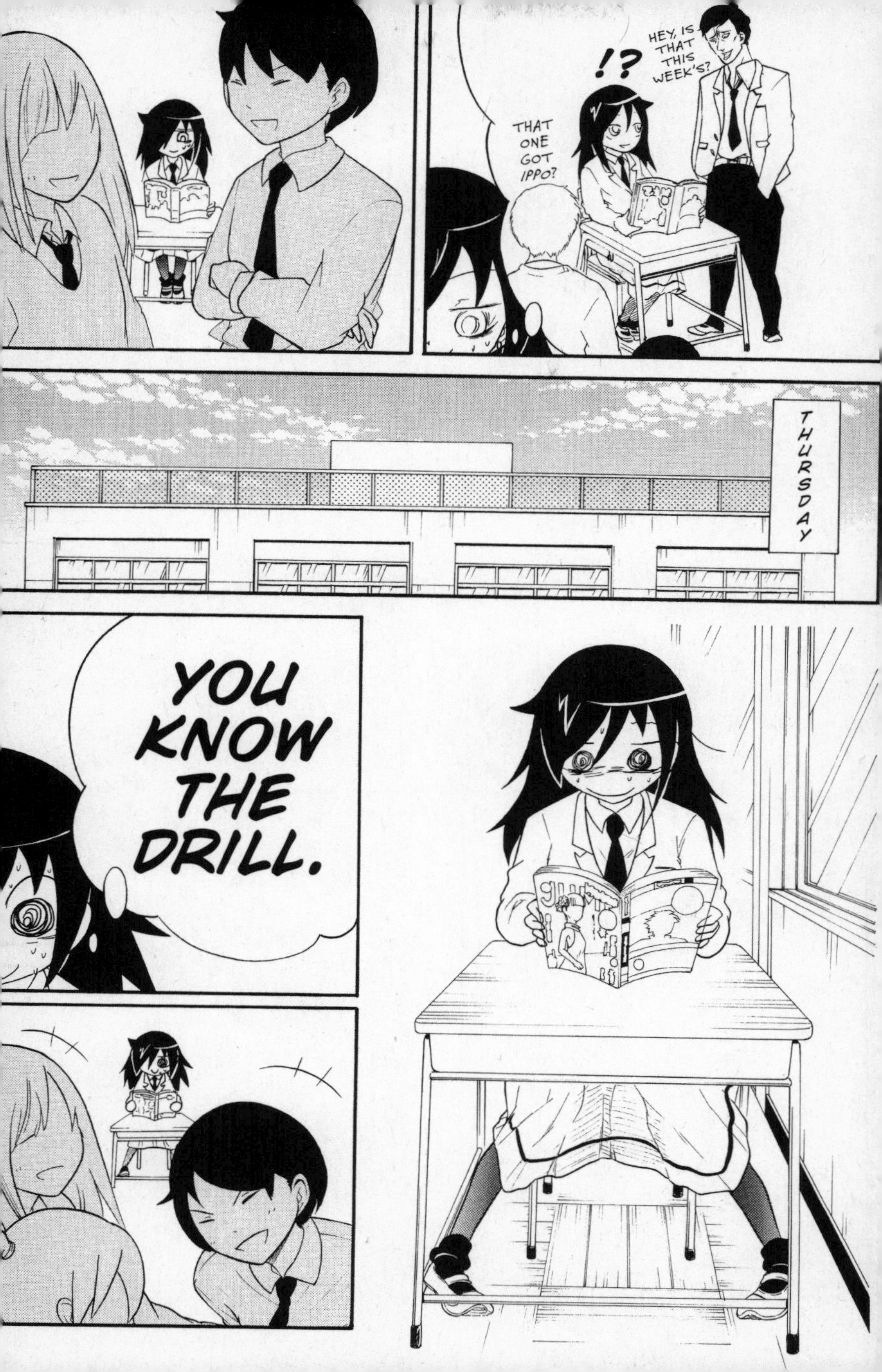
HEY, IS THAT THIS WEEK'S?
!?
THAT ONE GOT IPPO?
THURSDAY
YOU KNOW THE DRILL.

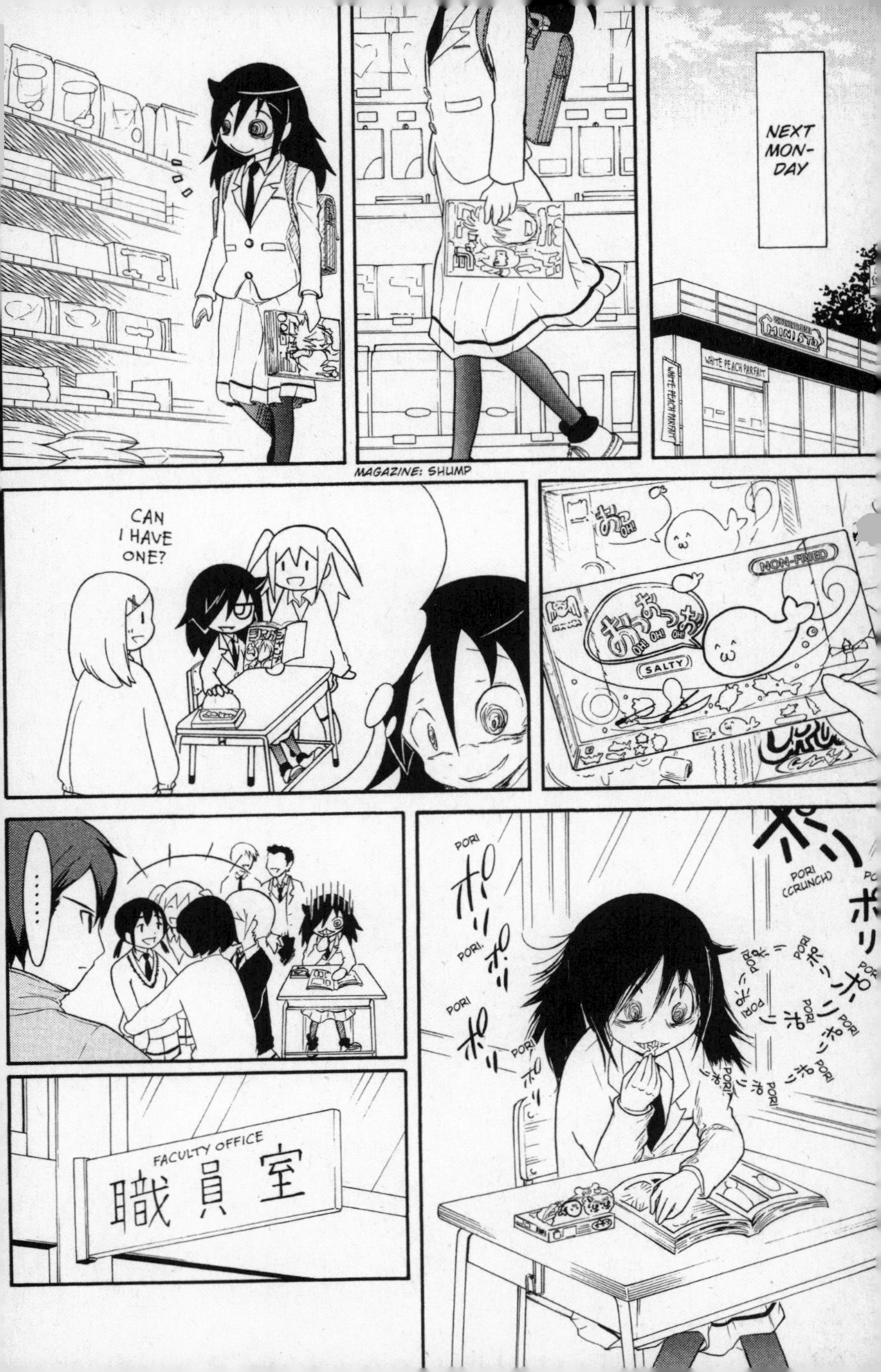

NEXT MON-DAY
WHITE PEACH PARFAIT
WHITE PEACH PARFAIT
MAGAZINE: SHUMP
NON-FRIED
おっおっおっ
OH! OH! OH!
SALTY
CAN I HAVE ONE?
ポリ
PORI (CRUNCH)
PORI
PORI
PORI
PORI
PORI
PORI
PORI
PORI
PORI
PORI
......
FACULTY OFFICE
職員室

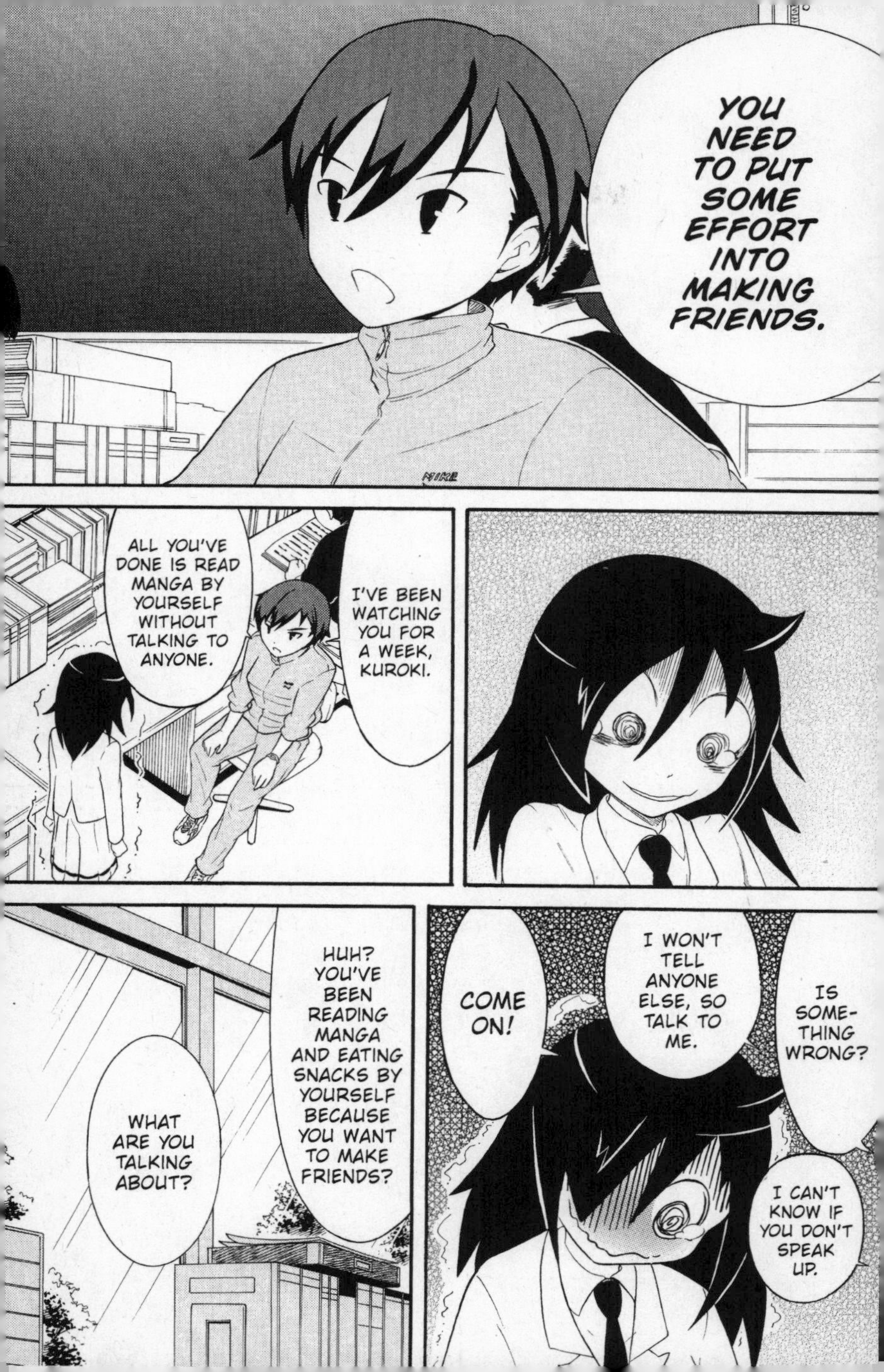
YOU NEED TO PUT SOME EFFORT INTO MAKING FRIENDS.
I'VE BEEN WATCHING YOU FOR A WEEK, KUROKI.
ALL YOU'VE DONE IS READ MANGA BY YOURSELF WITHOUT TALKING TO ANYONE.
IS SOME-THING WRONG?
I WON'T TELL ANYONE ELSE, SO TALK TO ME.
COME ON!
I CAN'T KNOW IF YOU DON'T SPEAK UP.
HUH? YOU'VE BEEN READING MANGA AND EATING SNACKS BY YOURSELF BECAUSE YOU WANT TO MAKE FRIENDS?
WHAT ARE YOU TALKING ABOUT?

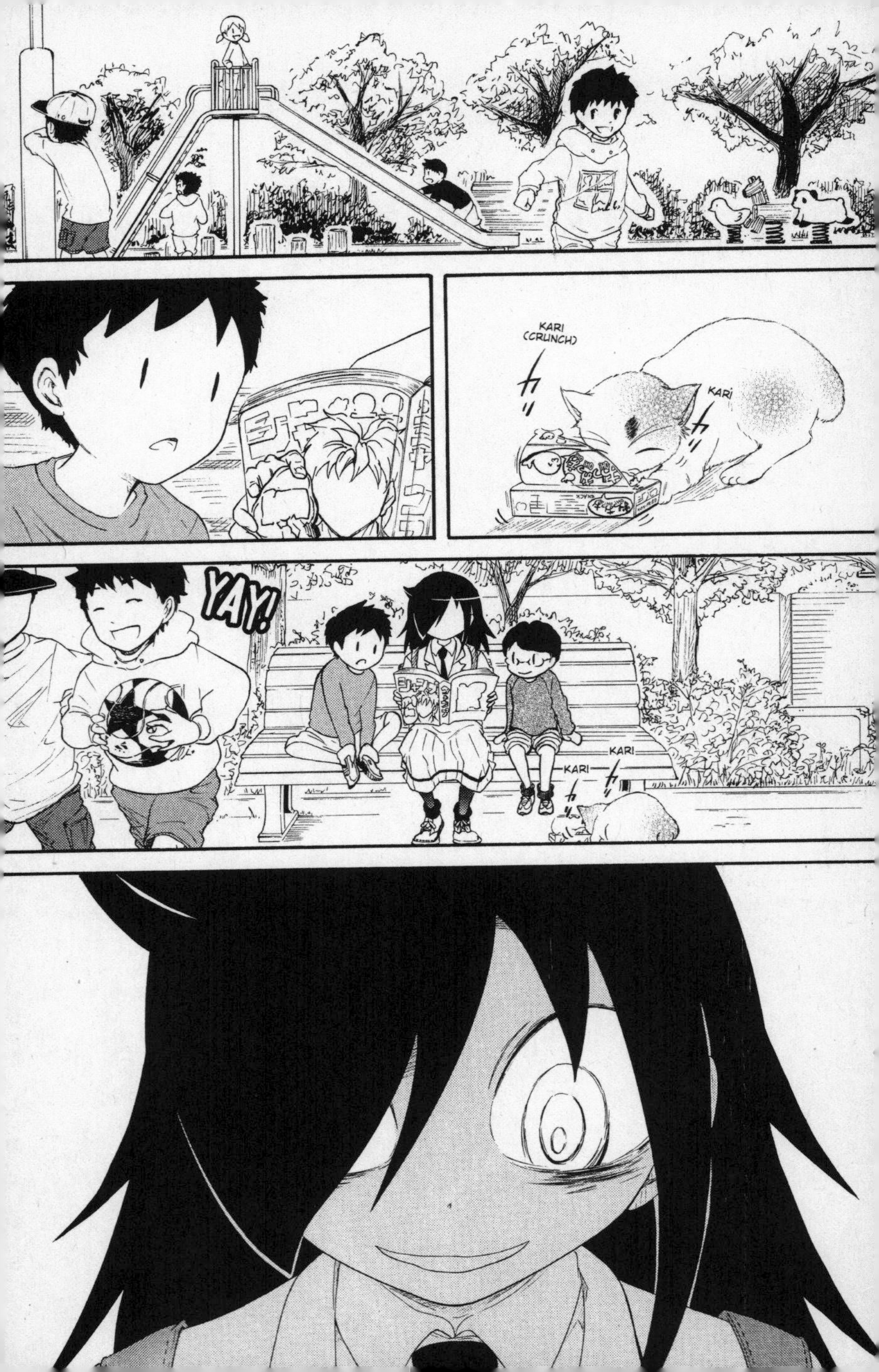
KARI
(CRUNCH)
KARI
YAY!
KARI
KARI

No Matter How I Look at It, It's You Guys' Fault I'm Not Popular!

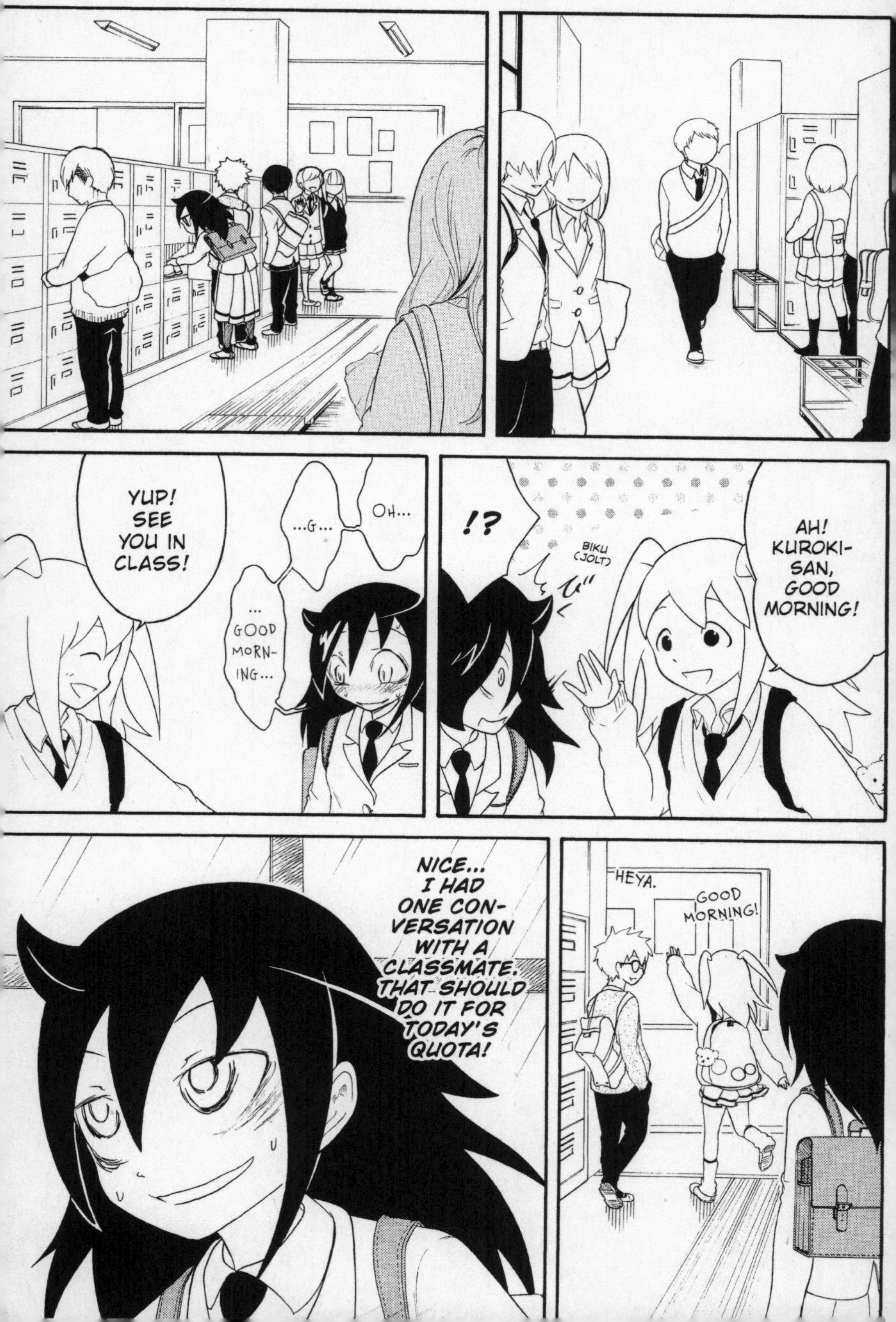
AH! KUROKI-SAN, GOOD MORNING!
BIKU (JOLT)
!?
OH...
...G...
... GOOD MORN-ING...
YUP! SEE YOU IN CLASS!
HEYA.
GOOD MORNING!
NICE... I HAD ONE CON-VERSATION WITH A CLASSMATE. THAT SHOULD DO IT FOR TODAY'S QUOTA!

FAIL 41: I'M NOT POPULAR, SO I'LL USE A POINT SYSTEM.

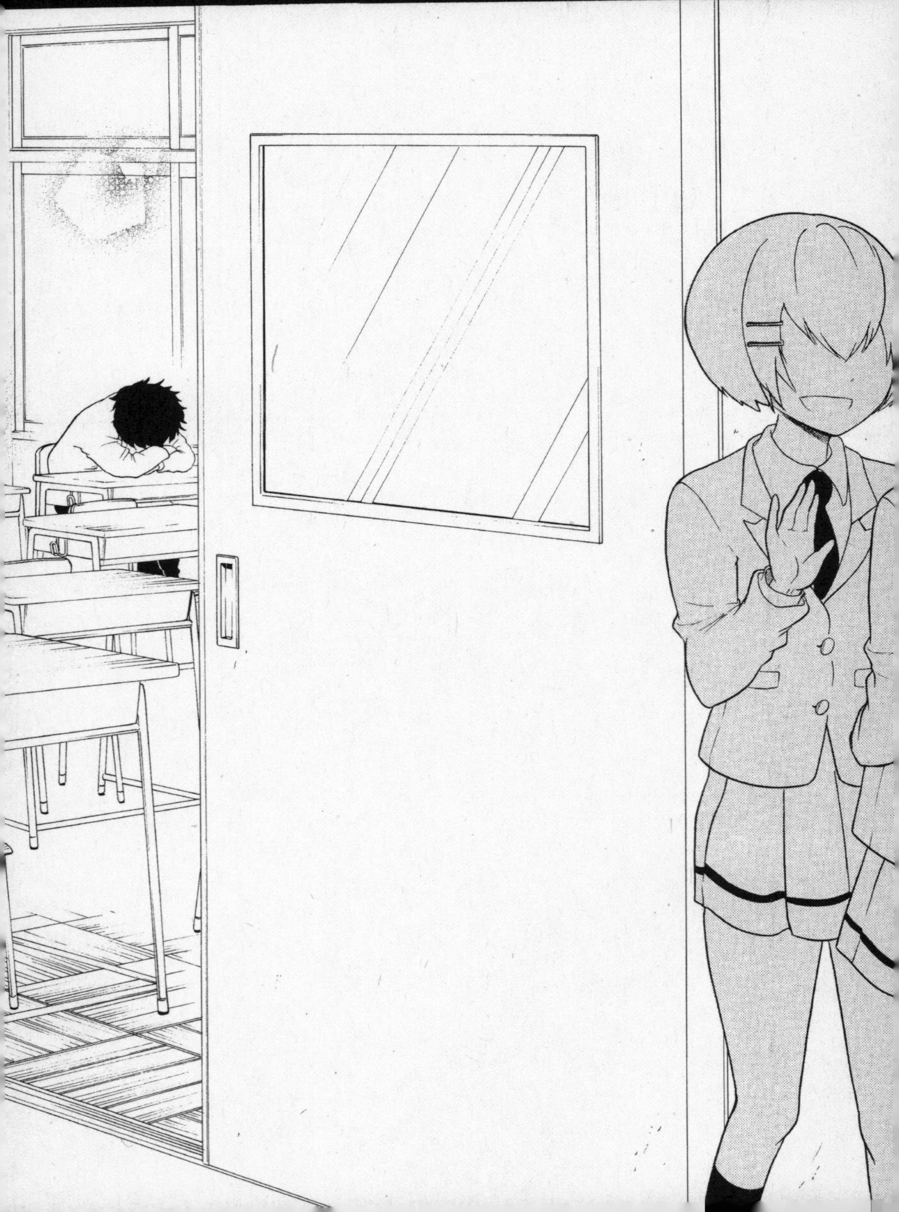

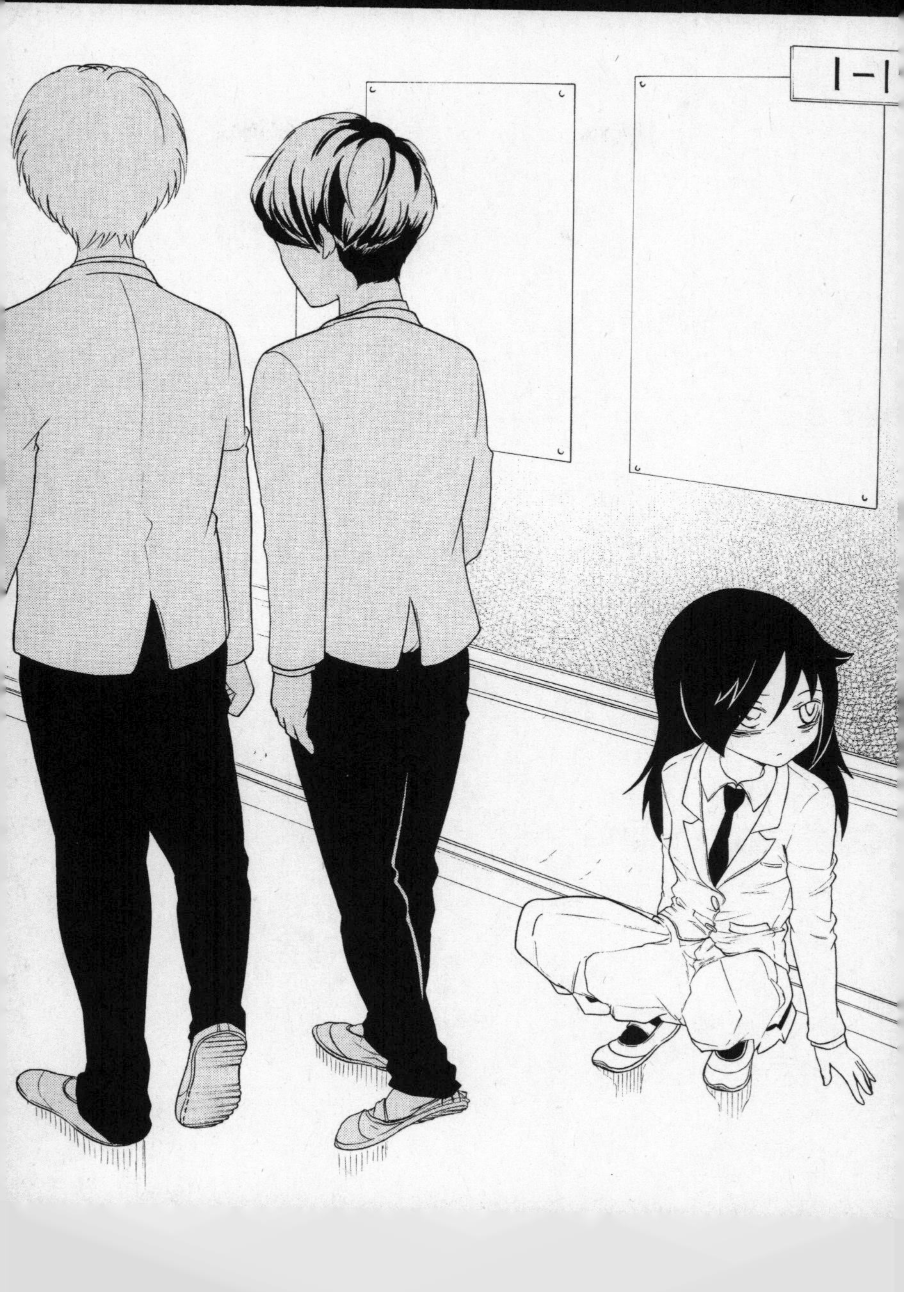
1-1

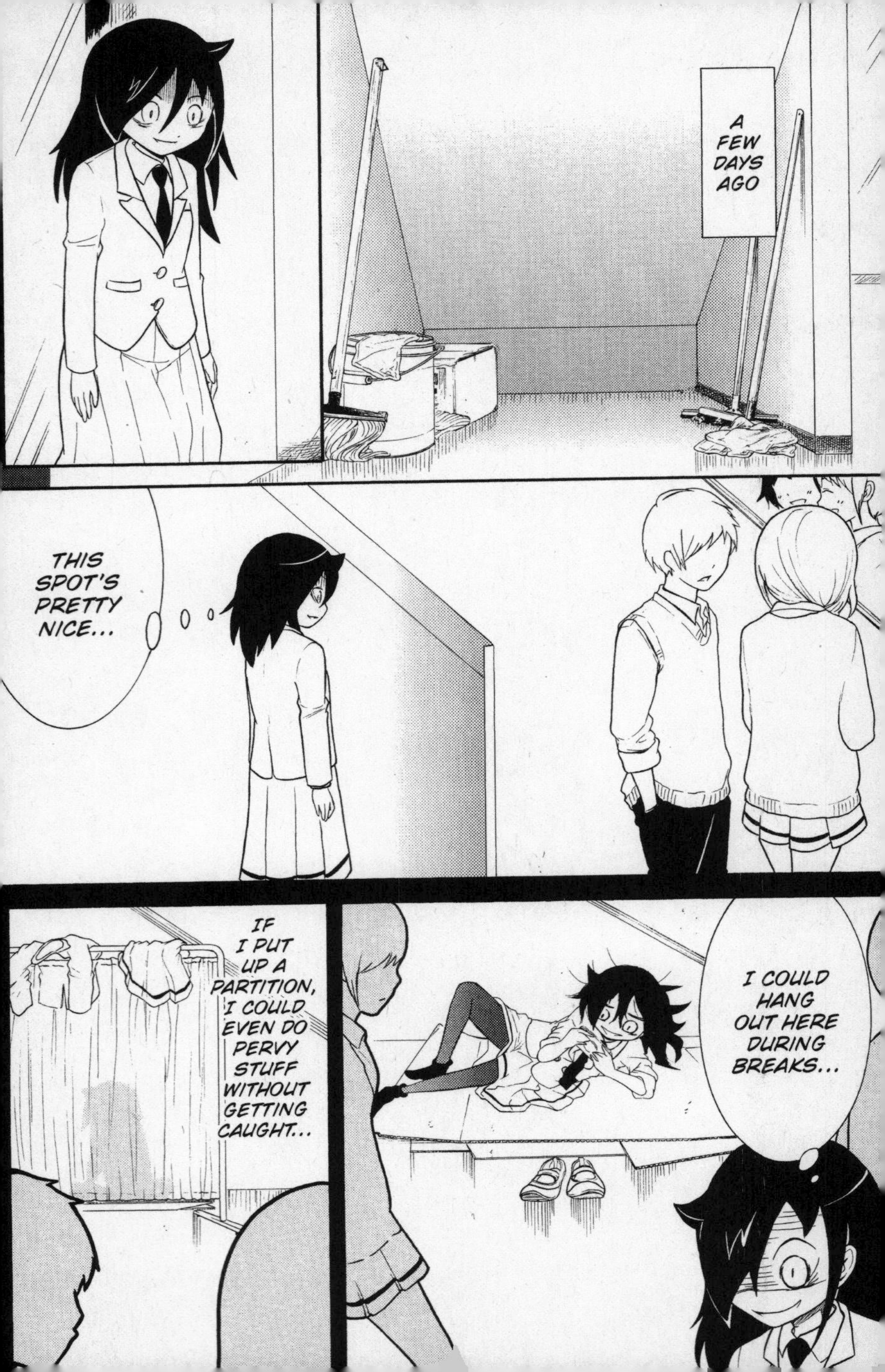
A FEW DAYS AGO
THIS SPOT'S PRETTY NICE...
I COULD HANG OUT HERE DURING BREAKS...
IF I PUT UP A PARTITION, I COULD EVEN DO PERVY STUFF WITHOUT GETTING CAUGHT...

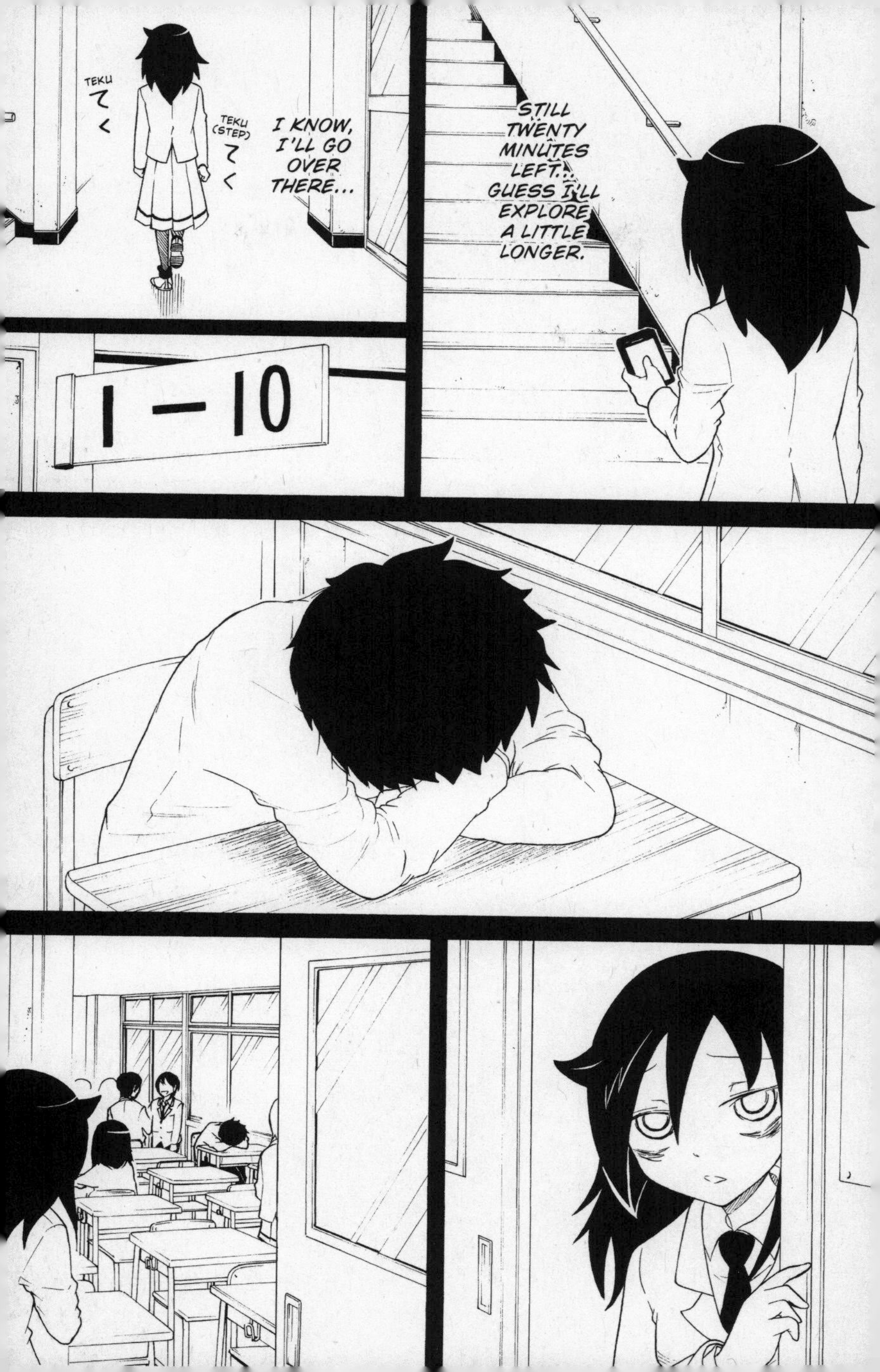
STILL TWENTY MINUTES LEFT... GUESS I'LL EXPLORE A LITTLE LONGER.
I KNOW, I'LL GO OVER THERE...
TEKU (STEP) てく
TEKU てく
1－10

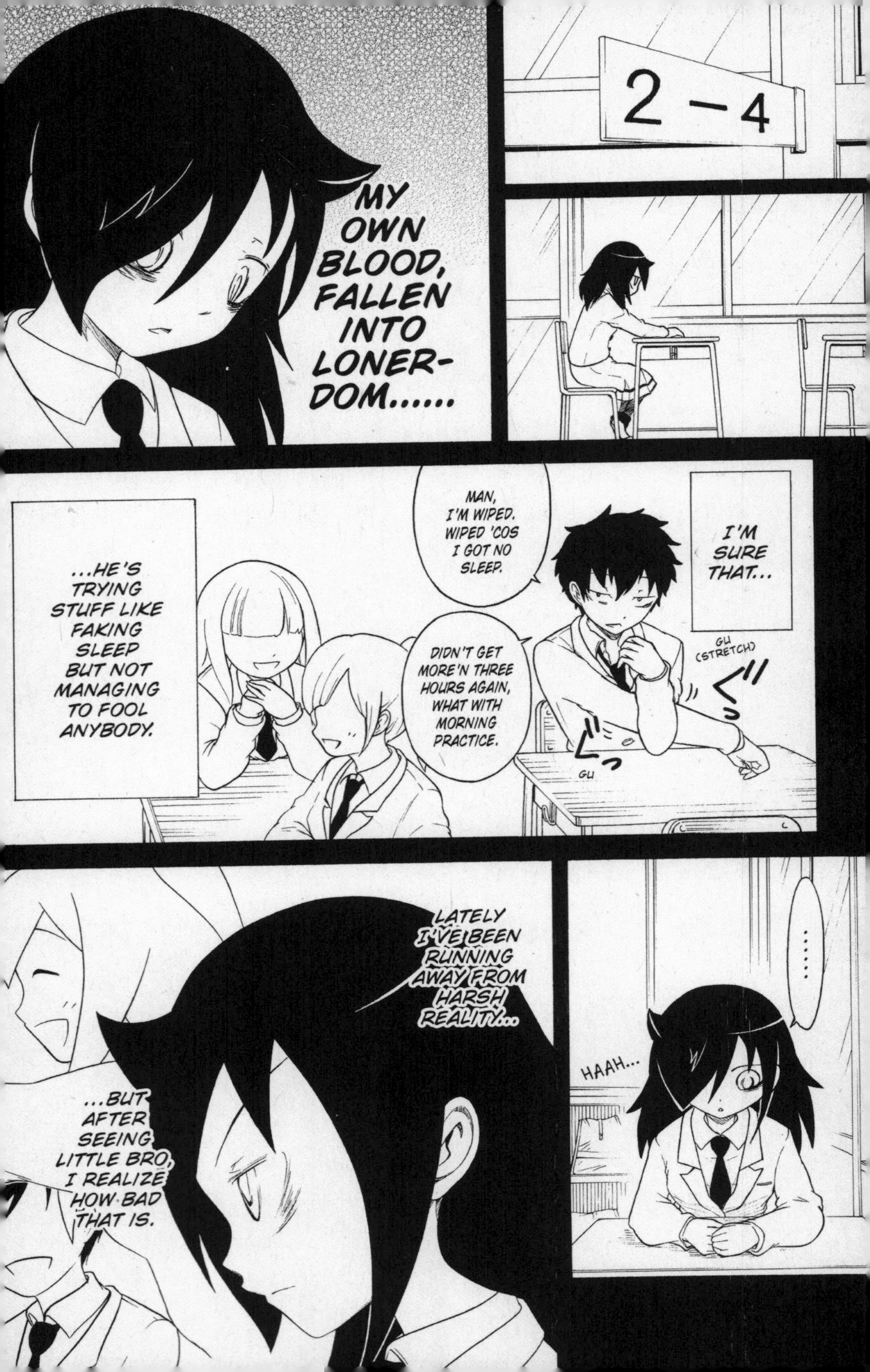
2-4
MY OWN BLOOD, FALLEN INTO LONER-DOM......
I'M SURE THAT...
GU (STRETCH)
MAN, I'M WIPED. WIPED 'COS I GOT NO SLEEP.
DIDN'T GET MORE'N THREE HOURS AGAIN, WHAT WITH MORNING PRACTICE.
GU
...HE'S TRYING STUFF LIKE FAKING SLEEP BUT NOT MANAGING TO FOOL ANYBODY.
......
HAAH...
LATELY I'VE BEEN RUNNING AWAY FROM HARSH REALITY...
...BUT AFTER SEEING LITTLE BRO, I REALIZE HOW BAD THAT IS.

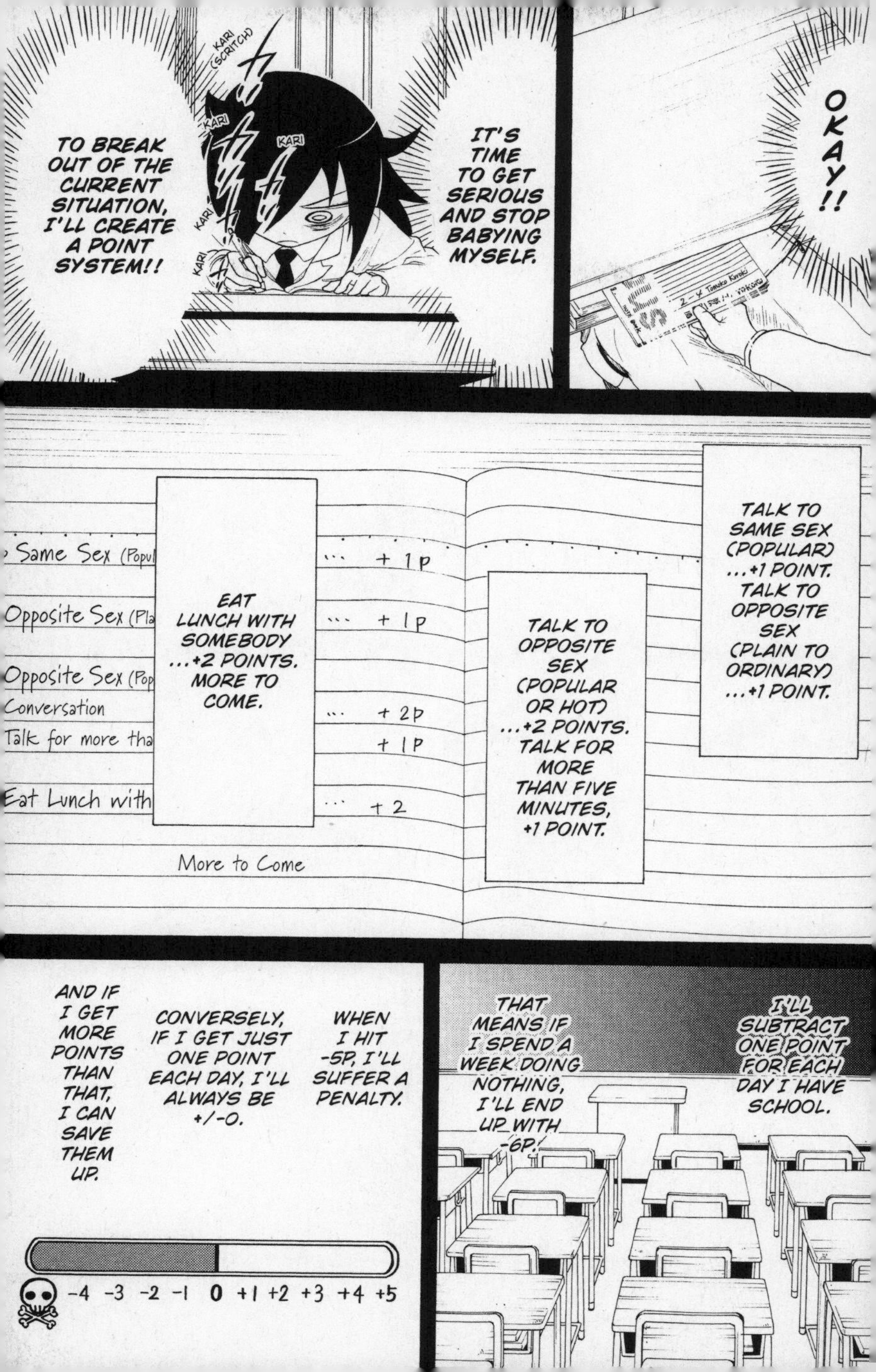

TO BREAK OUT OF THE CURRENT SITUATION, I'LL CREATE A POINT SYSTEM!!

IT'S TIME TO GET SERIOUS AND STOP BABYING MYSELF.

OKAY!!

KARI (SCRITCH)
KARI
KARI

Same Sex (Popul...	...	+ 1 P
Opposite Sex (Pla...	...	+ 1 P
Opposite Sex (Pop...		
Conversation	...	+ 2 P
Talk for more tha...		+ 1 P
Eat Lunch with...	...	+ 2

More to Come

EAT LUNCH WITH SOMEBODY ...+2 POINTS. MORE TO COME.

TALK TO OPPOSITE SEX (POPULAR OR HOT) ...+2 POINTS. TALK FOR MORE THAN FIVE MINUTES, +1 POINT.

TALK TO SAME SEX (POPULAR) ...+1 POINT. TALK TO OPPOSITE SEX (PLAIN TO ORDINARY) ...+1 POINT.

AND IF I GET MORE POINTS THAN THAT, I CAN SAVE THEM UP.

CONVERSELY, IF I GET JUST ONE POINT EACH DAY, I'LL ALWAYS BE +/-0.

WHEN I HIT -5P, I'LL SUFFER A PENALTY.

THAT MEANS IF I SPEND A WEEK DOING NOTHING, I'LL END UP WITH -6P!

I'LL SUBTRACT ONE POINT FOR EACH DAY I HAVE SCHOOL.

-4 -3 -2 -1 0 +1 +2 +3 +4 +5

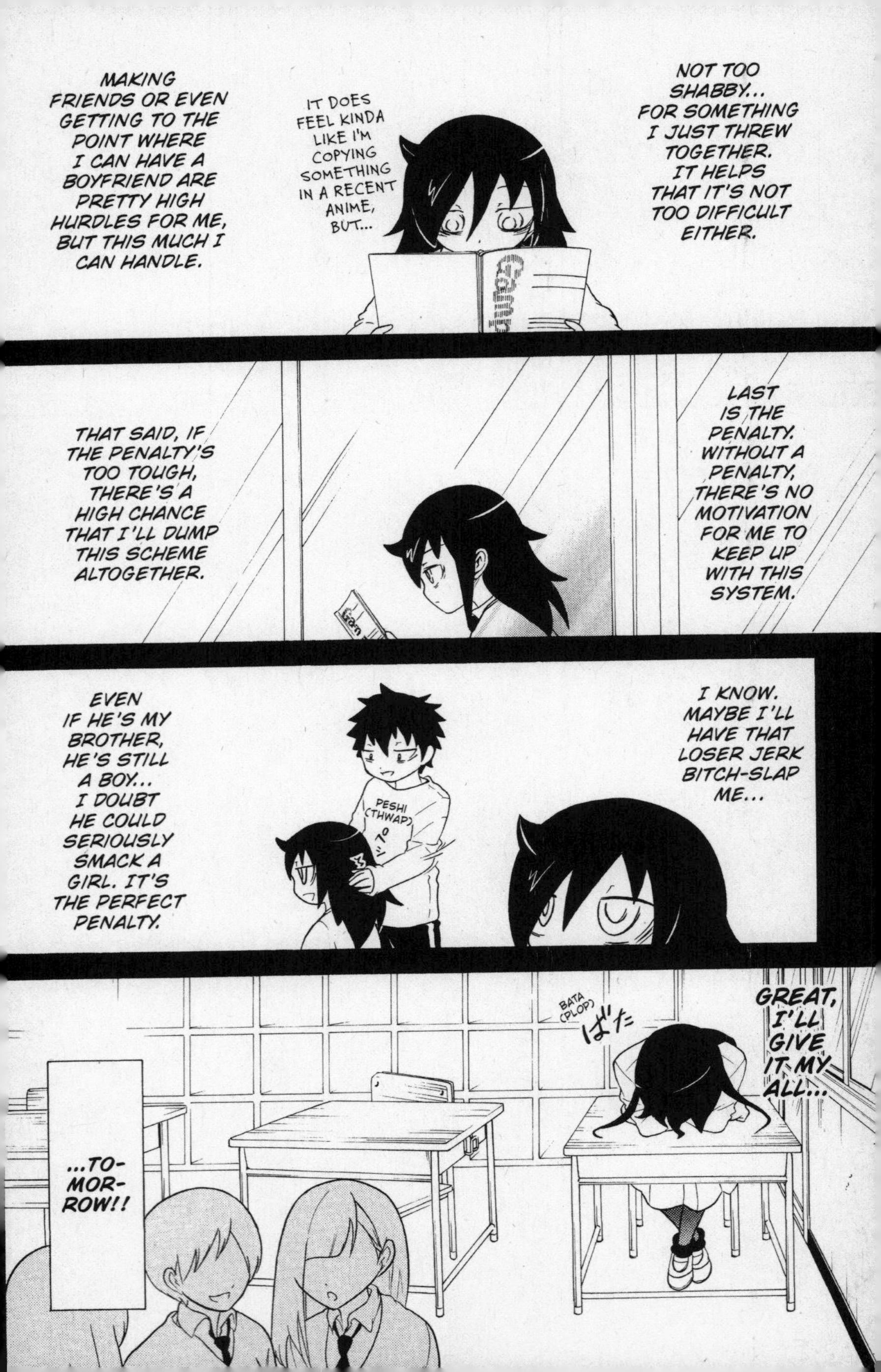
NOT TOO SHABBY... FOR SOMETHING I JUST THREW TOGETHER. IT HELPS THAT IT'S NOT TOO DIFFICULT EITHER.
IT DOES FEEL KINDA LIKE I'M COPYING SOMETHING IN A RECENT ANIME, BUT...
MAKING FRIENDS OR EVEN GETTING TO THE POINT WHERE I CAN HAVE A BOYFRIEND ARE PRETTY HIGH HURDLES FOR ME, BUT THIS MUCH I CAN HANDLE.
LAST IS THE PENALTY. WITHOUT A PENALTY, THERE'S NO MOTIVATION FOR ME TO KEEP UP WITH THIS SYSTEM.
THAT SAID, IF THE PENALTY'S TOO TOUGH, THERE'S A HIGH CHANCE THAT I'LL DUMP THIS SCHEME ALTOGETHER.
I KNOW. MAYBE I'LL HAVE THAT LOSER JERK BITCH-SLAP ME...
PESHI (THWAP)
EVEN IF HE'S MY BROTHER, HE'S STILL A BOY... I DOUBT HE COULD SERIOUSLY SMACK A GIRL. IT'S THE PERFECT PENALTY.
GREAT, I'LL GIVE IT MY ALL...
BATA (PLOP)
ばた
...TO-MORROW!!

		Subtotal	Total
4/17	Did nothing	−1	
			−1
4/18	Did nothing	−1	
			−2
4/19	〃	−1	
			−3
4/20	〃	−1	
			−4
4/22	Talked to Nemoto-san	+1	

...AND SO...

...I'VE REACHED THE PRESENT, BUT...

I DID TRY TO TALK TO PEOPLE!

.........NO, IT'S NOT MY FAULT.

IF I HADN'T TALKED TO HER THIS MORNING, I'D HAVE A PENALTY ALREADY...

BUT NEMOTO, WHO SEEMS LIKE SHE'D TALK TO ME, IS ALWAYS AWAY FROM HER DESK.

AND THE BOYS, DESPITE BEING MEN, ARE ALWAYS IN GROUPS, SO I CAN'T TALK TO THEM EITHER...

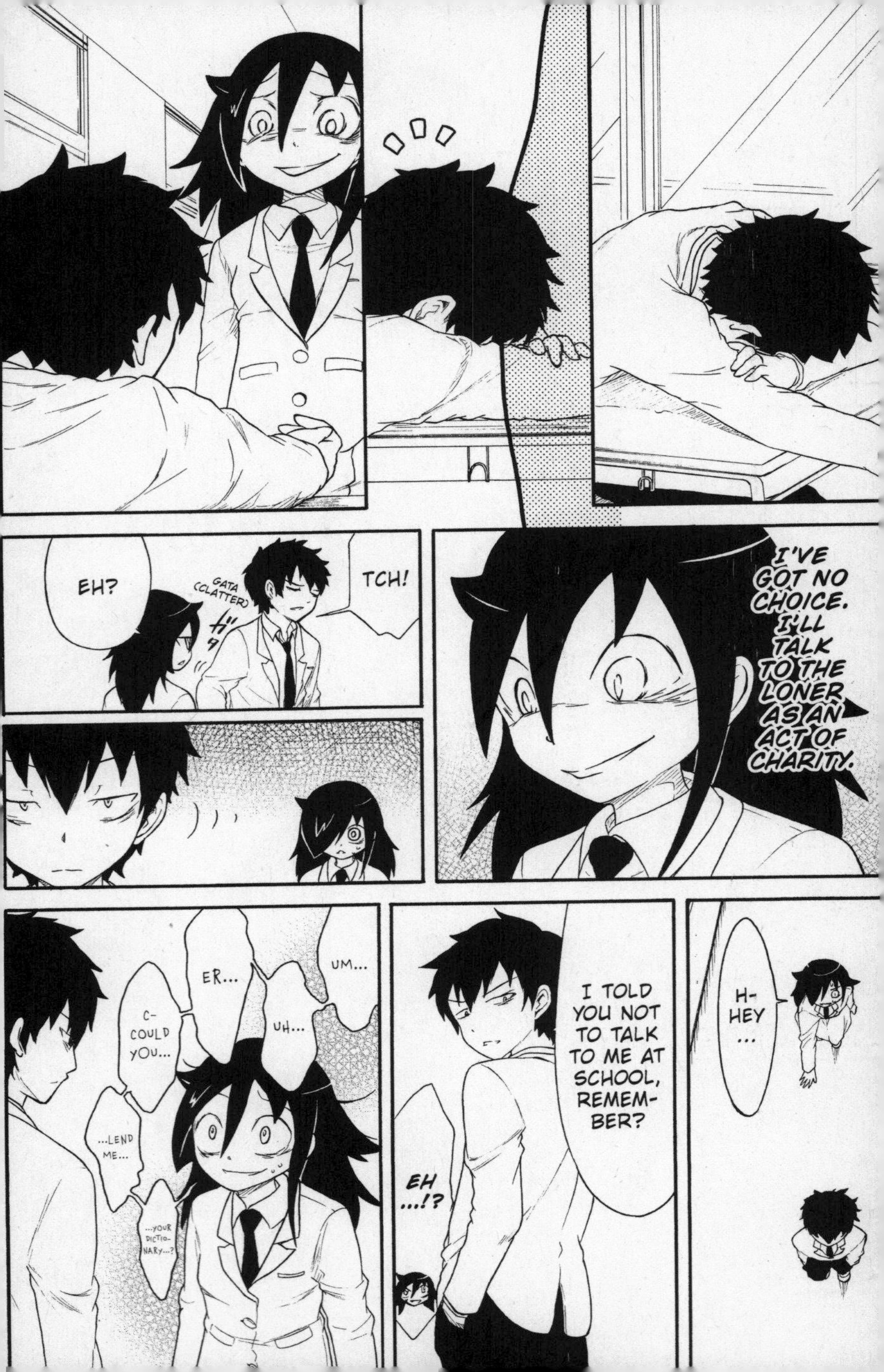
I'VE GOT NO CHOICE. I'LL TALK TO THE LONER AS AN ACT OF CHARITY.
TCH!
GATA (CLATTER)
ガタ
EH?
H-HEY ...
I TOLD YOU NOT TO TALK TO ME AT SCHOOL, REMEMBER?
EH ...!?
UM...
ER...
UH...
C-COULD YOU...
...LEND ME...
...YOUR DICTIONARY...?

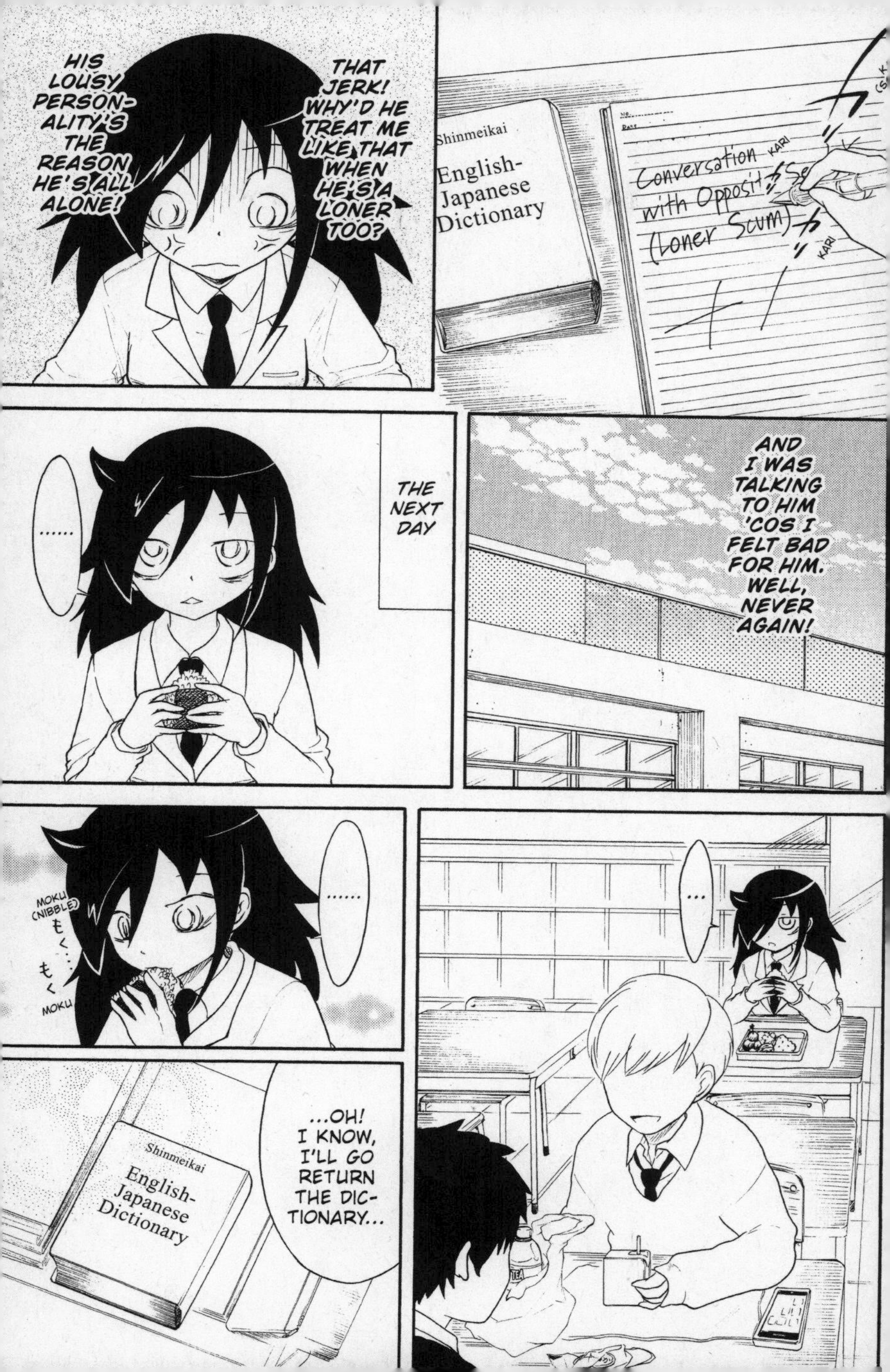

Shinmeikai English-Japanese Dictionary
No.
Date
Conversation with Opposit Se (Loner Scum)
KARI
KARI
THAT JERK! WHY'D HE TREAT ME LIKE THAT WHEN HE'S A LONER TOO?
HIS LOUSY PERSONALITY'S THE REASON HE'S ALL ALONE!
AND I WAS TALKING TO HIM 'COS I FELT BAD FOR HIM. WELL, NEVER AGAIN!
THE NEXT DAY
......
...
TEA
......
MOKU (NIBBLE)
もく…
もく
MOKU
...OH! I KNOW, I'LL GO RETURN THE DICTIONARY...
Shinmeikai English-Japanese Dictionary

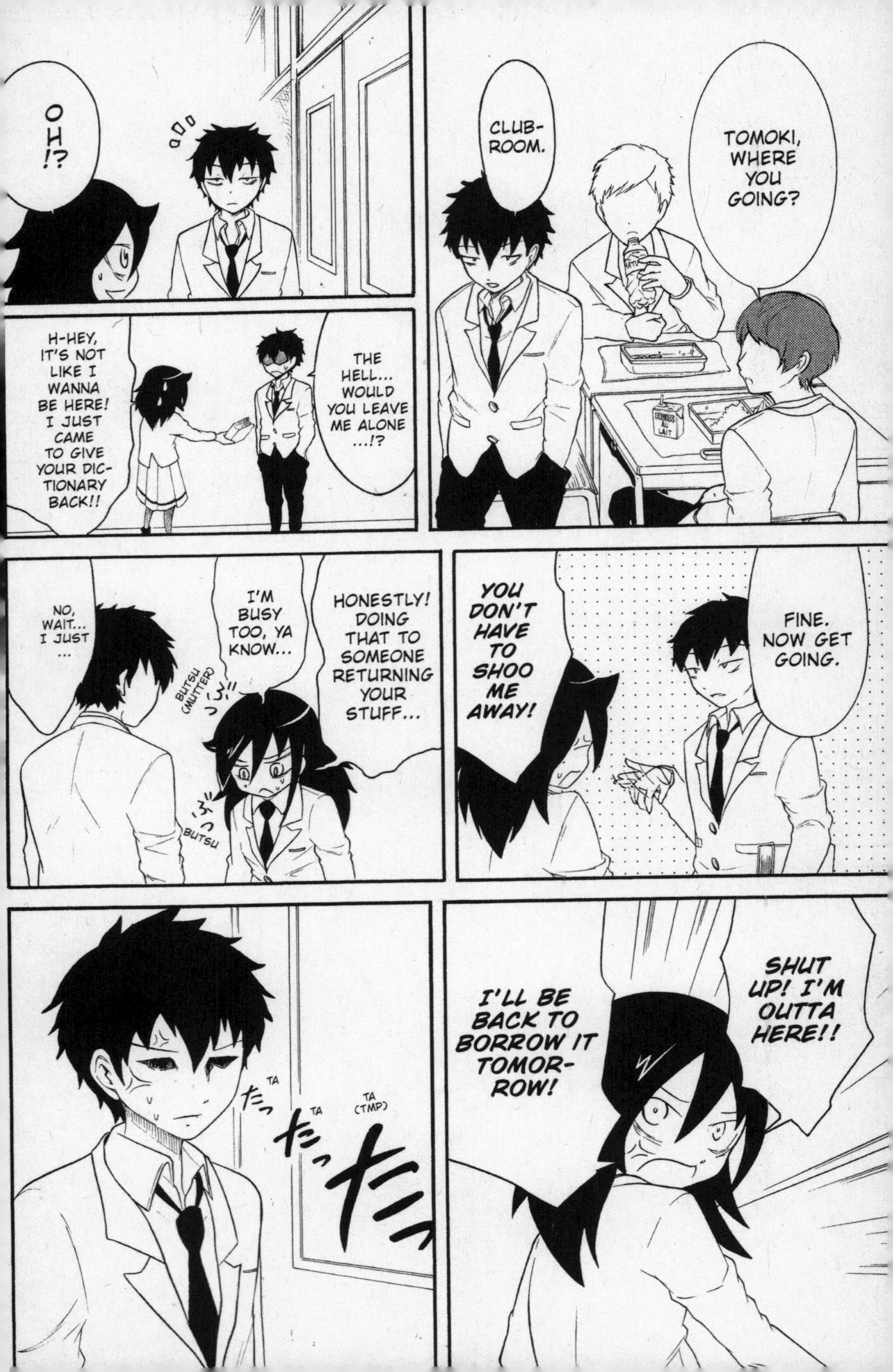
TOMOKI, WHERE YOU GOING?
CLUB-ROOM.
OH!?
THE HELL... WOULD YOU LEAVE ME ALONE ...!?
H-HEY, IT'S NOT LIKE I WANNA BE HERE! I JUST CAME TO GIVE YOUR DICTIONARY BACK!!
FINE. NOW GET GOING.
YOU DON'T HAVE TO SHOO ME AWAY!
HONESTLY! DOING THAT TO SOMEONE RETURNING YOUR STUFF...
I'M BUSY TOO, YA KNOW...
BUTSU (MUTTER)
BUTSU
NO, WAIT... I JUST ...
SHUT UP! I'M OUTTA HERE!!
I'LL BE BACK TO BORROW IT TOMOR-ROW!
TA
TA
TA (TMP)

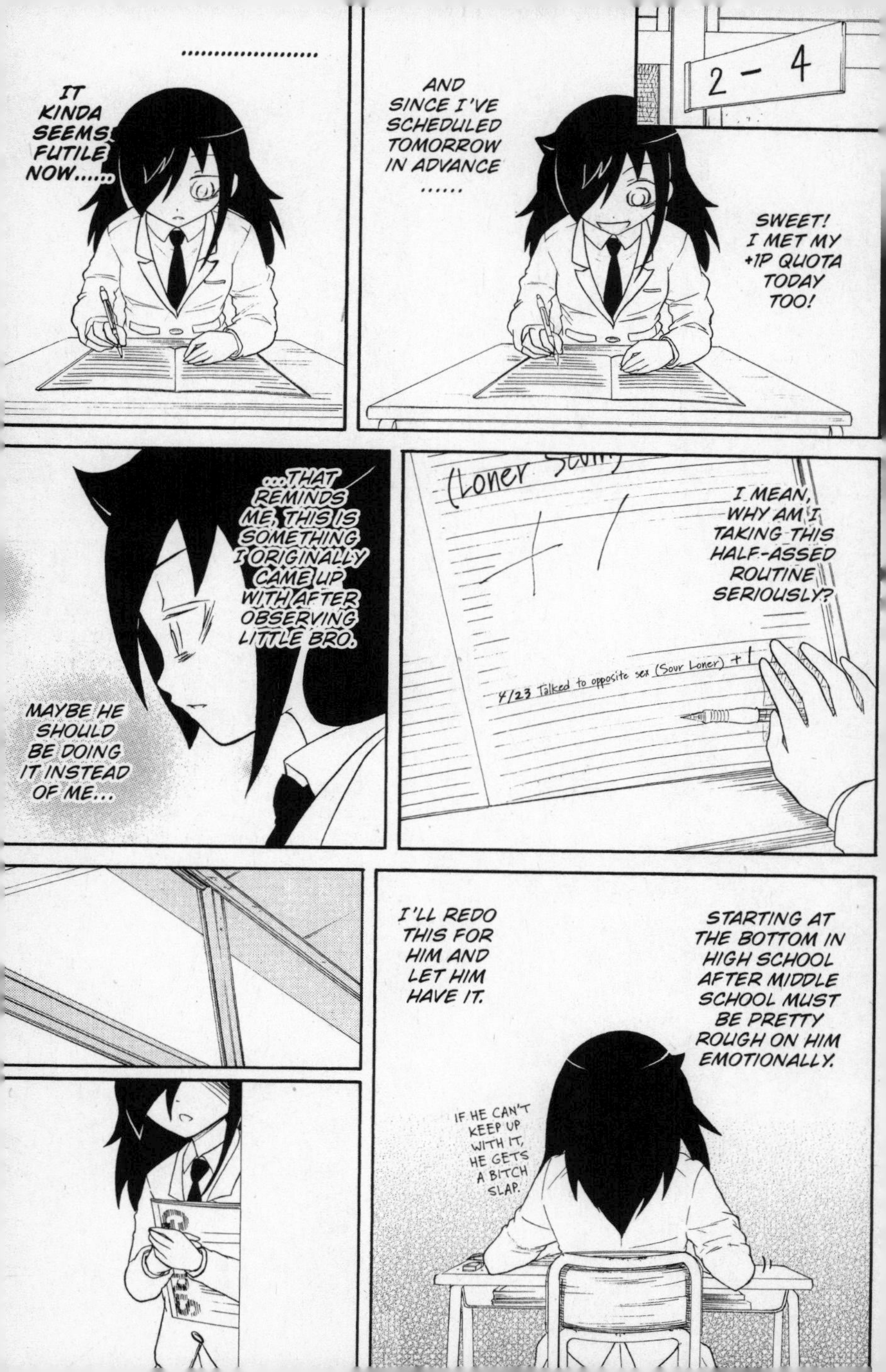
2 - 4
SWEET! I MET MY +1P QUOTA TODAY TOO!
AND SINCE I'VE SCHEDULED TOMORROW IN ADVANCE ......
....
IT KINDA SEEMS FUTILE NOW......
(Loner Scum)
I MEAN, WHY AM I TAKING THIS HALF-ASSED ROUTINE SERIOUSLY?
4/23 Talked to opposite sex (Sour Loner) +1
...THAT REMINDS ME, THIS IS SOMETHING I ORIGINALLY CAME UP WITH AFTER OBSERVING LITTLE BRO.
MAYBE HE SHOULD BE DOING IT INSTEAD OF ME...
STARTING AT THE BOTTOM IN HIGH SCHOOL AFTER MIDDLE SCHOOL MUST BE PRETTY ROUGH ON HIM EMOTIONALLY.
I'LL REDO THIS FOR HIM AND LET HIM HAVE IT.
IF HE CAN'T KEEP UP WITH IT, HE GETS A BITCH SLAP.

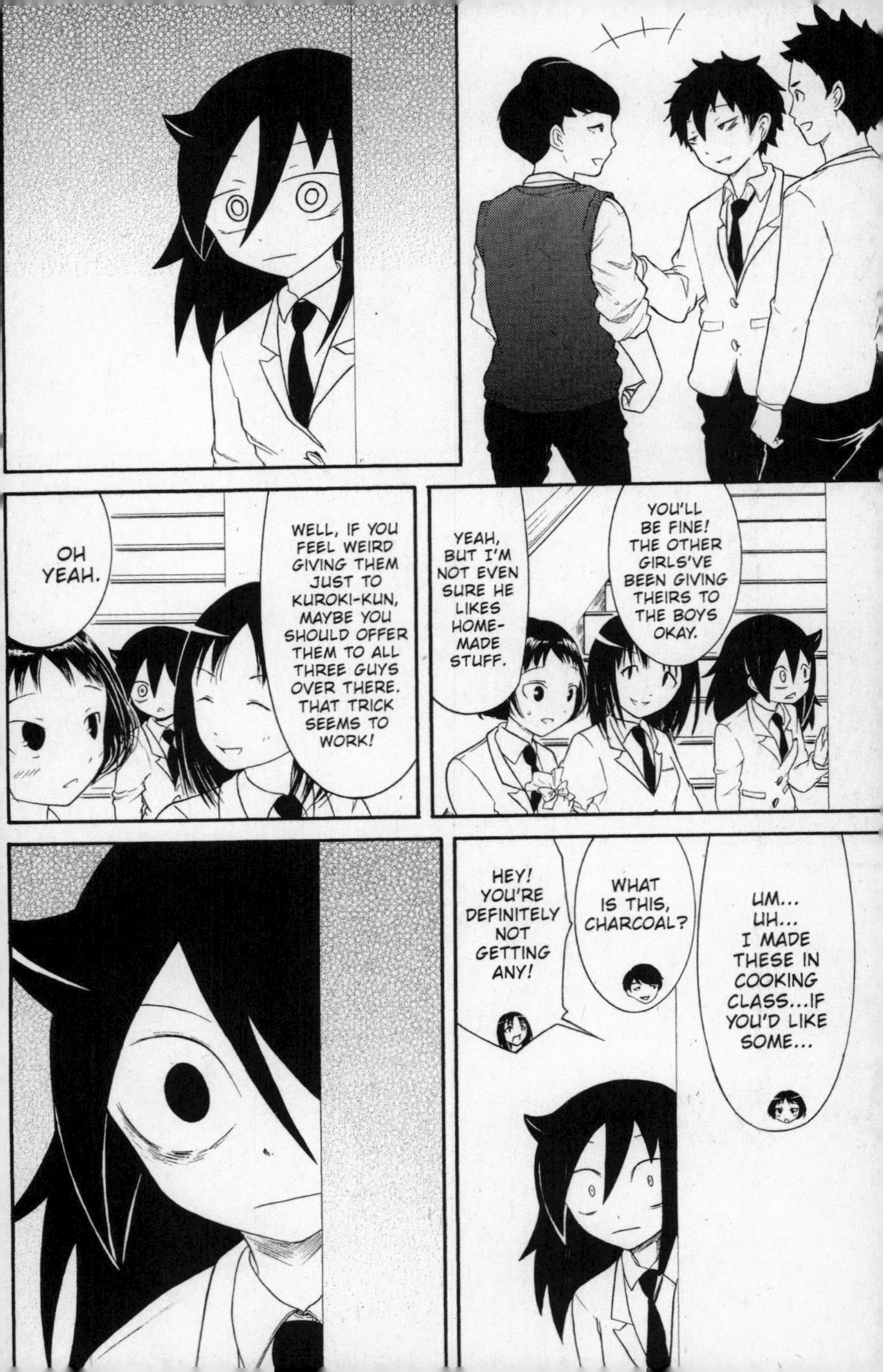
YOU'LL BE FINE! THE OTHER GIRLS'VE BEEN GIVING THEIRS TO THE BOYS OKAY.
YEAH, BUT I'M NOT EVEN SURE HE LIKES HOME-MADE STUFF.
WELL, IF YOU FEEL WEIRD GIVING THEM JUST TO KUROKI-KUN, MAYBE YOU SHOULD OFFER THEM TO ALL THREE GUYS OVER THERE. THAT TRICK SEEMS TO WORK!
OH YEAH.
UM... UH... I MADE THESE IN COOKING CLASS...IF YOU'D LIKE SOME...
WHAT IS THIS, CHARCOAL?
HEY! YOU'RE DEFINITELY NOT GETTING ANY!

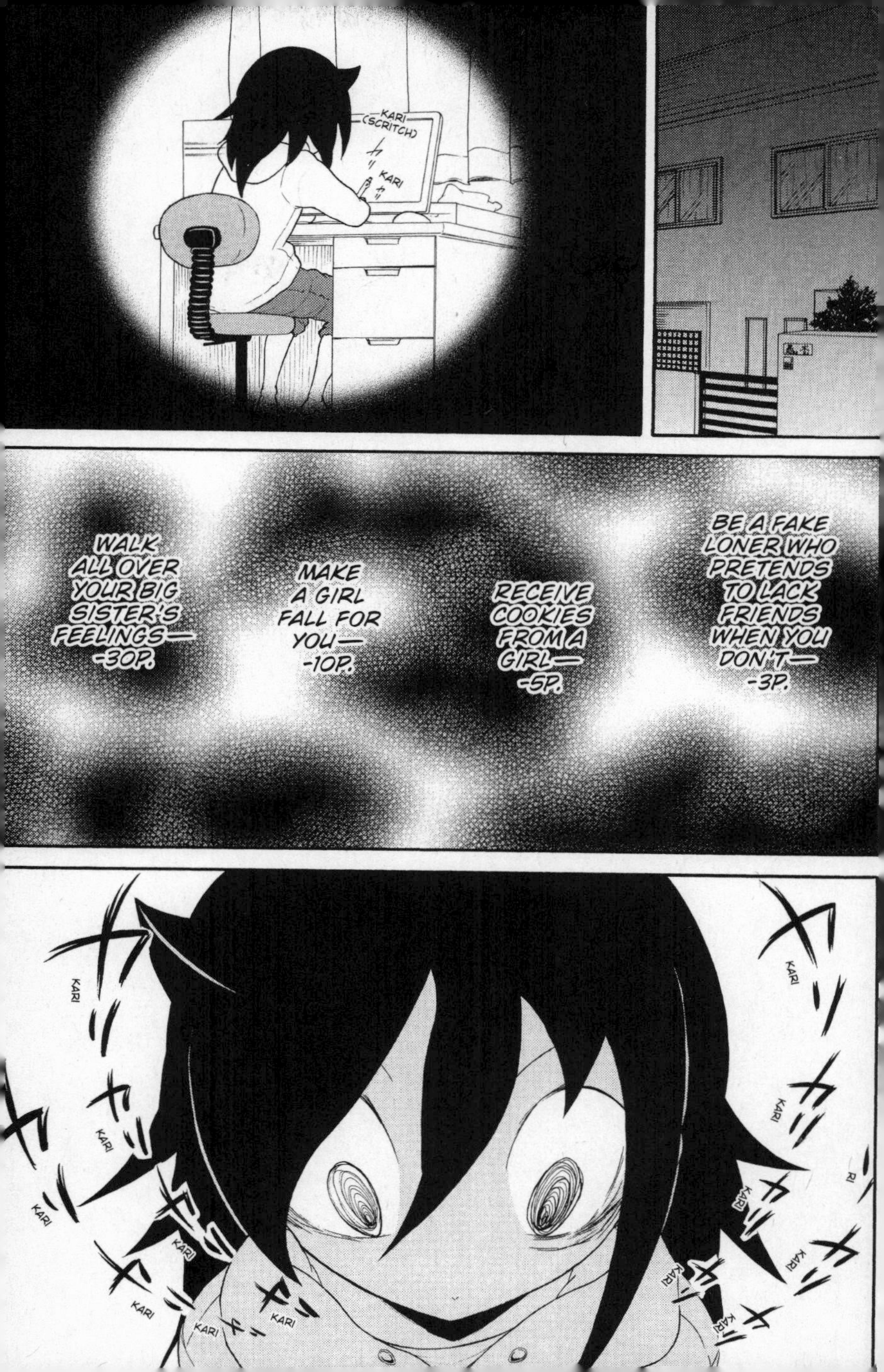
KARI (SCRITCH)
KARI
BE A FAKE LONER WHO PRETENDS TO LACK FRIENDS WHEN YOU DON'T— -3P.
RECEIVE COOKIES FROM A GIRL— -5P.
MAKE A GIRL FALL FOR YOU— -10P.
WALK ALL OVER YOUR BIG SISTER'S FEELINGS— -30P.
KARI
KARI
KARI
KARI
KARI
KARI
KARI
KARI
KARI
KARI
KARI
KARI
KARI

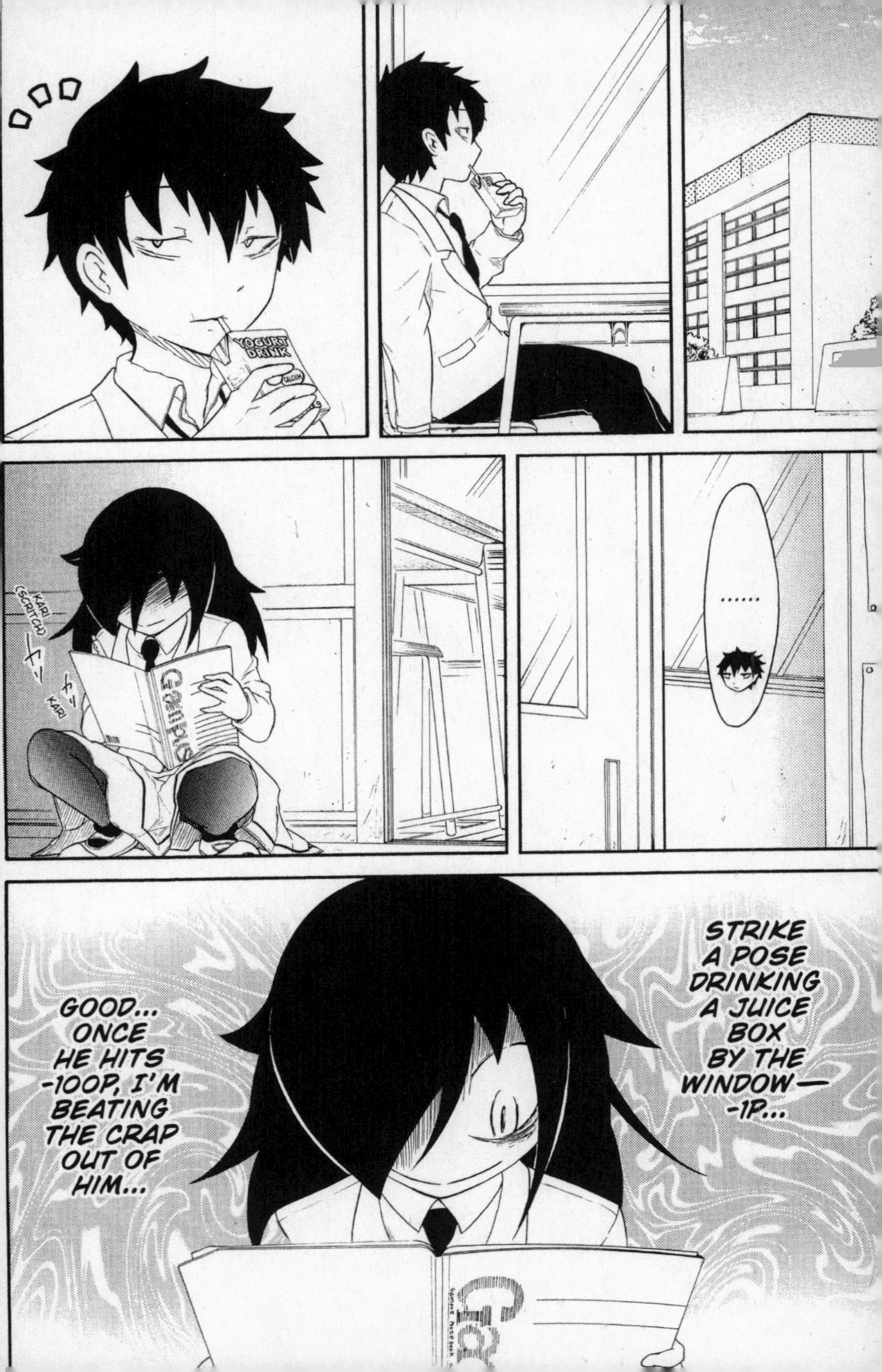

YOGURT DRINK
CALCIUM
......
KARI (SCRITCH)
カリ
カリ KARI
STRIKE A POSE DRINKING A JUICE BOX BY THE WINDOW— -1P...
GOOD... ONCE HE HITS -100P, I'M BEATING THE CRAP OUT OF HIM...

No Matter How I Look at It, It's You Guys' Fault I'm Not Popular!

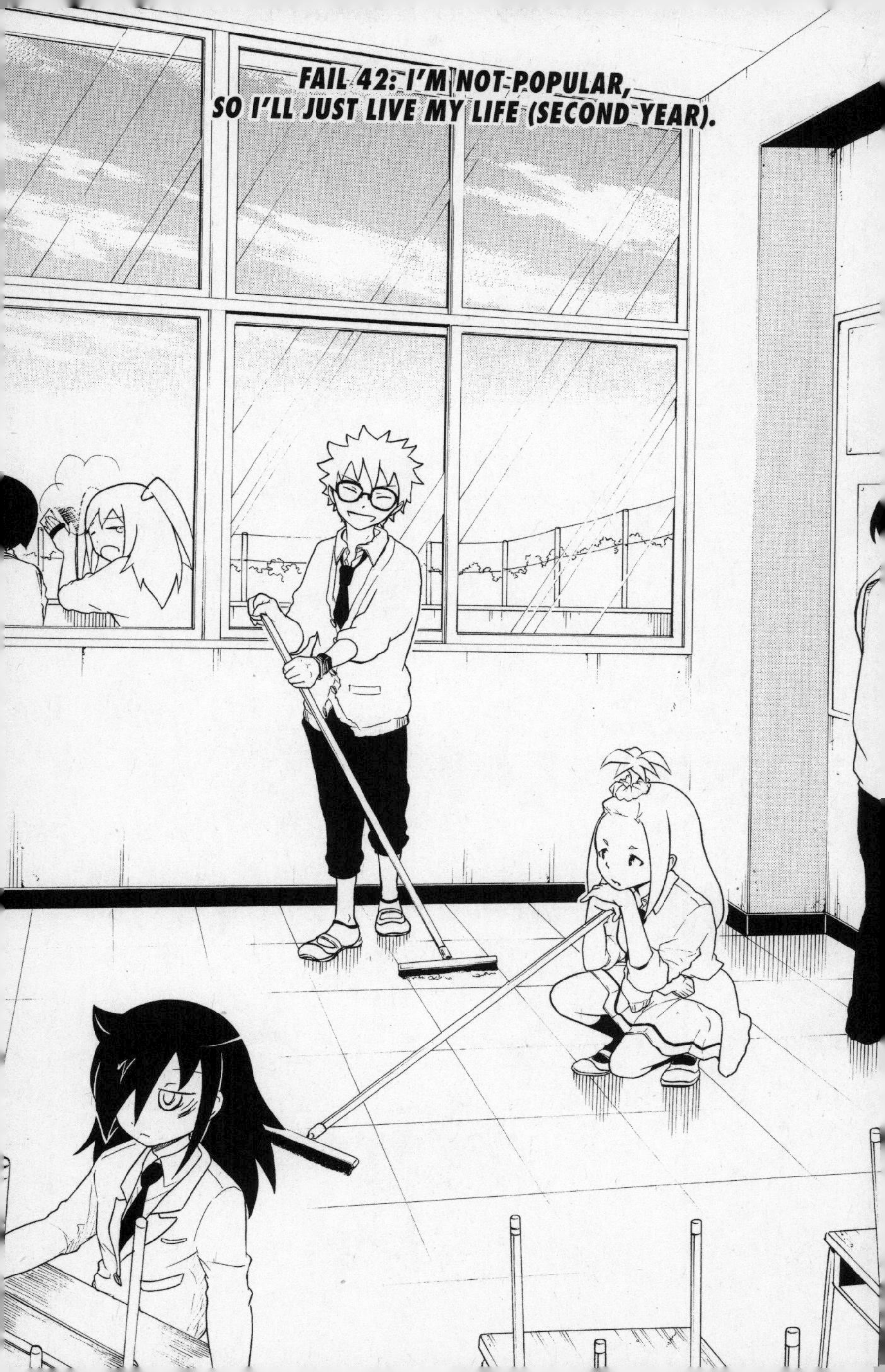
FAIL 42: I'M NOT POPULAR, SO I'LL JUST LIVE MY LIFE (SECOND YEAR).

GREETING EXERCISES

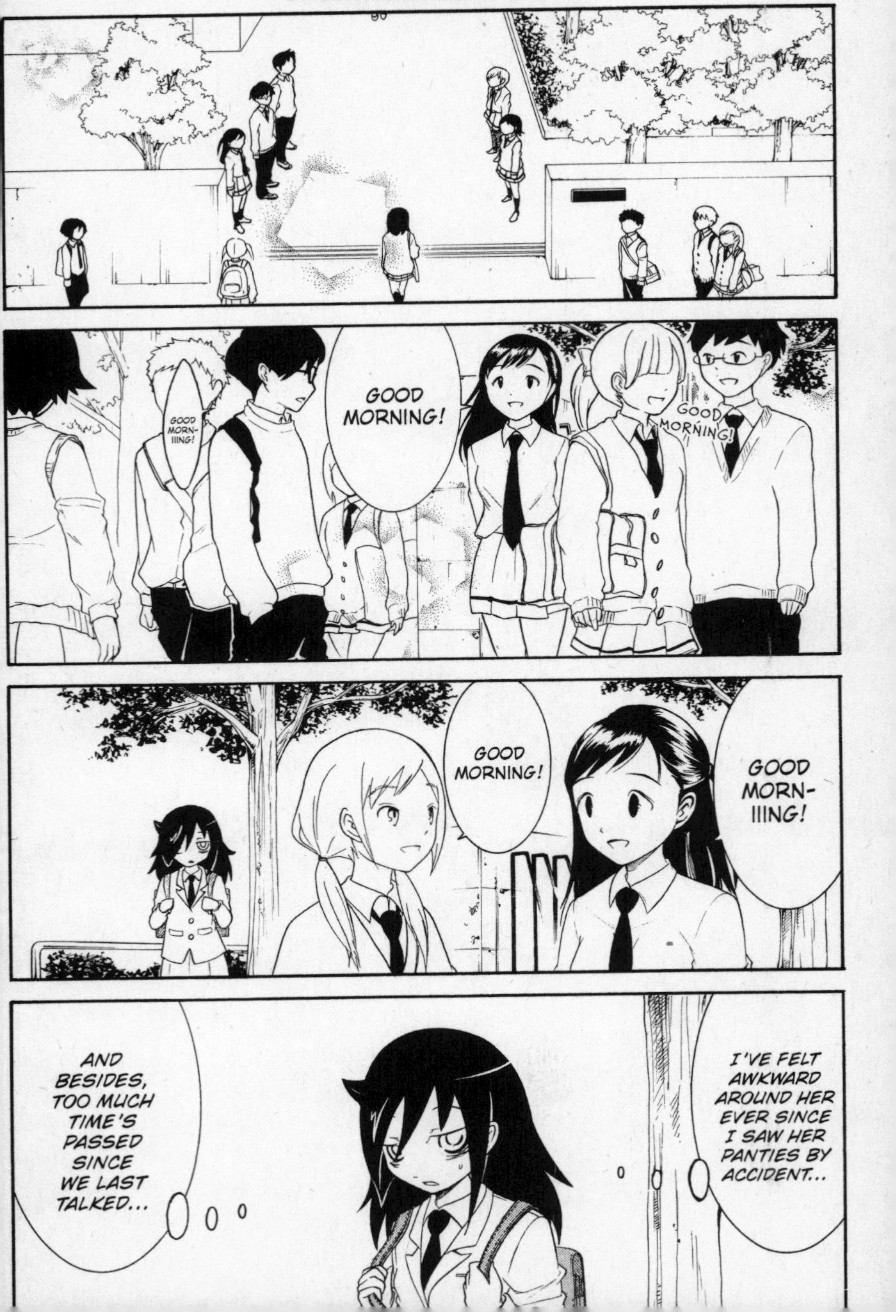
GOOD MORNING!
GOOD MORNING!
GOOD MORN-IIING!
GOOD MORN-IIING!
GOOD MORNING!
I'VE FELT AWKWARD AROUND HER EVER SINCE I SAW HER PANTIES BY ACCIDENT...
AND BESIDES, TOO MUCH TIME'S PASSED SINCE WE LAST TALKED...

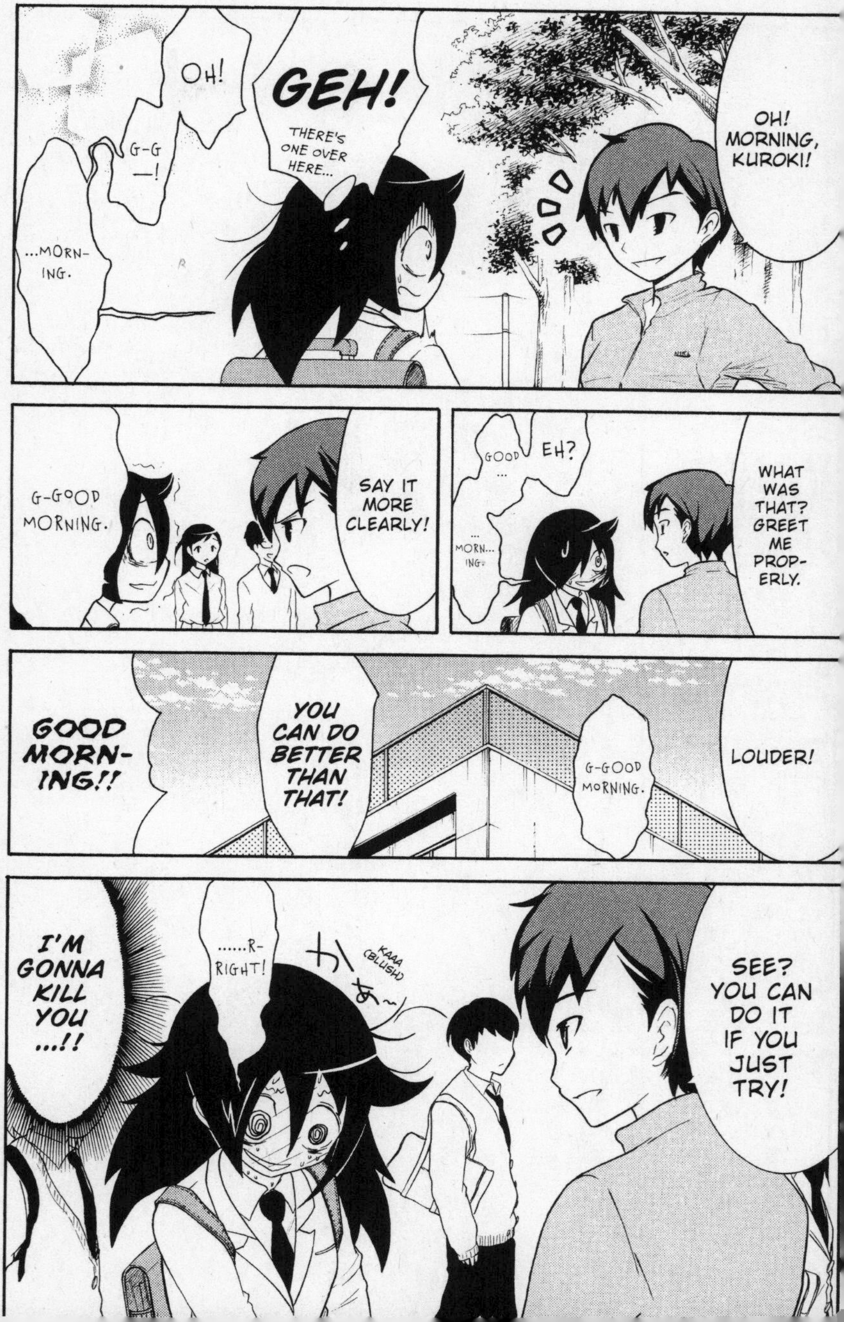
OH! MORNING, KUROKI!
GEH!
THERE'S ONE OVER HERE...
OH!
G-G —!
...MORN-ING.
WHAT WAS THAT? GREET ME PROPERLY.
EH?
GOOD ...
... MORN... ING.
SAY IT MORE CLEARLY!
G-GOOD MORNING.
LOUDER!
G-GOOD MORNING.
YOU CAN DO BETTER THAN THAT!
GOOD MORN-ING!!
SEE? YOU CAN DO IT IF YOU JUST TRY!
KAAA (BLUSH)
......R-RIGHT!
I'M GONNA KILL YOU ...!!

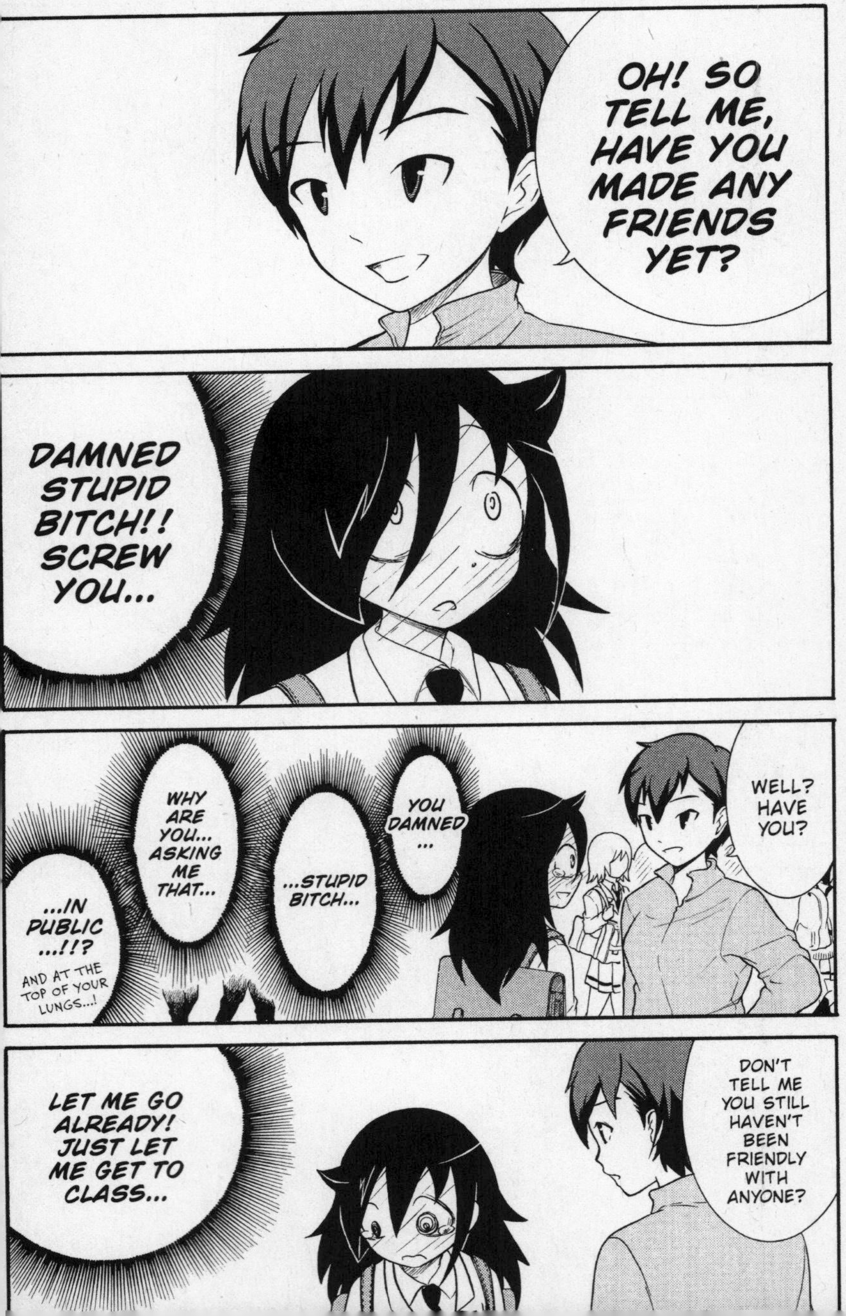
OH! SO TELL ME, HAVE YOU MADE ANY FRIENDS YET?
DAMNED STUPID BITCH!! SCREW YOU...
WELL? HAVE YOU?
YOU DAMNED ...
...STUPID BITCH...
WHY ARE YOU... ASKING ME THAT...
...IN PUBLIC ...!!?
AND AT THE TOP OF YOUR LUNGS...!
DON'T TELL ME YOU STILL HAVEN'T BEEN FRIENDLY WITH ANYONE?
LET ME GO ALREADY! JUST LET ME GET TO CLASS...

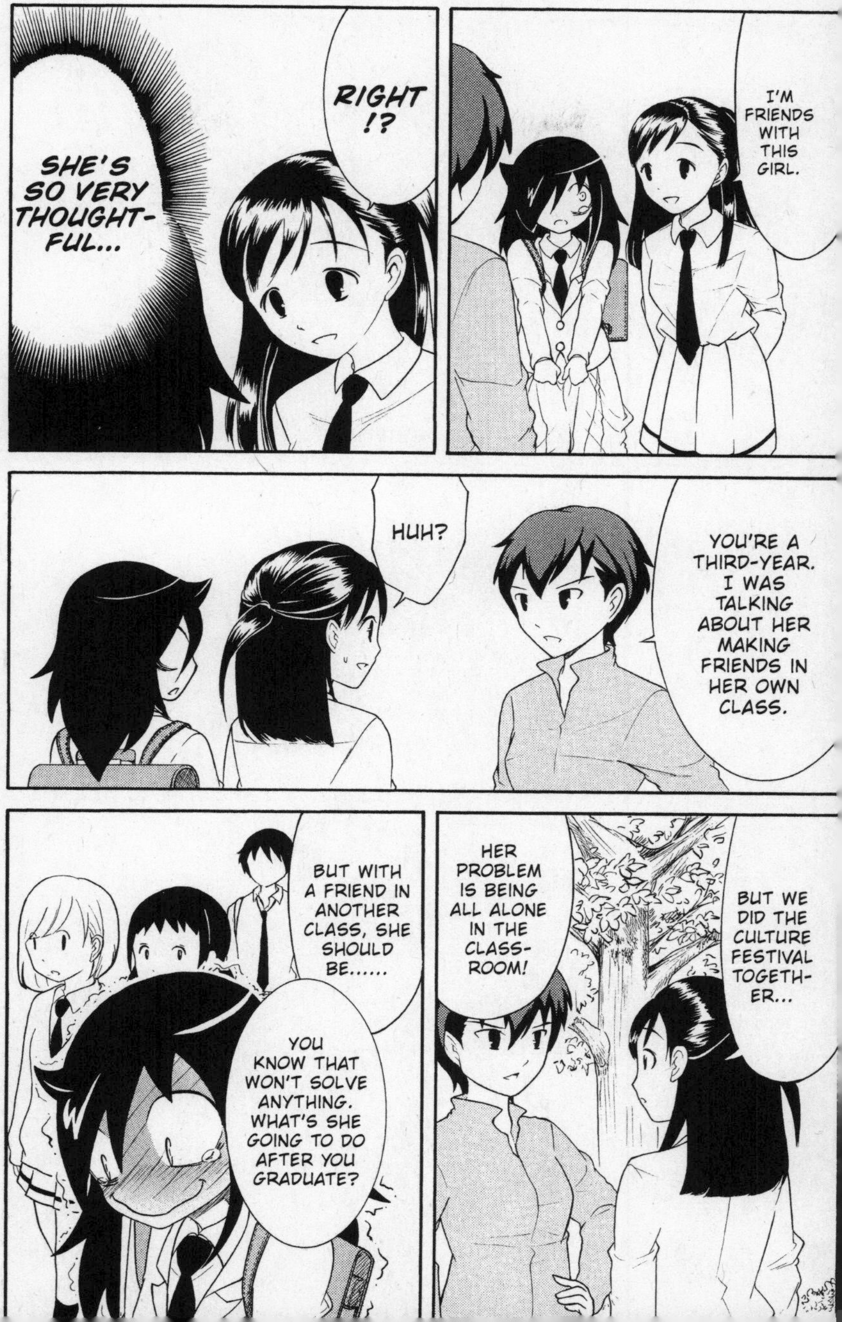
I'M FRIENDS WITH THIS GIRL.
RIGHT!?
SHE'S SO VERY THOUGHTFUL...
YOU'RE A THIRD-YEAR. I WAS TALKING ABOUT HER MAKING FRIENDS IN HER OWN CLASS.
HUH?
BUT WE DID THE CULTURE FESTIVAL TOGETHER...
HER PROBLEM IS BEING ALL ALONE IN THE CLASSROOM!
BUT WITH A FRIEND IN ANOTHER CLASS, SHE SHOULD BE......
YOU KNOW THAT WON'T SOLVE ANYTHING. WHAT'S SHE GOING TO DO AFTER YOU GRADUATE?

PERSONAL GROWTH

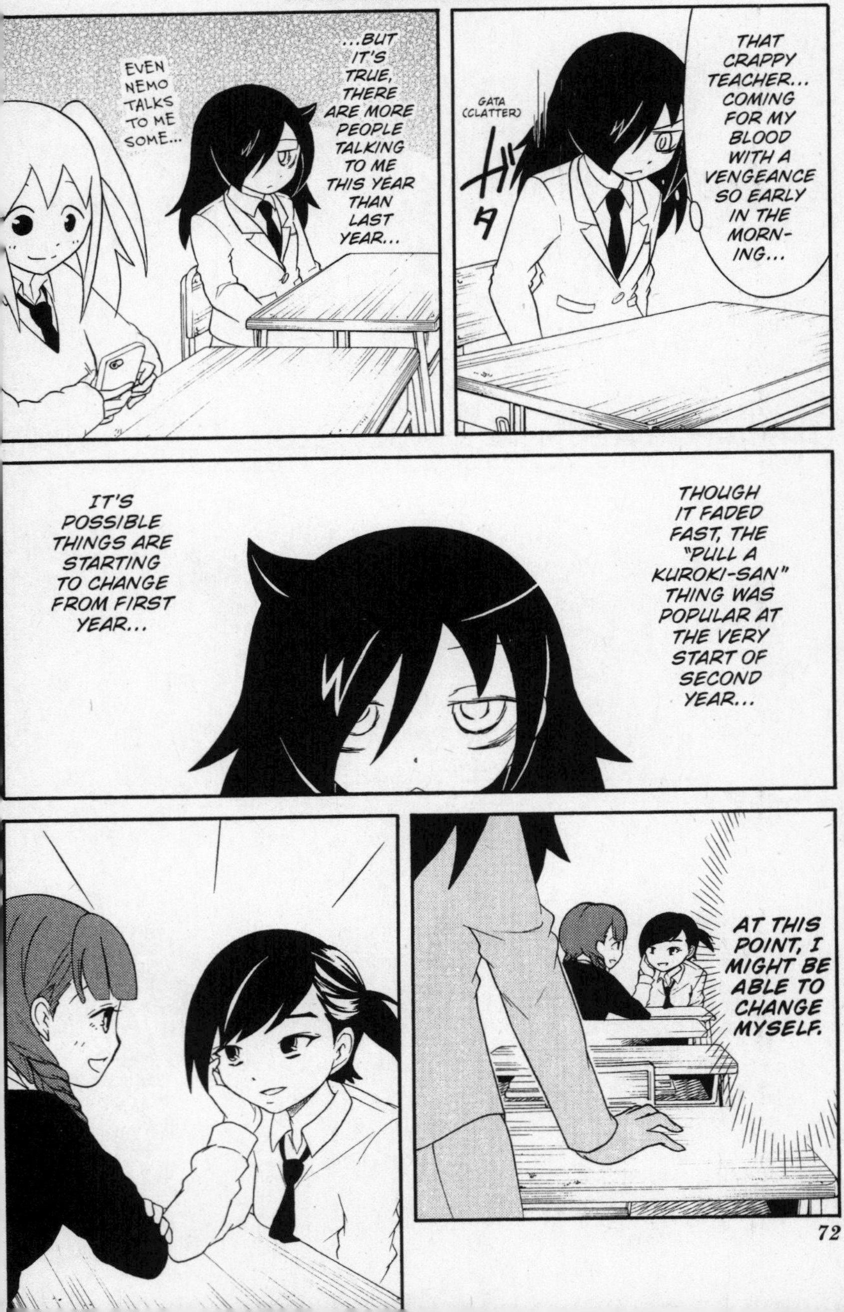
GATA (CLATTER)
THAT CRAPPY TEACHER... COMING FOR MY BLOOD WITH A VENGEANCE SO EARLY IN THE MORN-ING...
EVEN NEMO TALKS TO ME SOME...
...BUT IT'S TRUE, THERE ARE MORE PEOPLE TALKING TO ME THIS YEAR THAN LAST YEAR...
THOUGH IT FADED FAST, THE "PULL A KUROKI-SAN" THING WAS POPULAR AT THE VERY START OF SECOND YEAR...
IT'S POSSIBLE THINGS ARE STARTING TO CHANGE FROM FIRST YEAR...
AT THIS POINT, I MIGHT BE ABLE TO CHANGE MYSELF.

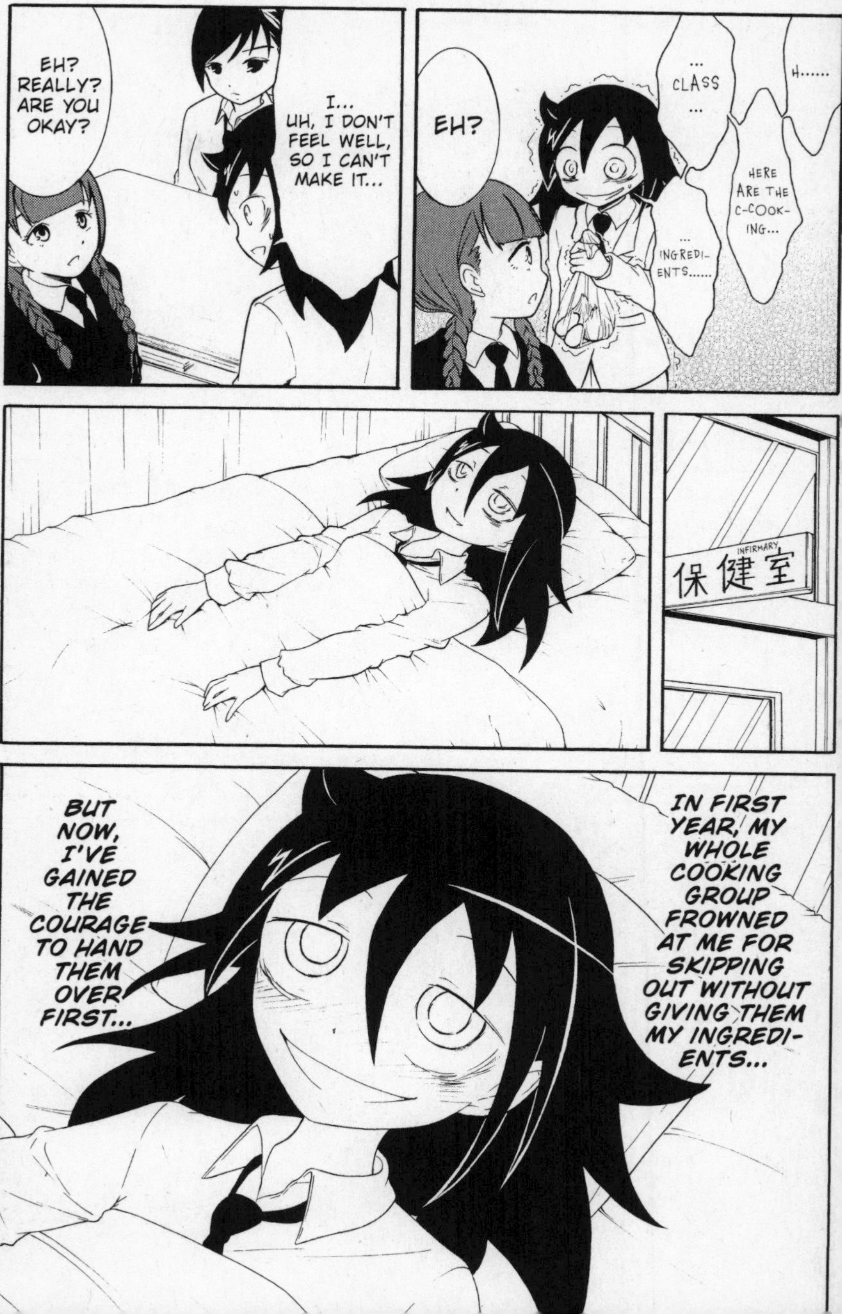
H......
... CLASS ...
HERE ARE THE C-COOK-ING...
... INGREDI-ENTS......
EH?
I... UH, I DON'T FEEL WELL, SO I CAN'T MAKE IT...
EH? REALLY? ARE YOU OKAY?
INFIRMARY
保健室
IN FIRST YEAR, MY WHOLE COOKING GROUP FROWNED AT ME FOR SKIPPING OUT WITHOUT GIVING THEM MY INGREDI-ENTS...
BUT NOW, I'VE GAINED THE COURAGE TO HAND THEM OVER FIRST...

SILHOUETTE

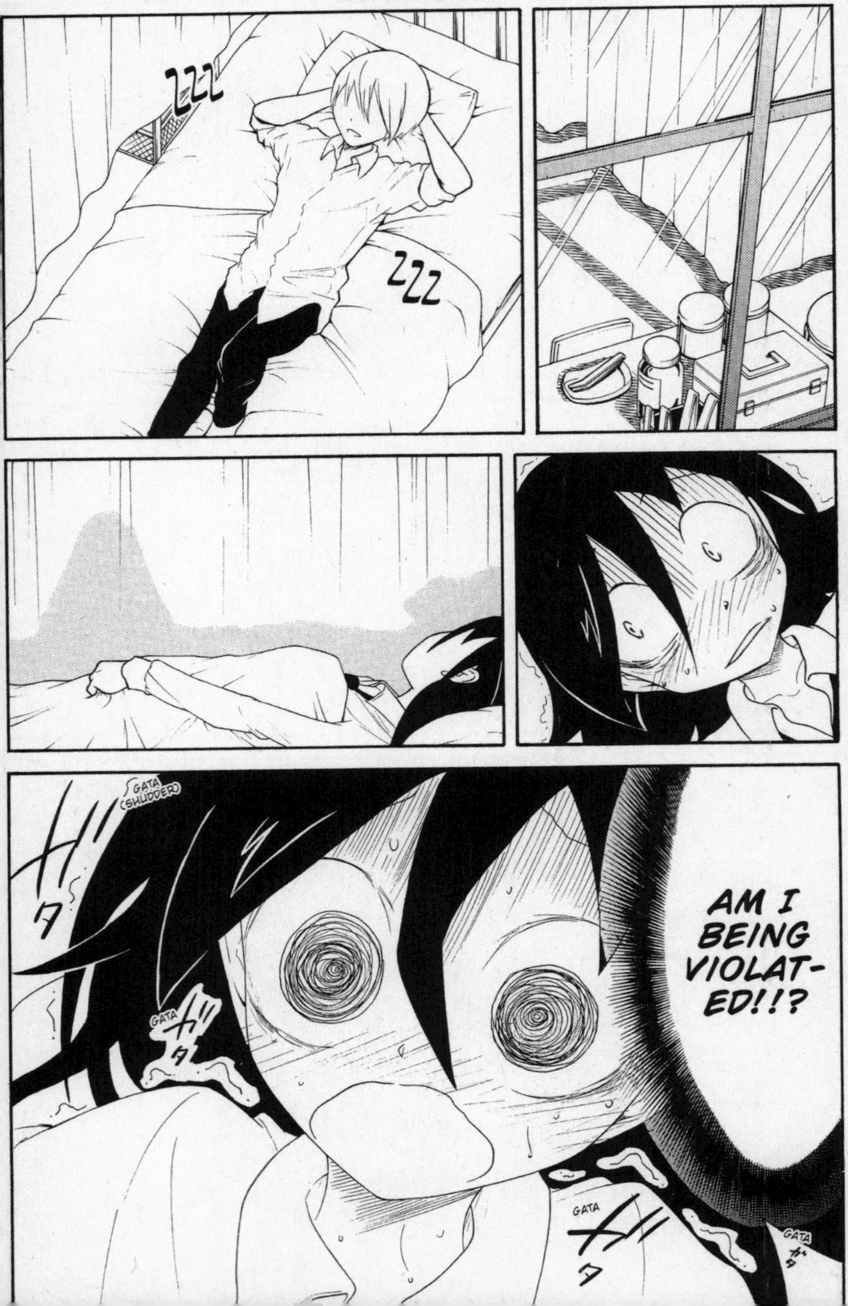
ZZZ
ZZZ
AM I BEING VIOLAT-ED!!?
GATA (SHUDDER)
ガタ
GATA
ガタ
GATA
ガタ
GATA
ガタ

EMOTIONAL ROLLER COASTER

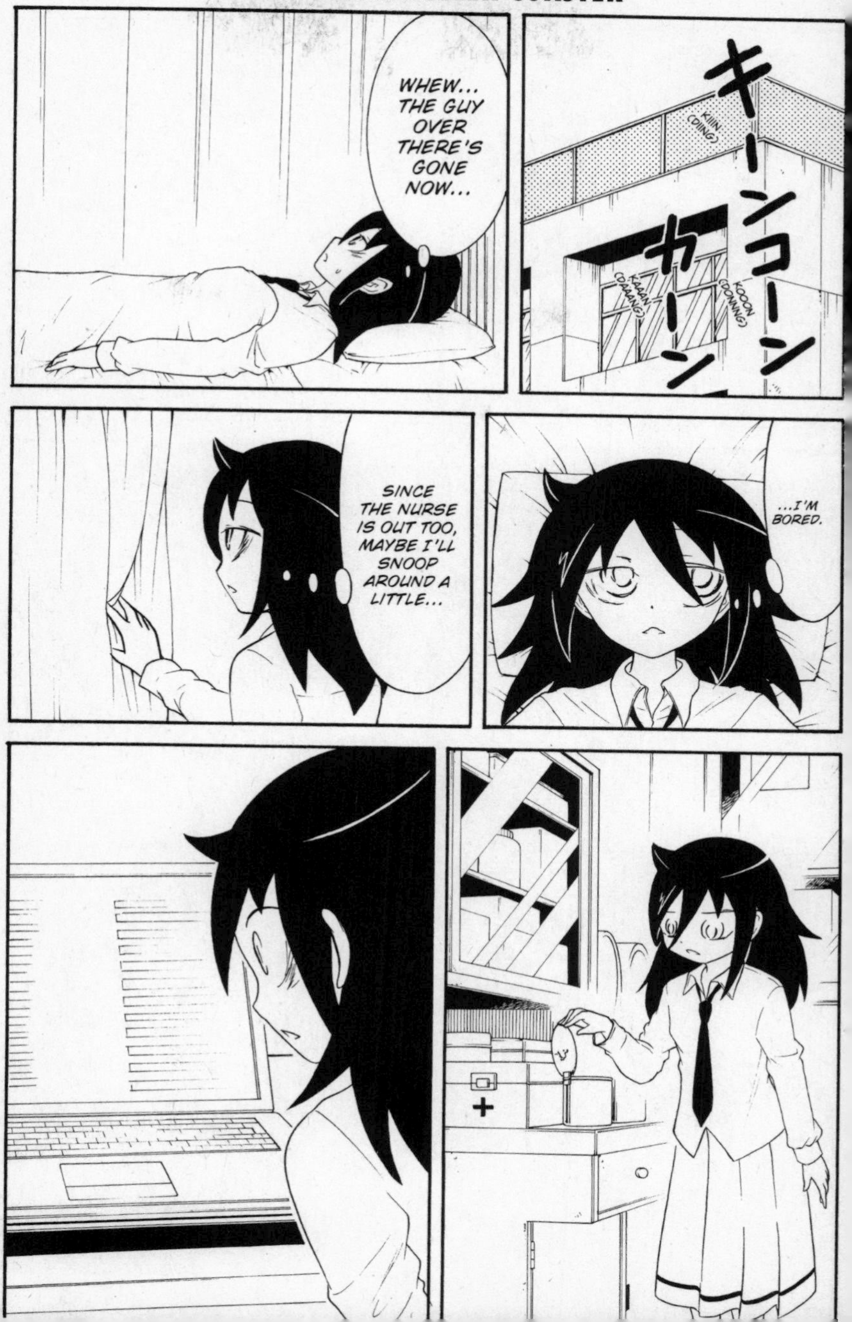
キーンコーン
KIIN (DIING)
KOON (DONNNG)
カーン
KAAAN (DAAANG)
WHEW... THE GUY OVER THERE'S GONE NOW...
...I'M BORED.
SINCE THE NURSE IS OUT TOO, MAYBE I'LL SNOOP AROUND A LITTLE...

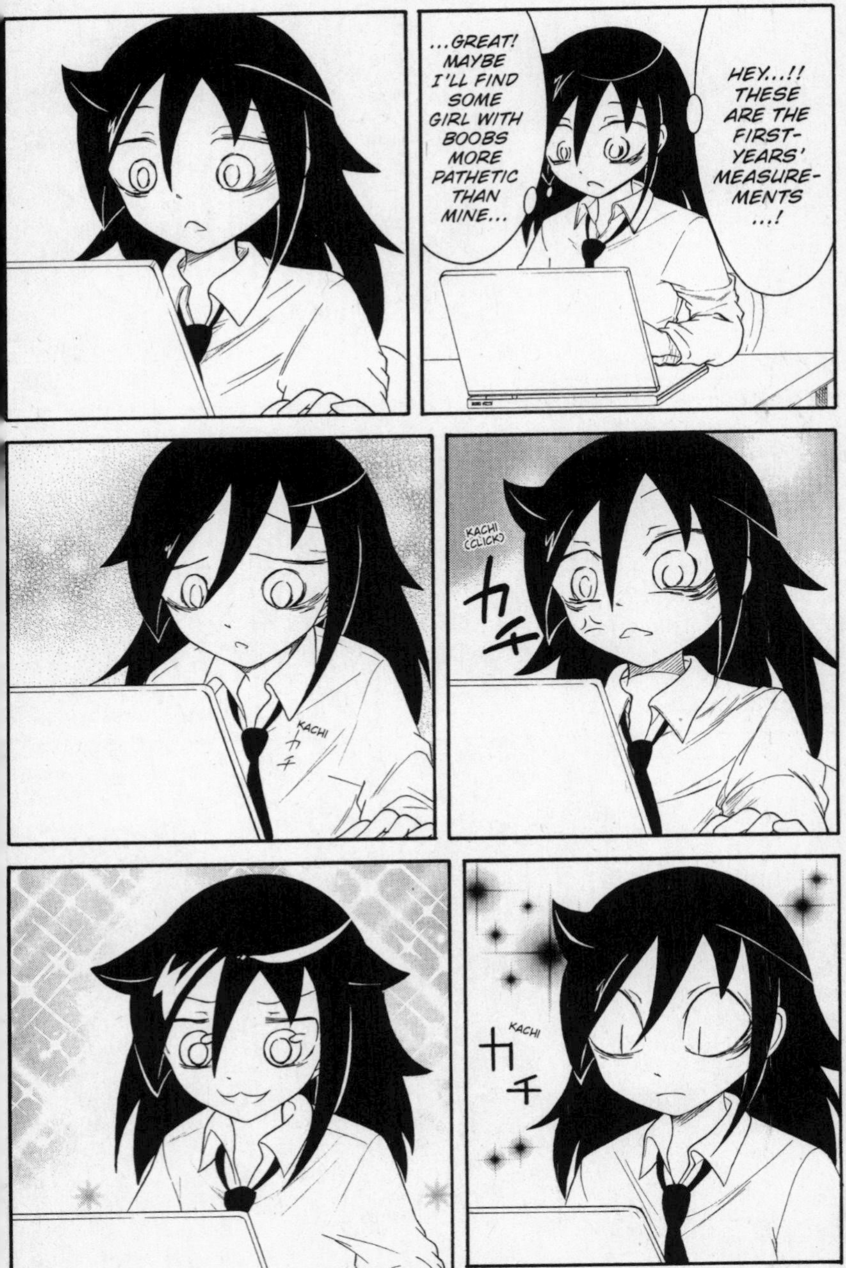
HEY...!! THESE ARE THE FIRST-YEARS' MEASUREMENTS...!
...GREAT! MAYBE I'LL FIND SOME GIRL WITH BOOBS MORE PATHETIC THAN MINE...
KACHI (CLICK)
カチ
KACHI
カチ
KACHI
カチ

HOMEMADE

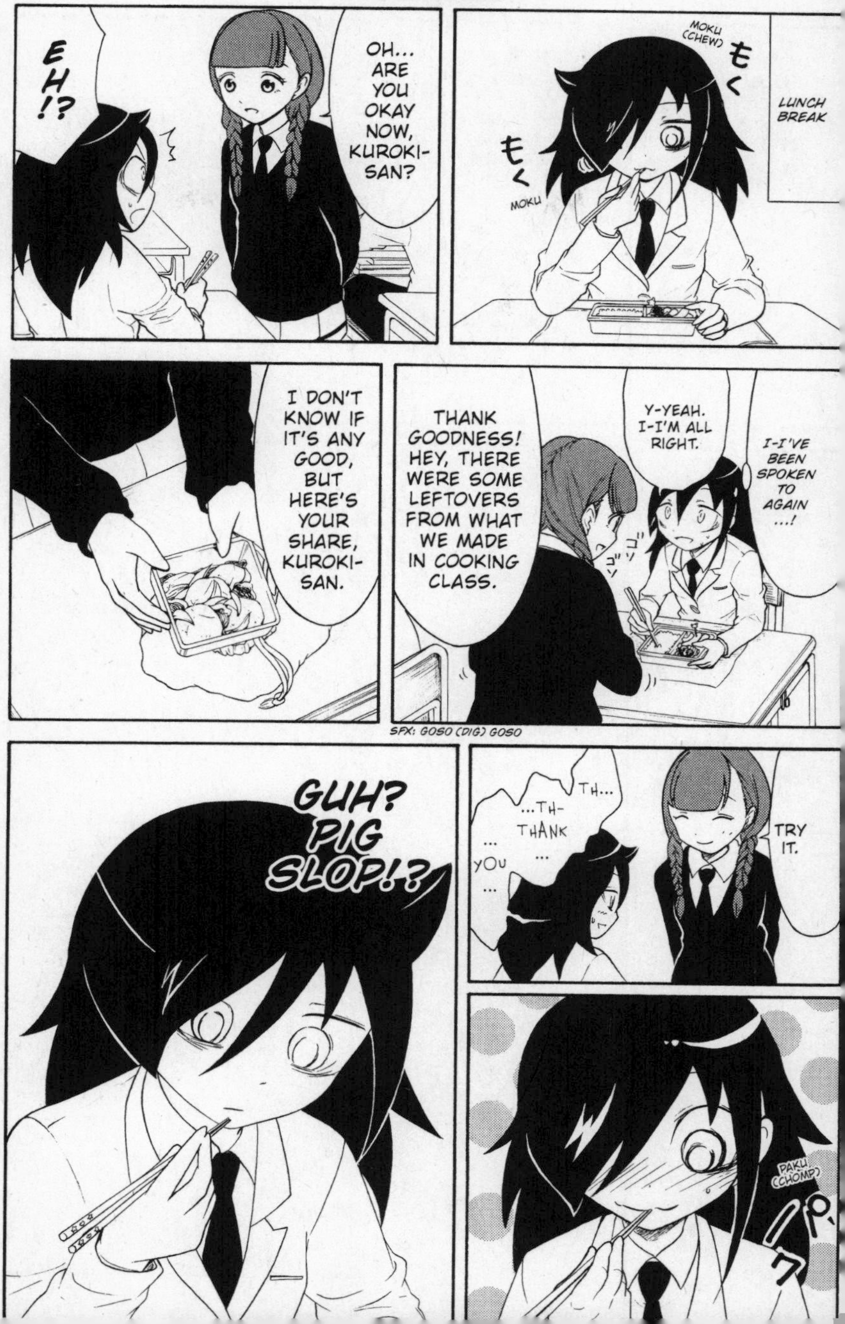
LUNCH BREAK
MOKU (CHEW)
MOKU
OH... ARE YOU OKAY NOW, KUROKI-SAN?
EH!?
Y-YEAH. I-I'M ALL RIGHT.
I-I'VE BEEN SPOKEN TO AGAIN ...!
THANK GOODNESS! HEY, THERE WERE SOME LEFTOVERS FROM WHAT WE MADE IN COOKING CLASS.
I DON'T KNOW IF IT'S ANY GOOD, BUT HERE'S YOUR SHARE, KUROKI-SAN.
SFX: GOSO (DIG) GOSO
TRY IT.
TH...
...TH- THANK ... YOU ...
PAKU (CHOMP)
GUH? PIG SLOP!?

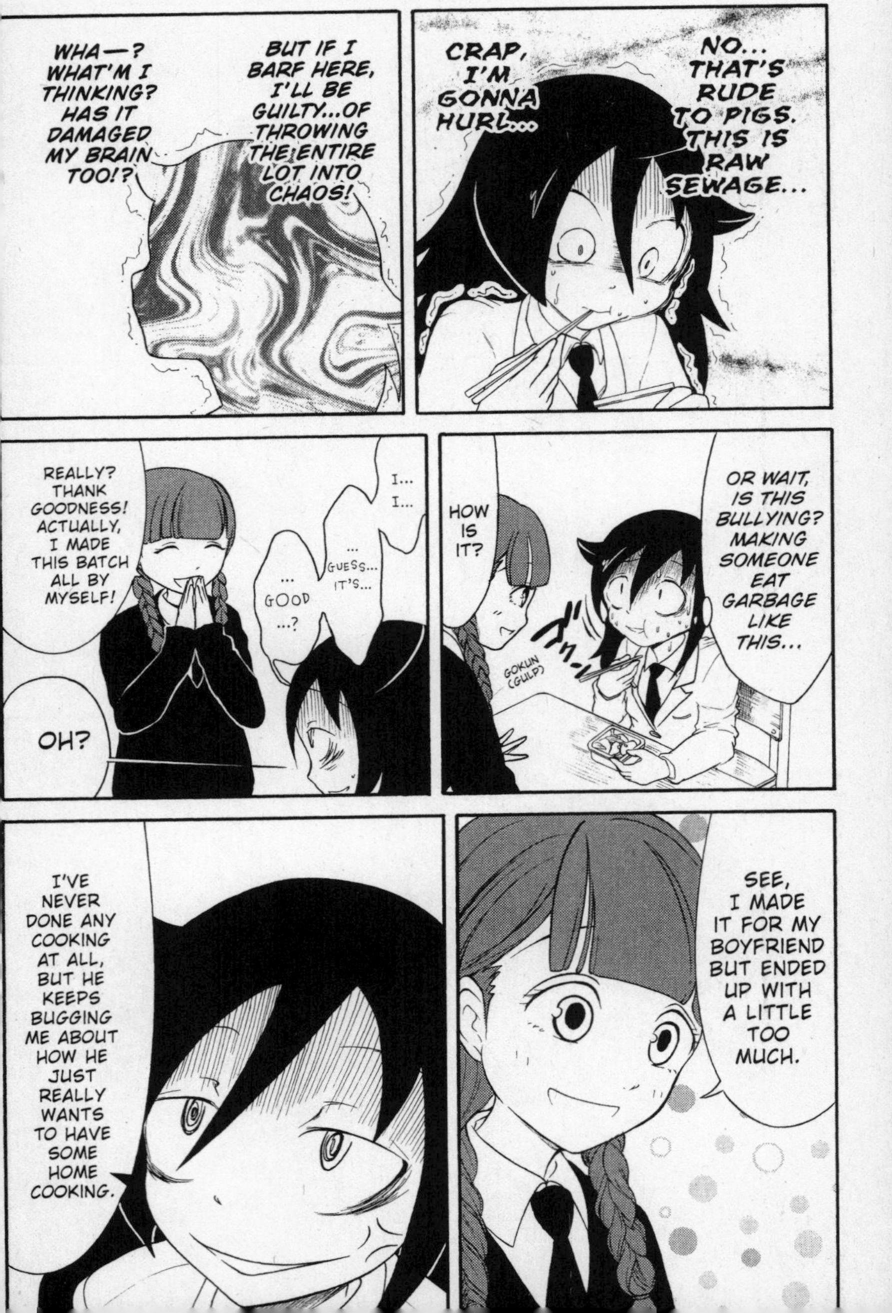
NO... THAT'S RUDE TO PIGS. THIS IS RAW SEWAGE...
CRAP, I'M GONNA HURL...
BUT IF I BARF HERE, I'LL BE GUILTY...OF THROWING THE ENTIRE LOT INTO CHAOS!
WHA—? WHAT'M I THINKING? HAS IT DAMAGED MY BRAIN TOO!?
OR WAIT, IS THIS BULLYING? MAKING SOMEONE EAT GARBAGE LIKE THIS...
HOW IS IT?
GOKUN (GULP)
I... I...
... GUESS... IT'S...
... GOOD ...?
REALLY? THANK GOODNESS! ACTUALLY, I MADE THIS BATCH ALL BY MYSELF!
OH?
SEE, I MADE IT FOR MY BOYFRIEND BUT ENDED UP WITH A LITTLE TOO MUCH.
I'VE NEVER DONE ANY COOKING AT ALL, BUT HE KEEPS BUGGING ME ABOUT HOW HE JUST REALLY WANTS TO HAVE SOME HOME COOKING.

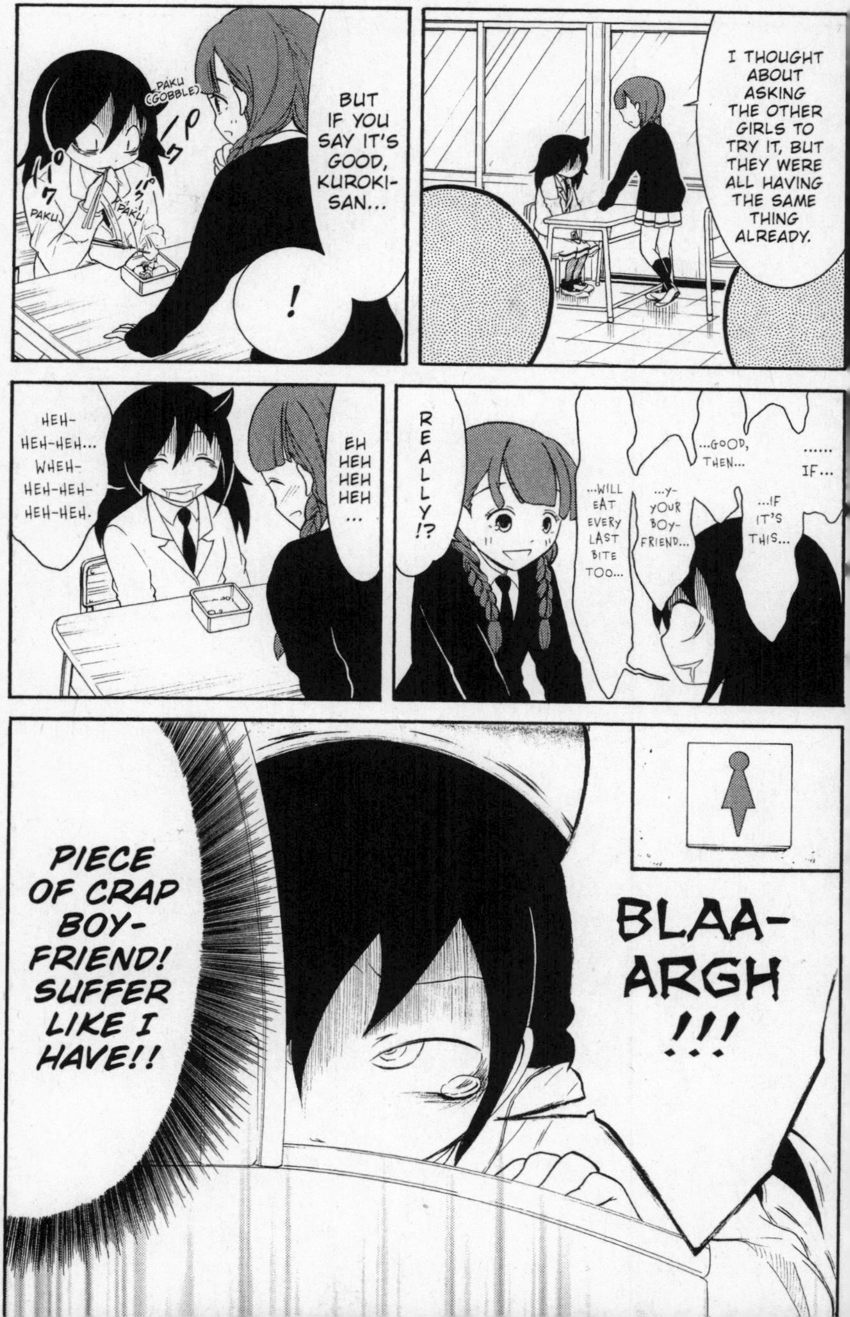
I THOUGHT ABOUT ASKING THE OTHER GIRLS TO TRY IT, BUT THEY WERE ALL HAVING THE SAME THING ALREADY.
BUT IF YOU SAY IT'S GOOD, KUROKI-SAN...
!
PAKU (GOBBLE)
PAKU
PAKU
...... IF...
...GOOD, THEN...
...IF IT'S THIS...
...Y-YOUR BOY-FRIEND...
...WILL EAT EVERY LAST BITE TOO...
REALLY!?
EH HEH HEH HEH...
HEH-HEH-HEH... WHEH-HEH-HEH-HEH-HEH.
BLAA-ARGH!!!
PIECE OF CRAP BOY-FRIEND! SUFFER LIKE I HAVE!!

ON HOLD

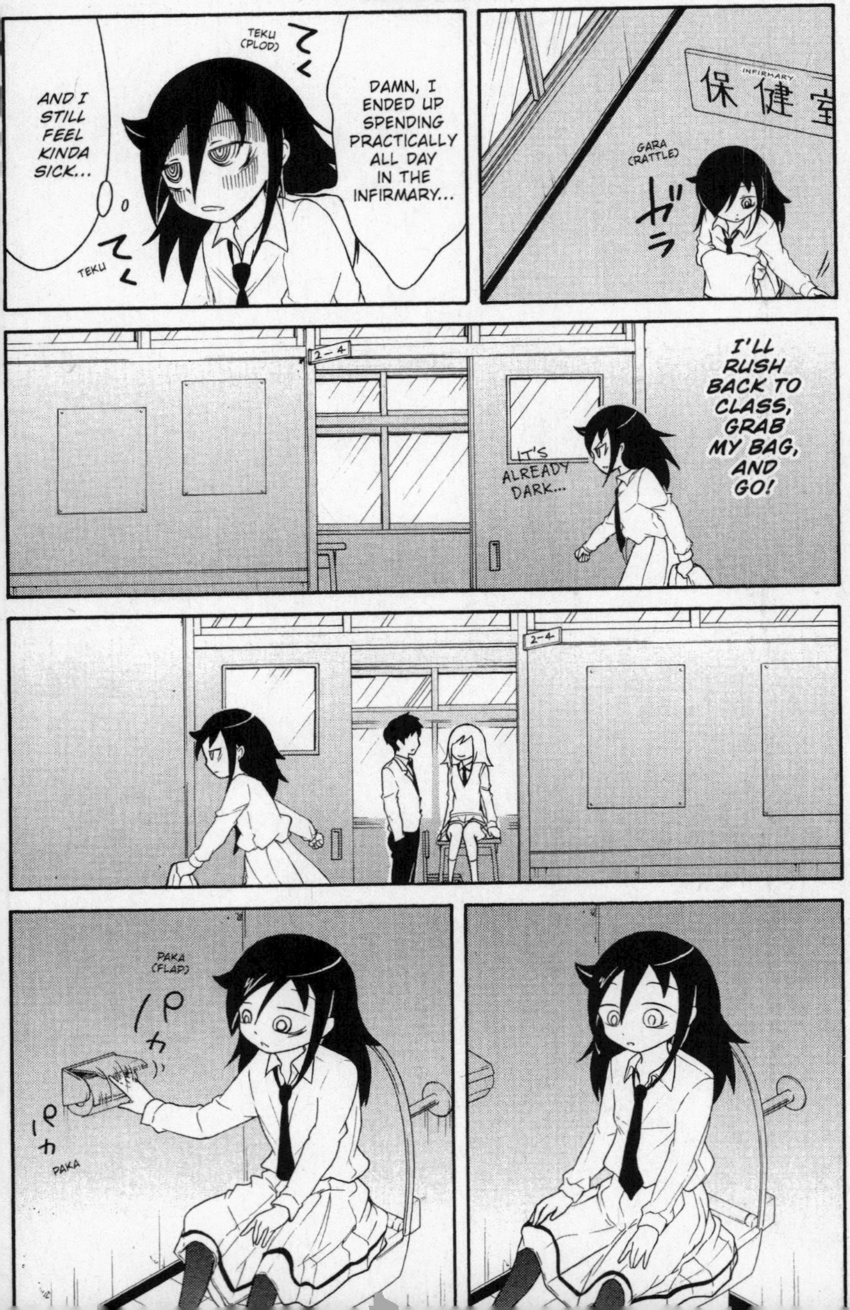

保健室
INFIRMARY
ガラ
GARA (RATTLE)
てく
TEKU (PLOD)
DAMN, I ENDED UP SPENDING PRACTICALLY ALL DAY IN THE INFIRMARY...
AND I STILL FEEL KINDA SICK...
てく
TEKU
2-4
I'LL RUSH BACK TO CLASS, GRAB MY BAG, AND GO!
IT'S ALREADY DARK...
2-4
パカ
PAKA (FLAP)
パカ
PAKA

AFTER-SCHOOL SOUNDS

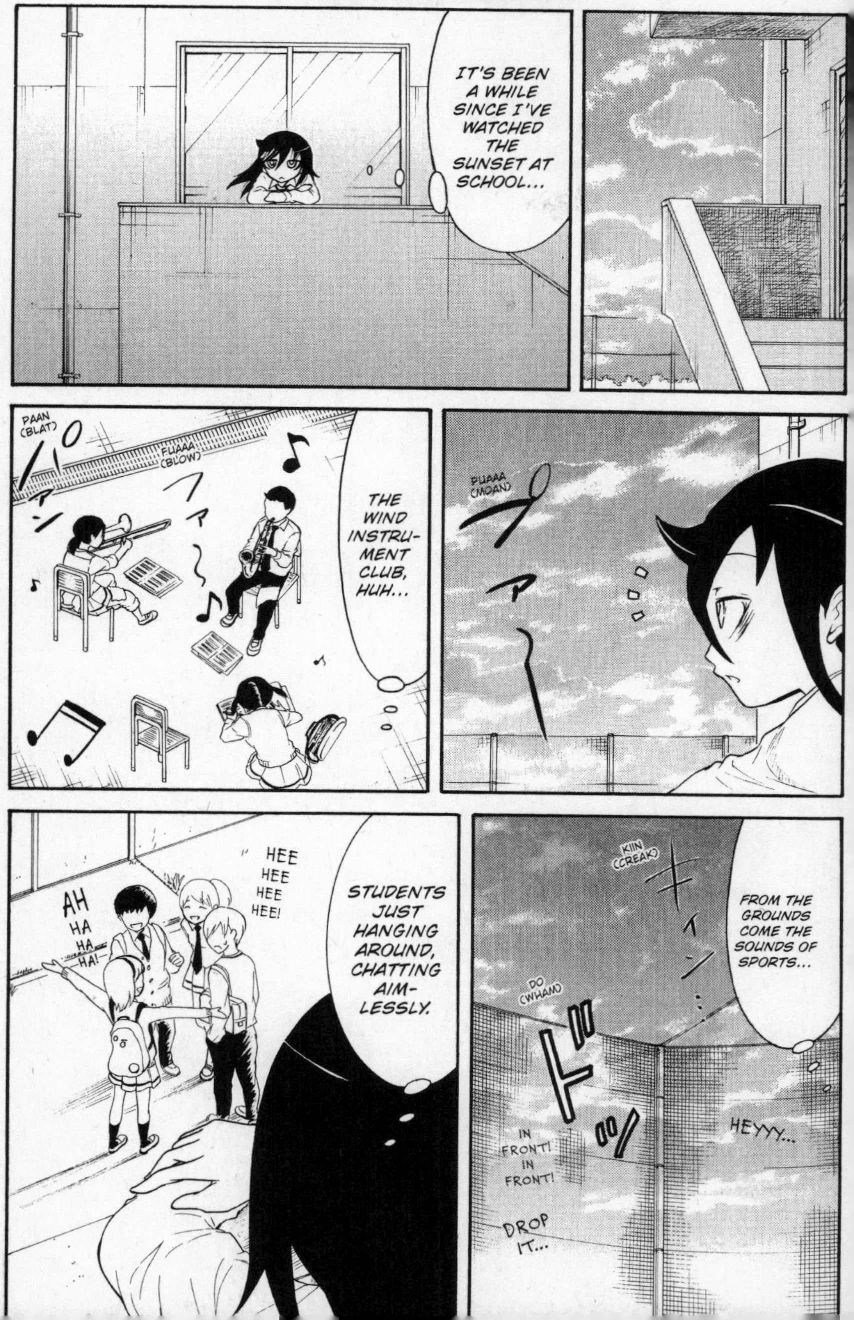
IT'S BEEN A WHILE SINCE I'VE WATCHED THE SUNSET AT SCHOOL...
PUAAA (MOAN)
PAAN (BLAT)
FUAAA (BLOW)
THE WIND INSTRUMENT CLUB, HUH...
KIIN (CREAK)
DO (WHAM)
FROM THE GROUNDS COME THE SOUNDS OF SPORTS...
HEYYY...
IN FRONT! IN FRONT!
DROP IT...
STUDENTS JUST HANGING AROUND, CHATTING AIMLESSLY.
HEE HEE HEE HEE!
AH HA HA HA!

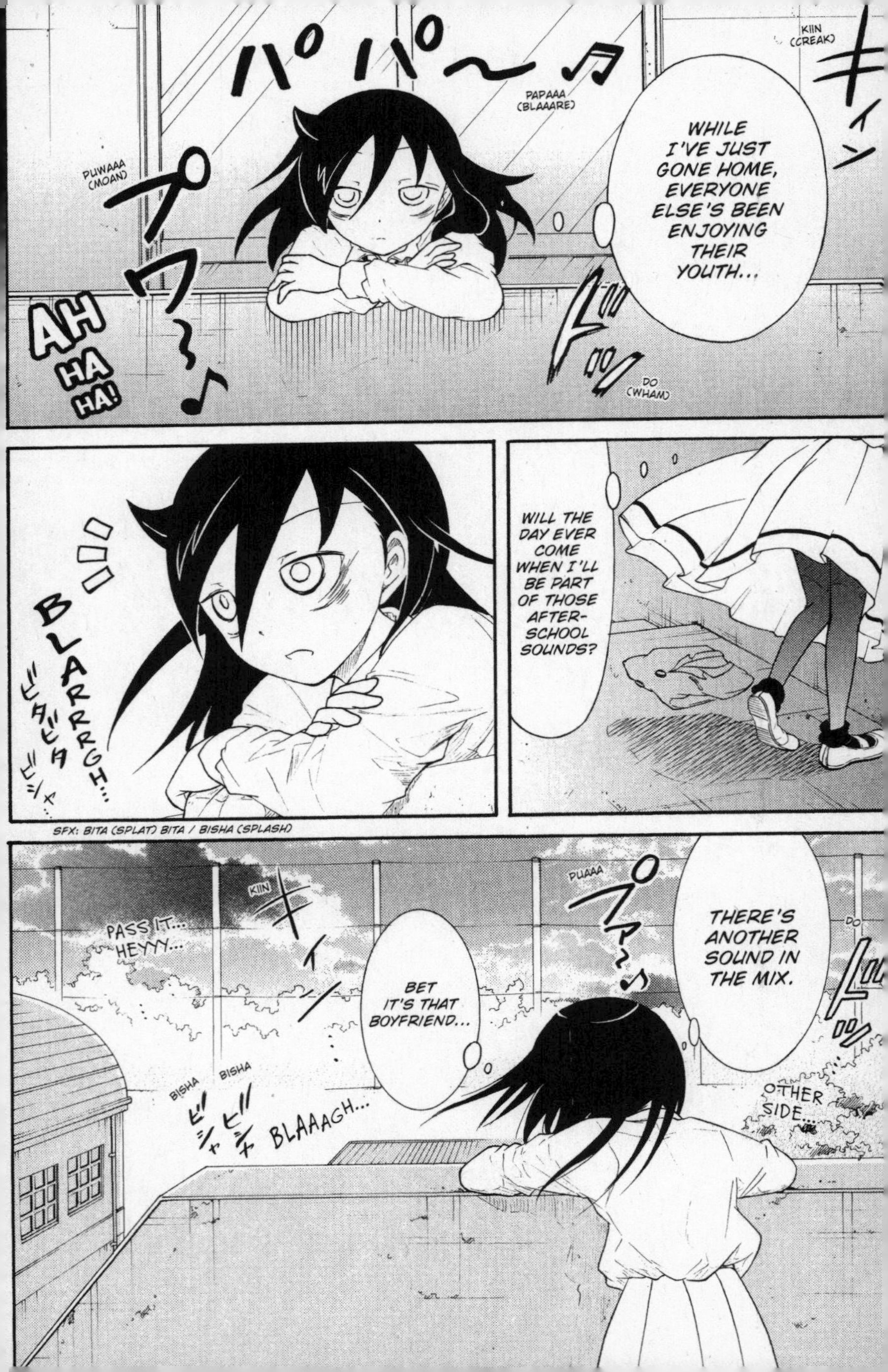
キィン
KIIN (CREAK)
WHILE I'VE JUST GONE HOME, EVERYONE ELSE'S BEEN ENJOYING THEIR YOUTH...
パパ～♫
PAPAAA (BLAAARE)
ドッ
DO (WHAM)
プワ～♪
PUWAAA (MOAN)
AH HA HA!
WILL THE DAY EVER COME WHEN I'LL BE PART OF THOSE AFTER-SCHOOL SOUNDS?
BLARRRGH...
ビタビタ
ビシャ...
SFX: BITA (SPLAT) BITA / BISHA (SPLASH)
THERE'S ANOTHER SOUND IN THE MIX.
DO
ドッ
OTHER SIDE...
プァ～♪
PUAAA
BET IT'S THAT BOYFRIEND...
キィン
KIIN
PASS IT... HEYYY...
BISHA BISHA
ビシャビシャ
BLAAAGH...

No Matter How I Look at It, It's You Guys' Fault I'm Not Popular!

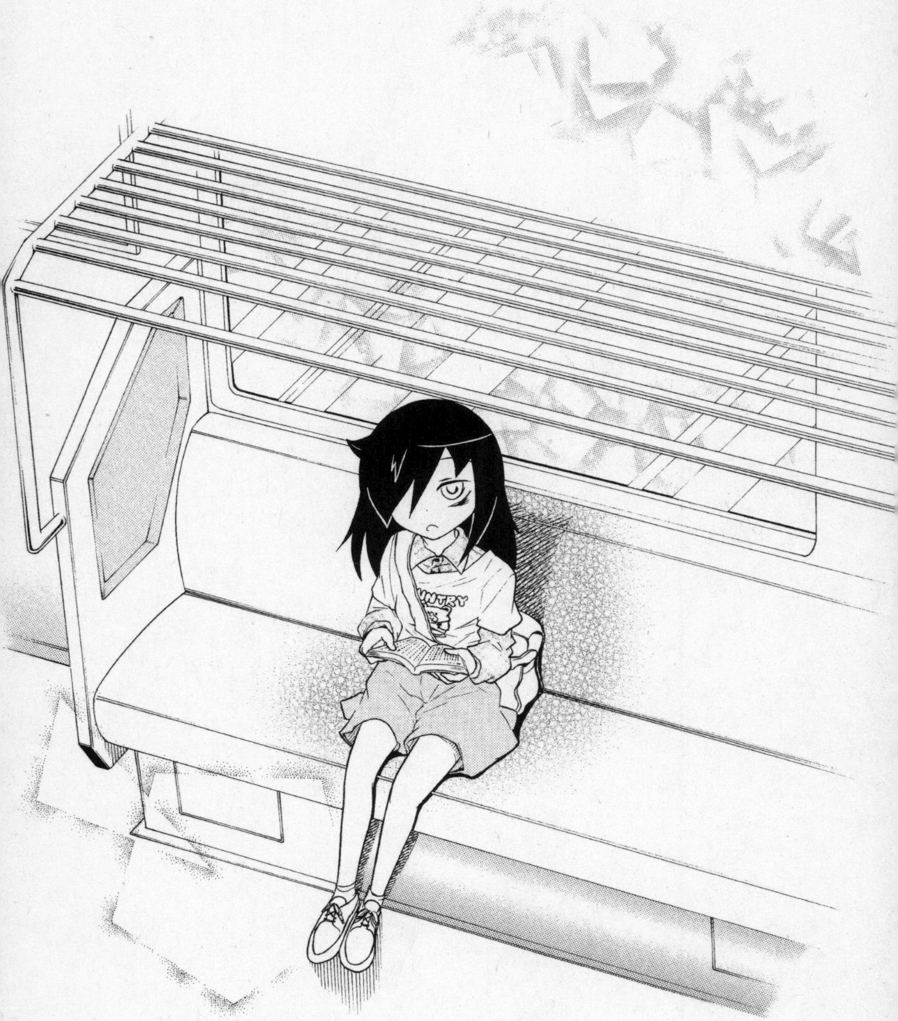

FAIL 43: I'M NOT POPULAR, SO I'LL DEVELOP AN INTEREST IN NUDITY.

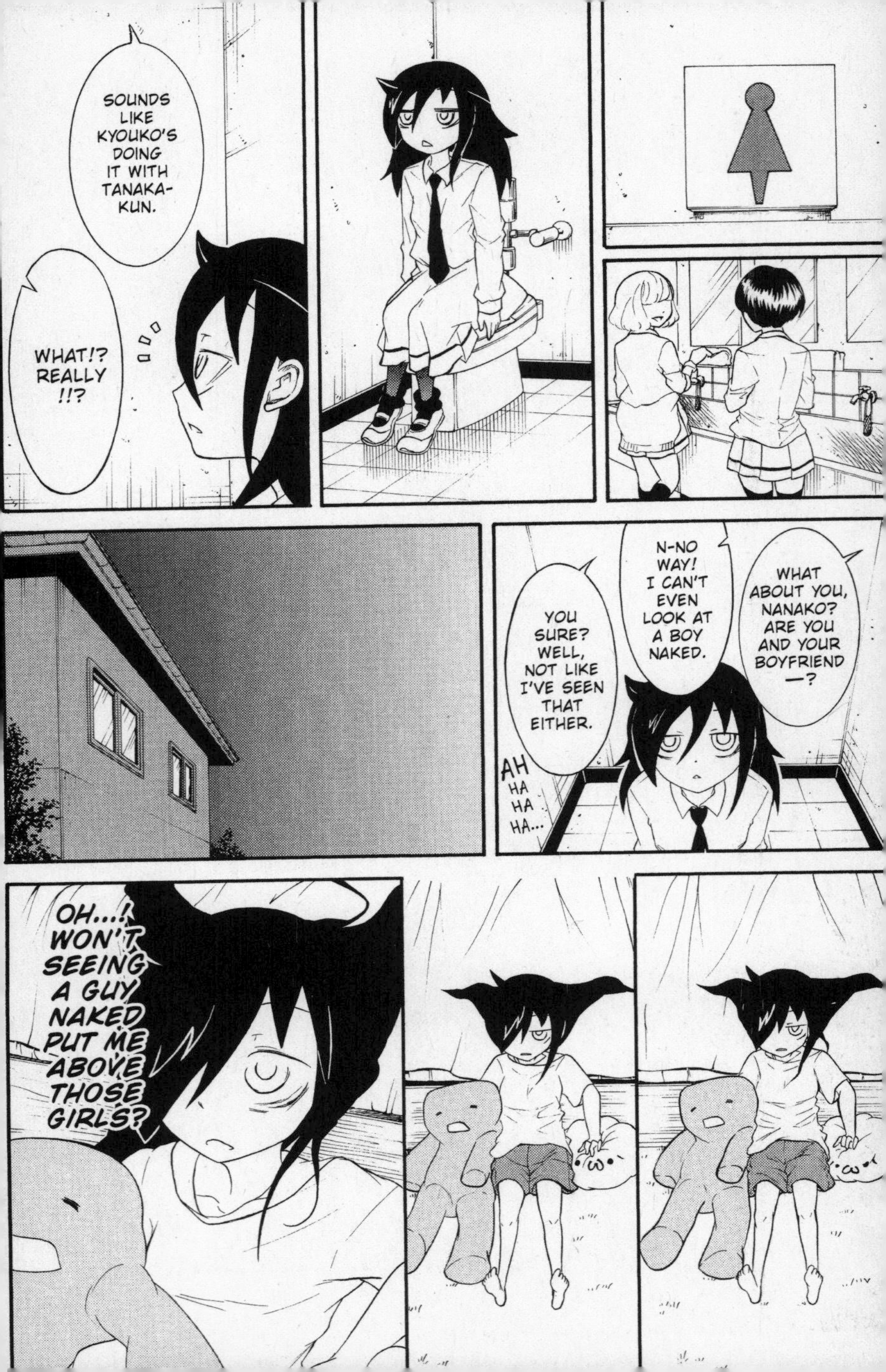
SOUNDS LIKE KYOUKO'S DOING IT WITH TANAKA-KUN.
WHAT!? REALLY !!?
WHAT ABOUT YOU, NANAKO? ARE YOU AND YOUR BOYFRIEND —?
N-NO WAY! I CAN'T EVEN LOOK AT A BOY NAKED.
YOU SURE? WELL, NOT LIKE I'VE SEEN THAT EITHER.
AH HA HA HA...
OH...! WON'T SEEING A GUY NAKED PUT ME ABOVE THOSE GIRLS?

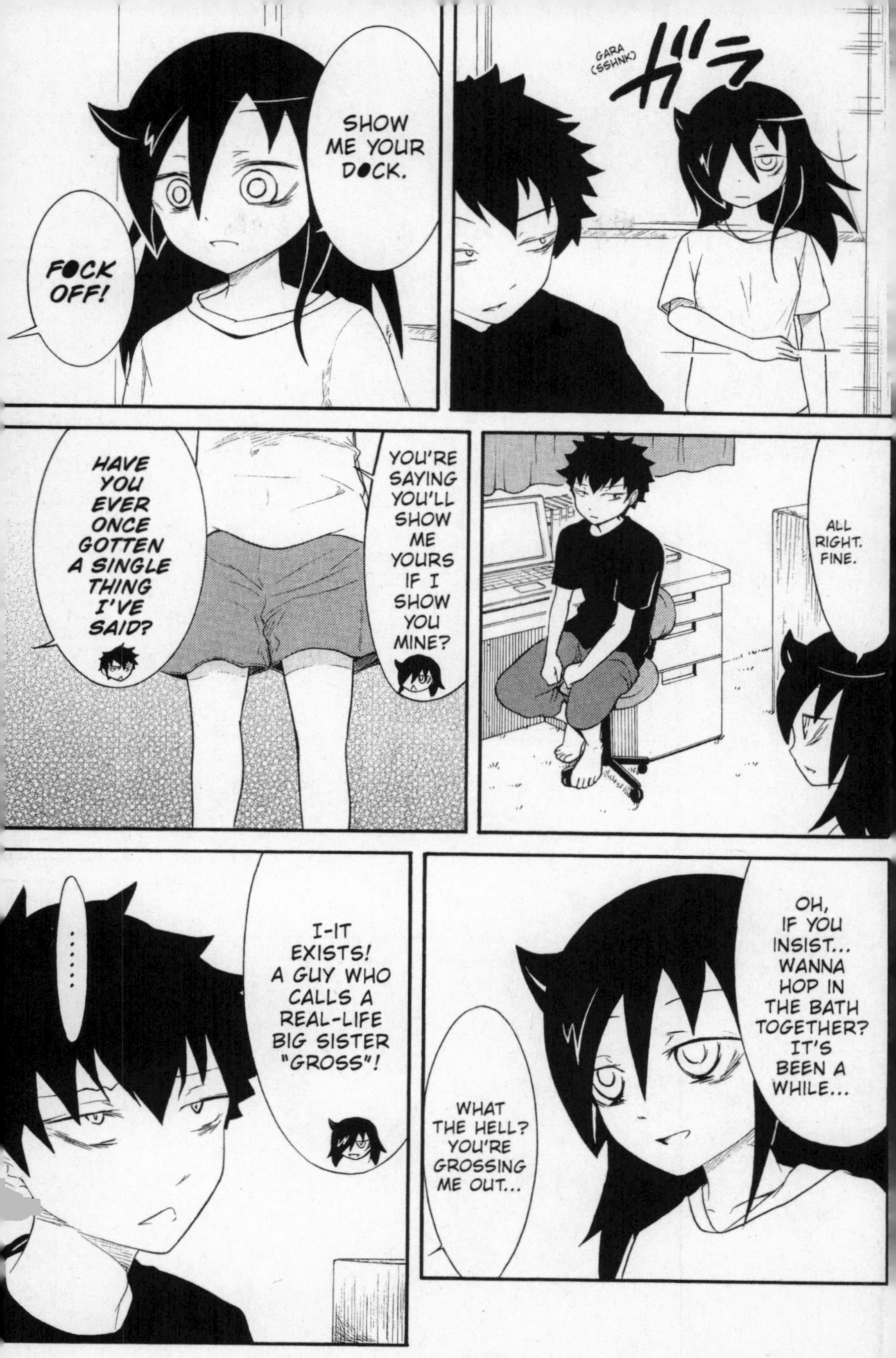

ガラ
GARA (SSHNK)
SHOW ME YOUR DOCK.
FOCK OFF!
ALL RIGHT. FINE.
YOU'RE SAYING YOU'LL SHOW ME YOURS IF I SHOW YOU MINE?
HAVE YOU EVER ONCE GOTTEN A SINGLE THING I'VE SAID?
OH, IF YOU INSIST... WANNA HOP IN THE BATH TOGETHER? IT'S BEEN A WHILE...
WHAT THE HELL? YOU'RE GROSSING ME OUT...
I-IT EXISTS! A GUY WHO CALLS A REAL-LIFE BIG SISTER "GROSS"!
......

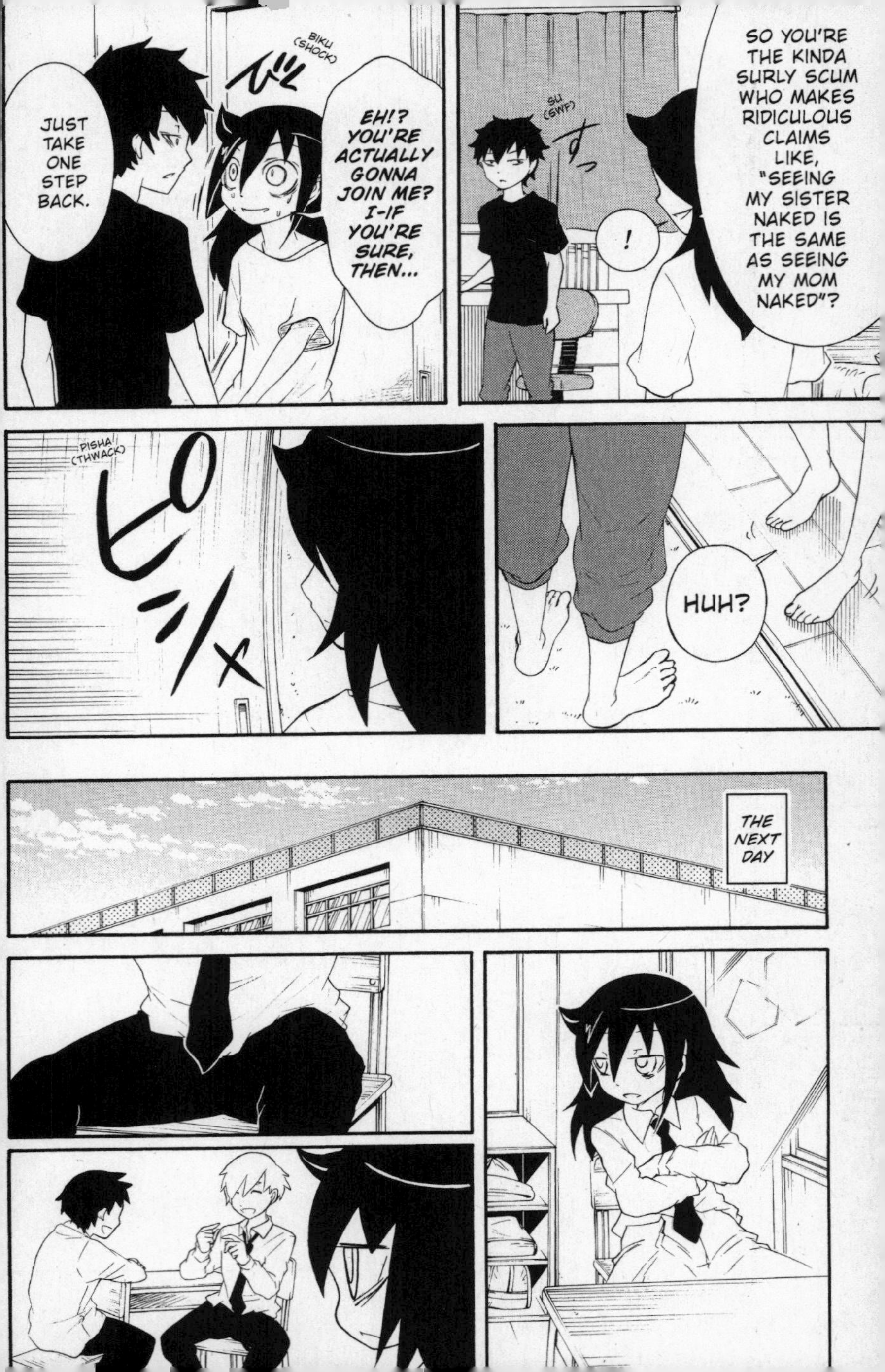
SO YOU'RE THE KINDA SURLY SCUM WHO MAKES RIDICULOUS CLAIMS LIKE, "SEEING MY SISTER NAKED IS THE SAME AS SEEING MY MOM NAKED"?
SU (SWF)
!
BIKU (SHOCK)
JUST TAKE ONE STEP BACK.
EH!? YOU'RE ACTUALLY GONNA JOIN ME? I-IF YOU'RE SURE, THEN...
HUH?
PISHA (THWACK)
THE NEXT DAY

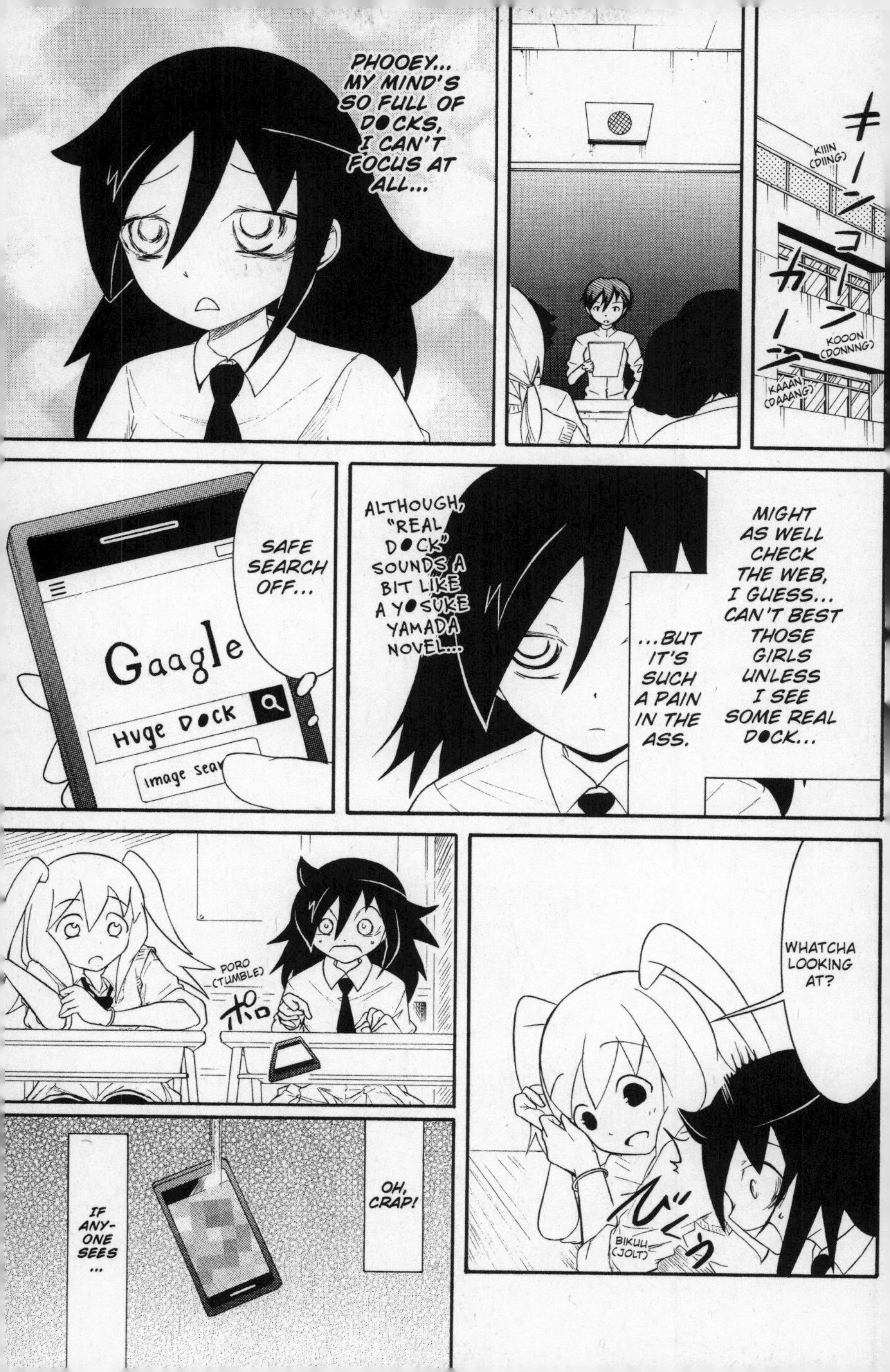
KIIN (DIING)
KOOON (DONNNG)
KAAAN (DAAANG)
PHOOEY... MY MIND'S SO FULL OF DOCKS, I CAN'T FOCUS AT ALL...
MIGHT AS WELL CHECK THE WEB, I GUESS... CAN'T BEST THOSE GIRLS UNLESS I SEE SOME REAL DOCK...
...BUT IT'S SUCH A PAIN IN THE ASS.
ALTHOUGH, "REAL DOCK" SOUNDS A BIT LIKE A YOSUKE YAMADA NOVEL...
SAFE SEARCH OFF...
Gaagle
Huge Dock
image sear
WHATCHA LOOKING AT?
BIKUU (JOLT)
PORO (TUMBLE)
OH, CRAP!
IF ANY-ONE SEES ...

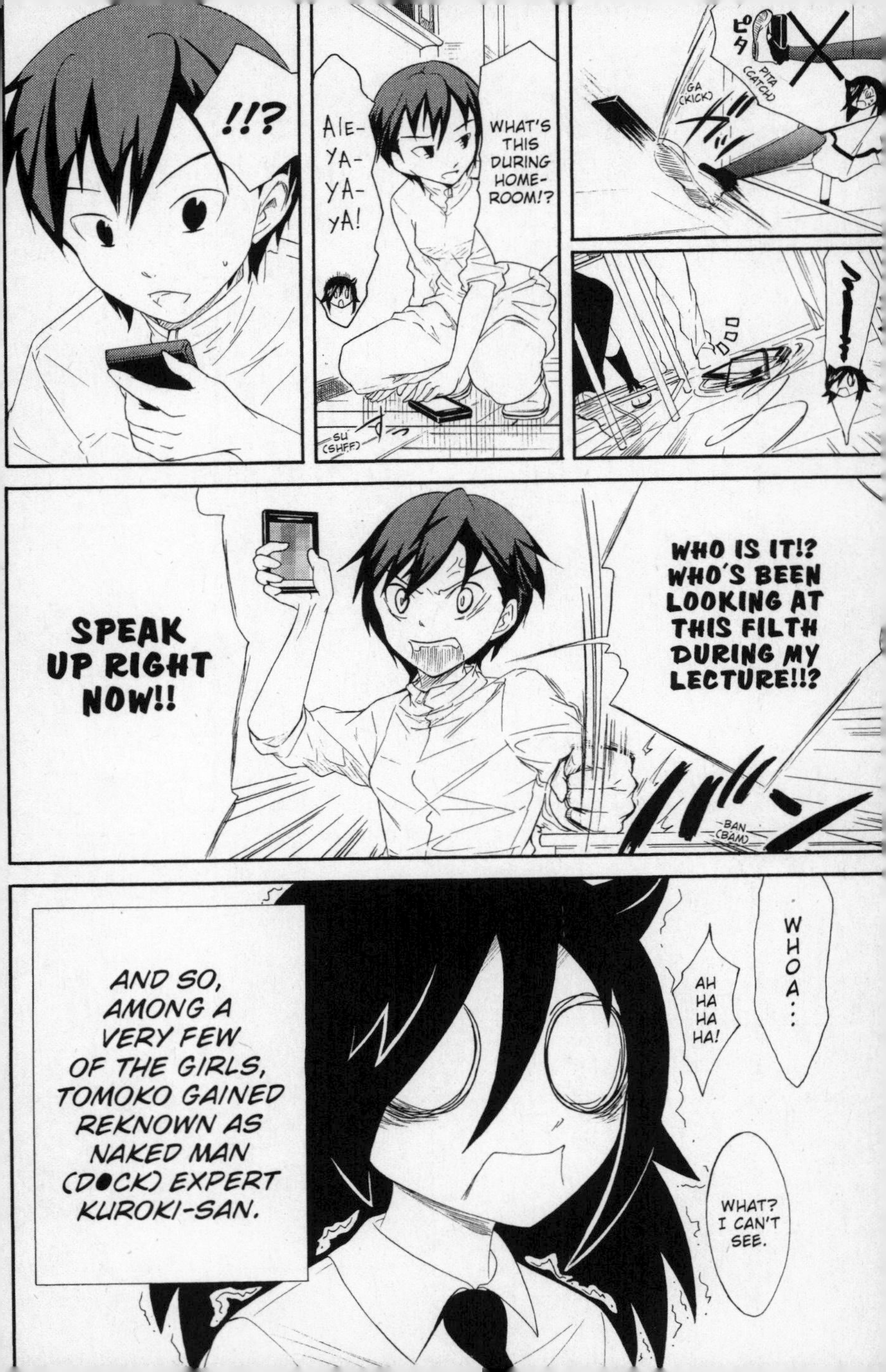

ピタ
PITA (CATCH)
GA (KICK)
WHAT'S THIS DURING HOME-ROOM!?
AIE-YA-YA-YA!
SU (SHFF)
!!?
WHO IS IT!? WHO'S BEEN LOOKING AT THIS FILTH DURING MY LECTURE!!?
SPEAK UP RIGHT NOW!!
BAN (BAM)
WHOA...
AH HA HA HA!
WHAT? I CAN'T SEE.
AND SO, AMONG A VERY FEW OF THE GIRLS, TOMOKO GAINED REKNOWN AS NAKED MAN (DOCK) EXPERT KUROKI-SAN.

No Matter How I Look at It, It's You Guys' Fault I'm Not Popular!

FAIL 44: I'M NOT POPULAR, SO I'LL STUDY FOR EXAMS.

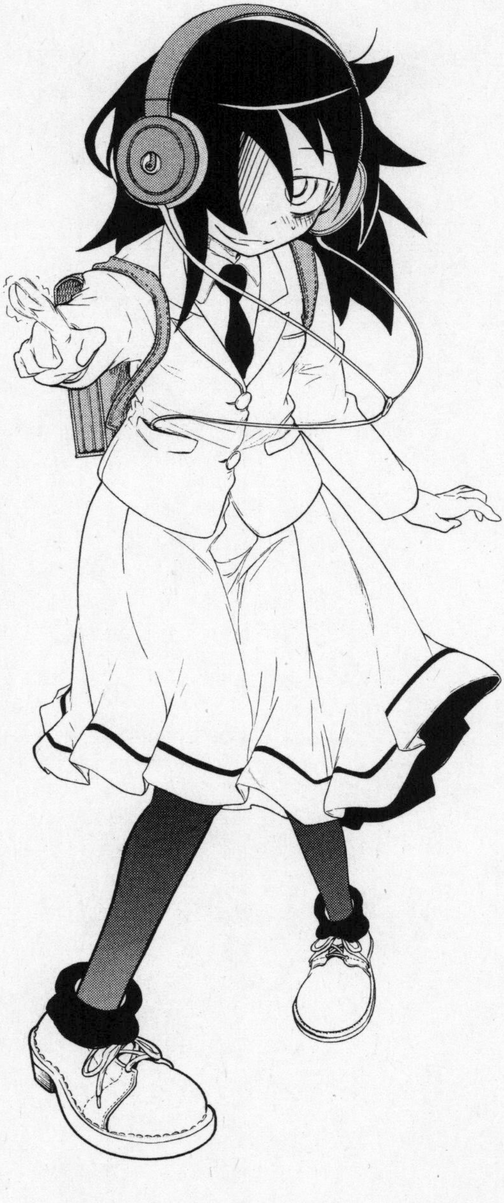

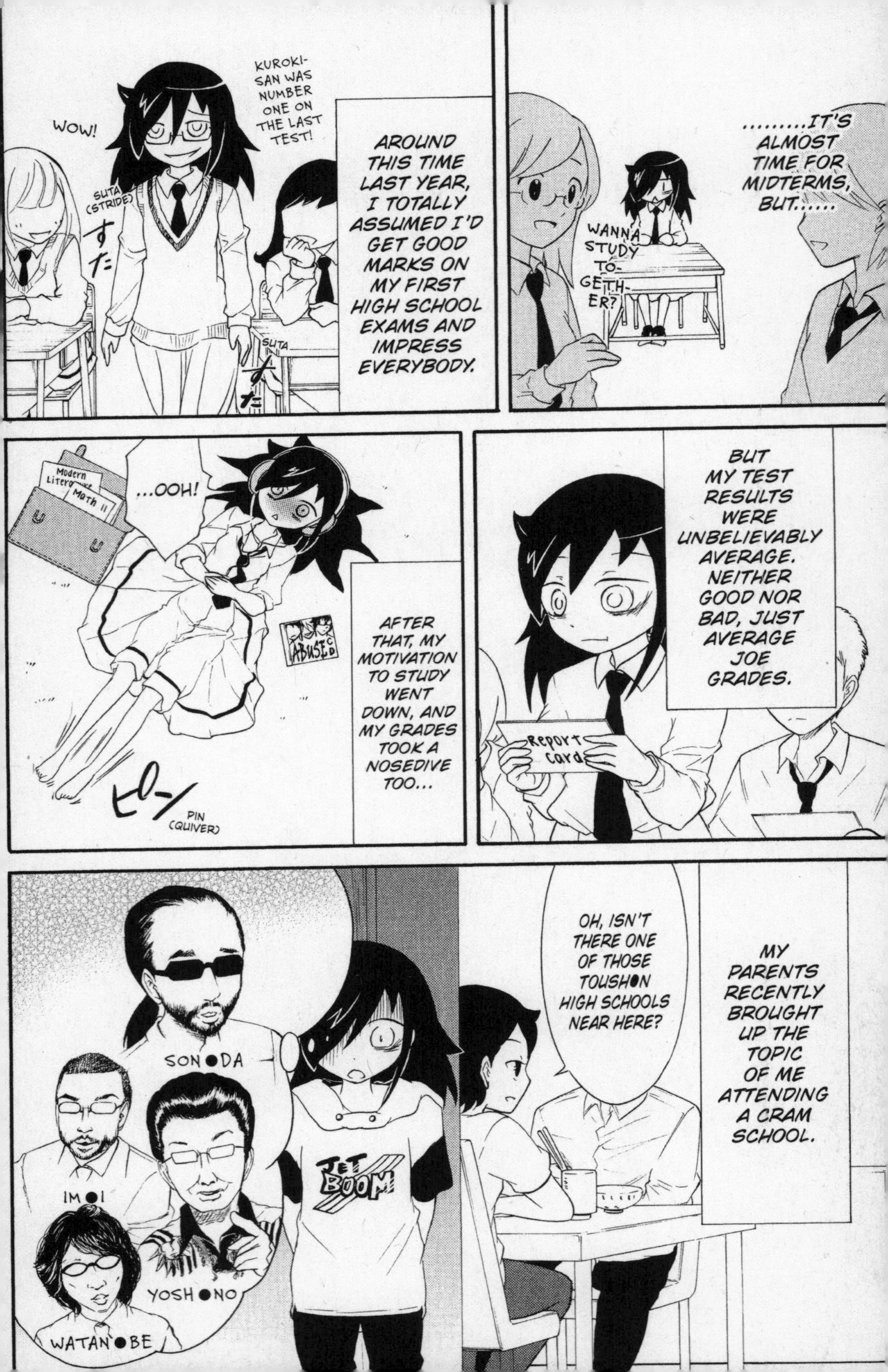
.........IT'S ALMOST TIME FOR MIDTERMS, BUT......
WANNA STUDY TO-GETH-ER?
AROUND THIS TIME LAST YEAR, I TOTALLY ASSUMED I'D GET GOOD MARKS ON MY FIRST HIGH SCHOOL EXAMS AND IMPRESS EVERYBODY.
KUROKI-SAN WAS NUMBER ONE ON THE LAST TEST!
WOW!
SUTA (STRIDE)
すた
SUTA
すた
BUT MY TEST RESULTS WERE UNBELIEVABLY AVERAGE. NEITHER GOOD NOR BAD, JUST AVERAGE JOE GRADES.
Report card
AFTER THAT, MY MOTIVATION TO STUDY WENT DOWN, AND MY GRADES TOOK A NOSEDIVE TOO...
...OOH!
Modern Literature
Math II
ABUSE CD
ピー
PIN (QUIVER)
MY PARENTS RECENTLY BROUGHT UP THE TOPIC OF ME ATTENDING A CRAM SCHOOL.
OH, ISN'T THERE ONE OF THOSE TOUSH●N HIGH SCHOOLS NEAR HERE?
SON●DA
IM●I
YOSH●NO
WATAN●BE
JET BOOM

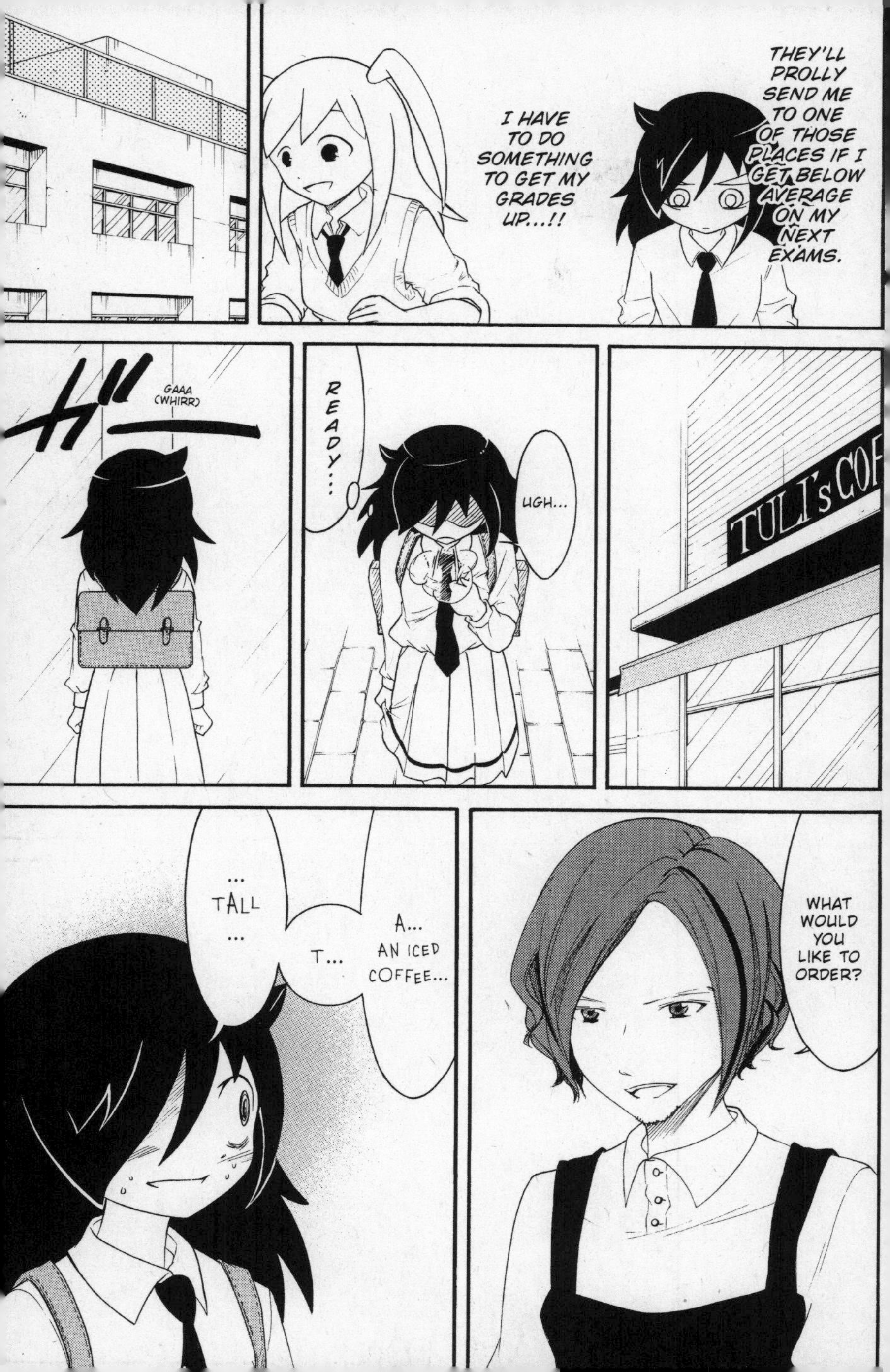
THEY'LL PROLLY SEND ME TO ONE OF THOSE PLACES IF I GET BELOW AVERAGE ON MY NEXT EXAMS.
I HAVE TO DO SOMETHING TO GET MY GRADES UP...!!
TULI's COF
UGH...
READY...
GAAA (WHIRR)
WHAT WOULD YOU LIKE TO ORDER?
A... AN ICED COFFEE...
T...
... TALL ...

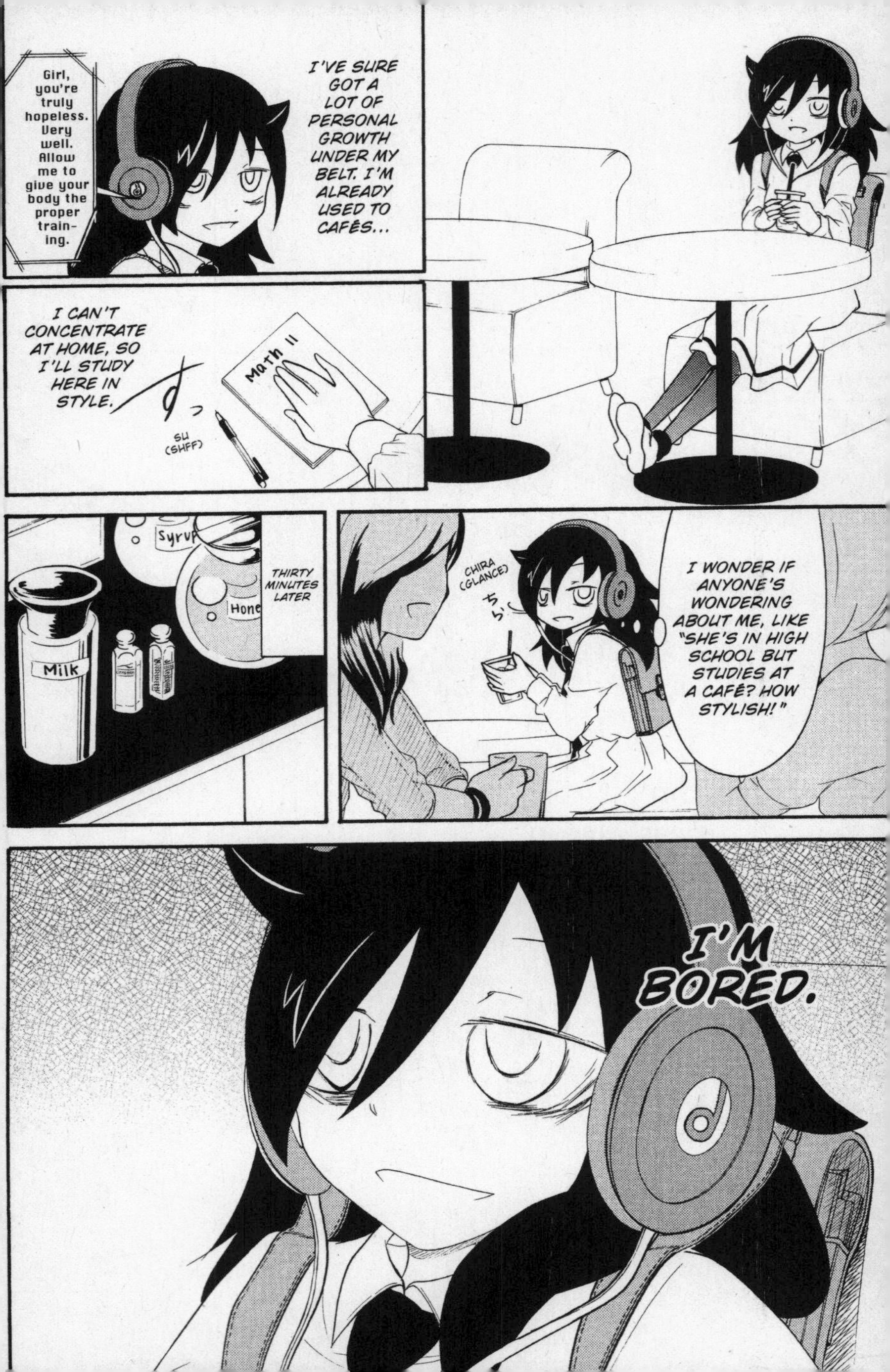
I'VE SURE GOT A LOT OF PERSONAL GROWTH UNDER MY BELT. I'M ALREADY USED TO CAFÉS...
Girl, you're truly hopeless. Very well. Allow me to give your body the proper training.
I CAN'T CONCENTRATE AT HOME, SO I'LL STUDY HERE IN STYLE.
Math II
SU (SHFF)
Syrup
Hone
Milk
THIRTY MINUTES LATER
CHIRA (GLANCE)
I WONDER IF ANYONE'S WONDERING ABOUT ME, LIKE "SHE'S IN HIGH SCHOOL BUT STUDIES AT A CAFÉ? HOW STYLISH!"
I'M BORED.

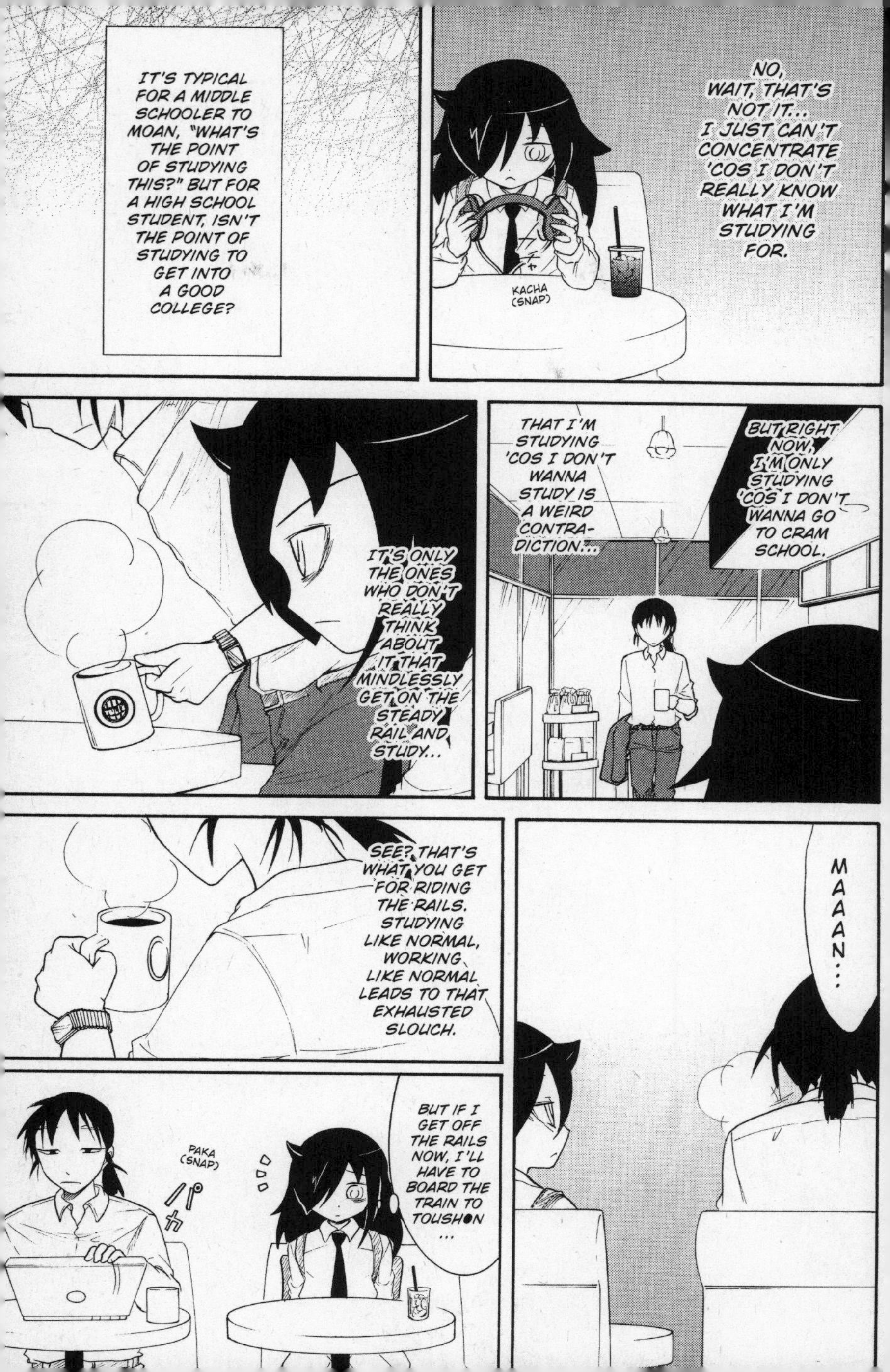
NO, WAIT, THAT'S NOT IT... I JUST CAN'T CONCENTRATE 'COS I DON'T REALLY KNOW WHAT I'M STUDYING FOR.
KACHA (SNAP)
IT'S TYPICAL FOR A MIDDLE SCHOOLER TO MOAN, "WHAT'S THE POINT OF STUDYING THIS?" BUT FOR A HIGH SCHOOL STUDENT, ISN'T THE POINT OF STUDYING TO GET INTO A GOOD COLLEGE?
BUT RIGHT NOW, I'M ONLY STUDYING 'COS I DON'T WANNA GO TO CRAM SCHOOL.
THAT I'M STUDYING 'COS I DON'T WANNA STUDY IS A WEIRD CONTRA-DICTION...
IT'S ONLY THE ONES WHO DON'T REALLY THINK ABOUT IT THAT MINDLESSLY GET ON THE STEADY RAIL AND STUDY...
SEE? THAT'S WHAT YOU GET FOR RIDING THE RAILS. STUDYING LIKE NORMAL, WORKING LIKE NORMAL LEADS TO THAT EXHAUSTED SLOUCH.
PAKA (SNAP)
BUT IF I GET OFF THE RAILS NOW, I'LL HAVE TO BOARD THE TRAIN TO TOUSH●N ...
MAAAN...

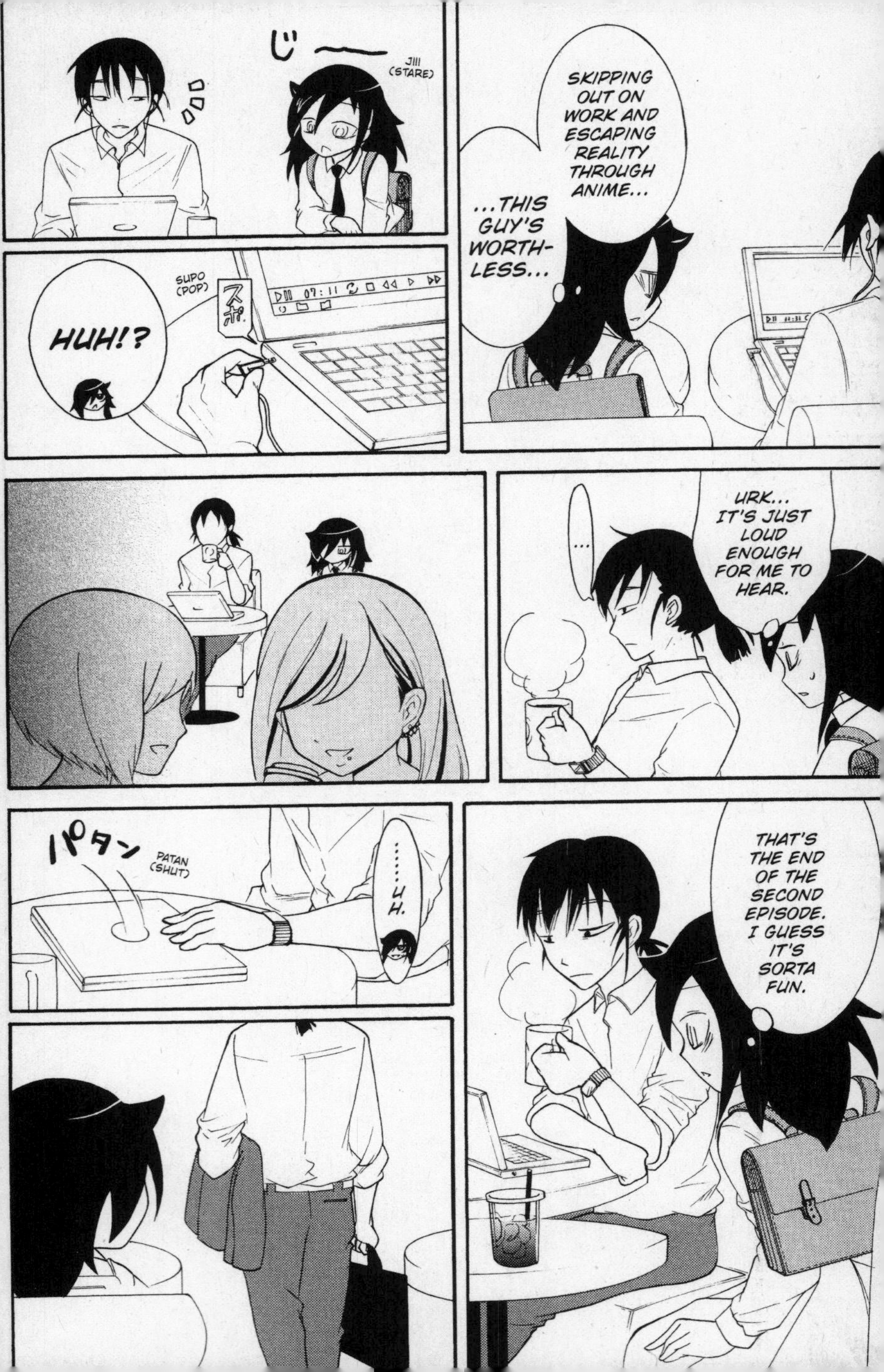
SKIPPING OUT ON WORK AND ESCAPING REALITY THROUGH ANIME...
...THIS GUY'S WORTH-LESS...
じー
JIII (STARE)
スポ
SUPO (POP)
HUH!?
...
URK... IT'S JUST LOUD ENOUGH FOR ME TO HEAR.
THAT'S THE END OF THE SECOND EPISODE. I GUESS IT'S SORTA FUN.
パタン
PATAN (SHUT)
......UH.

AHA, IT'S THIS ANIME...

I CAN WATCH THE NEXT EPISODE HERE...

SHUT DOWN

KACHI
(CLICK)

······

THE NEXT DAY

SA
(ZIP)

JURU
(SLURP)

JURU

CHIRA
(GLANCE)

ちら

CHIRA
ちら

HAAH
...

PAA
(BEAM)

ぱぁ...

I DON'T FEEL LIKE STUDYING. GUESS I'LL GO HOME...

JUST TWO EPISODES TODAY TOO? WELL, I GUESS IT'LL BE ODD FOR HIM TO SHOW ME ALL OF THEM...

TULI'S COFFEE

NEW ブルベリーラ
blue berry Lat

100

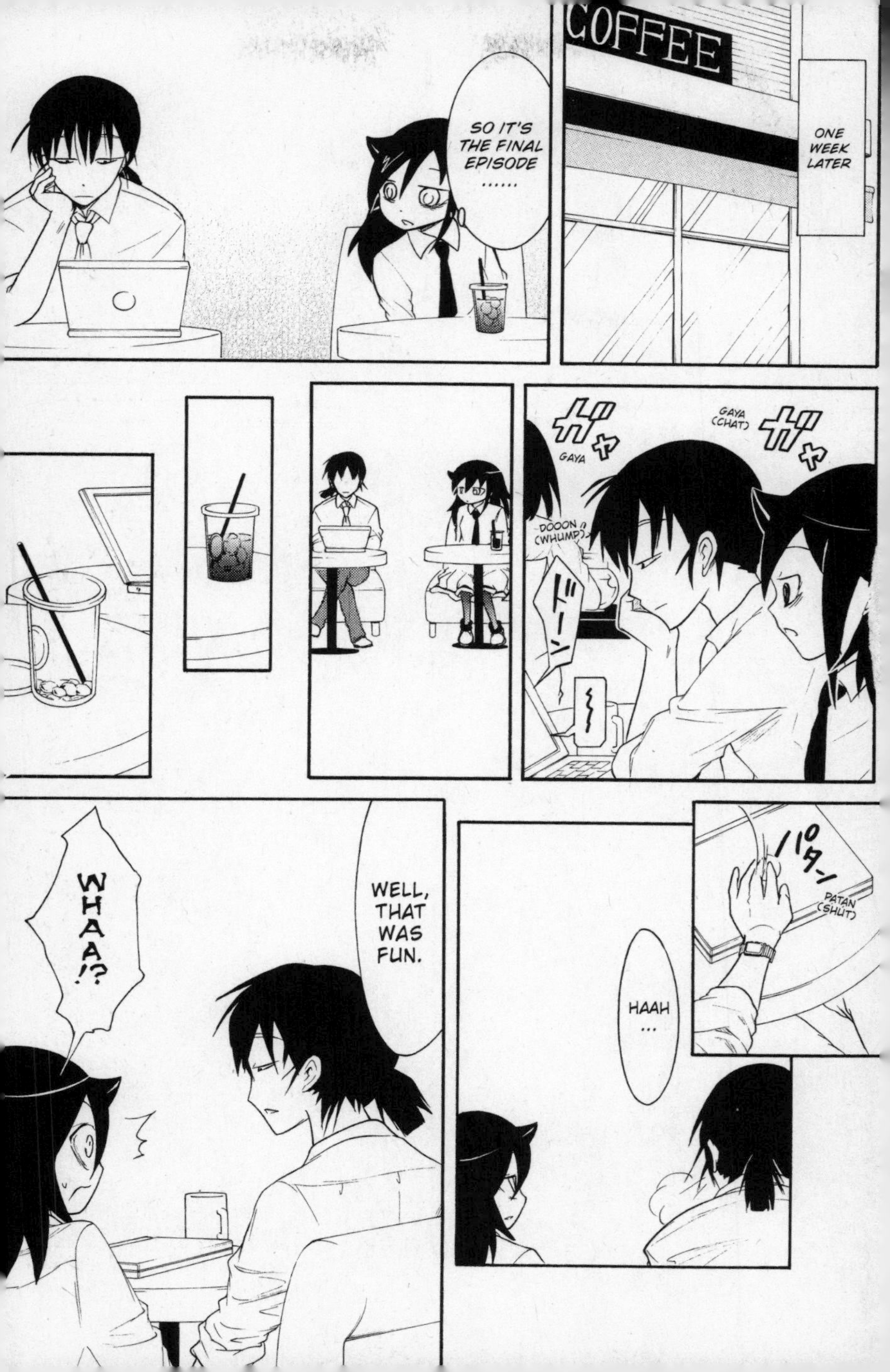

COFFEE
ONE WEEK LATER
SO IT'S THE FINAL EPISODE ......
GAYA (CHAT)
GAYA
DOOON (WHUMP)
PATAN (SHUT)
HAAH ...
WELL, THAT WAS FUN.
WHAA!?

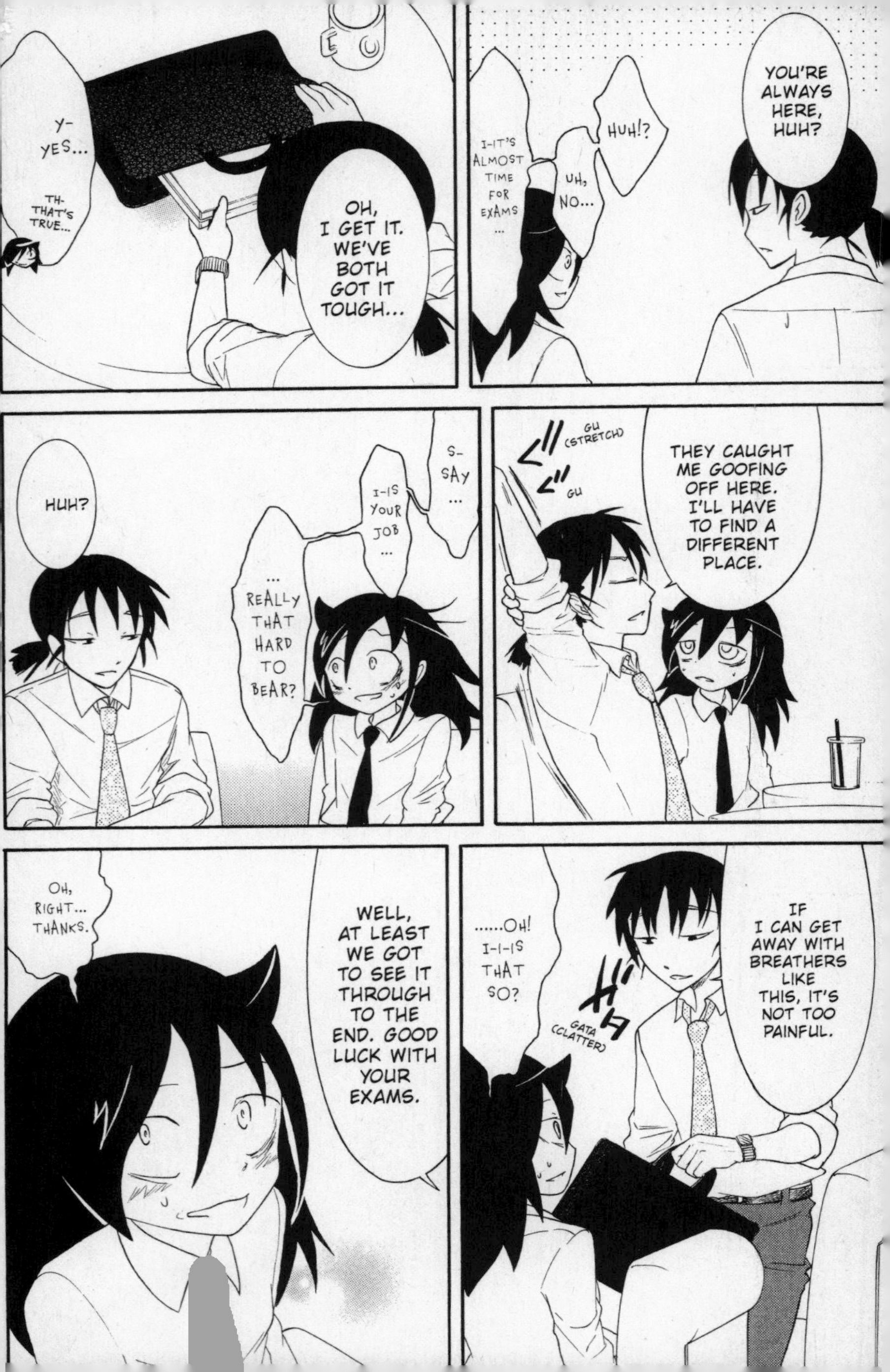
YOU'RE ALWAYS HERE, HUH?
HUH!?
UH, NO...
I-IT'S ALMOST TIME FOR EXAMS ...
OH, I GET IT. WE'VE BOTH GOT IT TOUGH...
Y-YES...
TH-THAT'S TRUE...
THEY CAUGHT ME GOOFING OFF HERE. I'LL HAVE TO FIND A DIFFERENT PLACE.
GU (STRETCH)
GU
S-SAY ...
I-IS YOUR JOB ...
... REALLY THAT HARD TO BEAR?
HUH?
IF I CAN GET AWAY WITH BREATHERS LIKE THIS, IT'S NOT TOO PAINFUL.
GATA (CLATTER)
......OH! I-I-IS THAT SO?
WELL, AT LEAST WE GOT TO SEE IT THROUGH TO THE END. GOOD LUCK WITH YOUR EXAMS.
OH, RIGHT... THANKS.

CHIRA
(GLANCE)
ち
ら

THE NEXT DAY

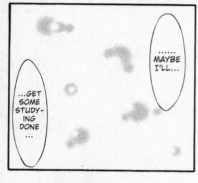

...GET SOME STUDYING DONE...

......MAYBE I'LL...

......

NO CRAM SCHOOL FOR ME!

GOOD, I GOT AVERAGE MARKS.

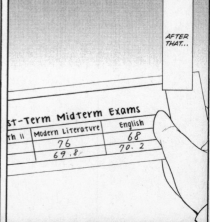

AFTER THAT...

st-Term Midterm Exams

th II	Modern Literature	English
	76	68
	69.8	70.2

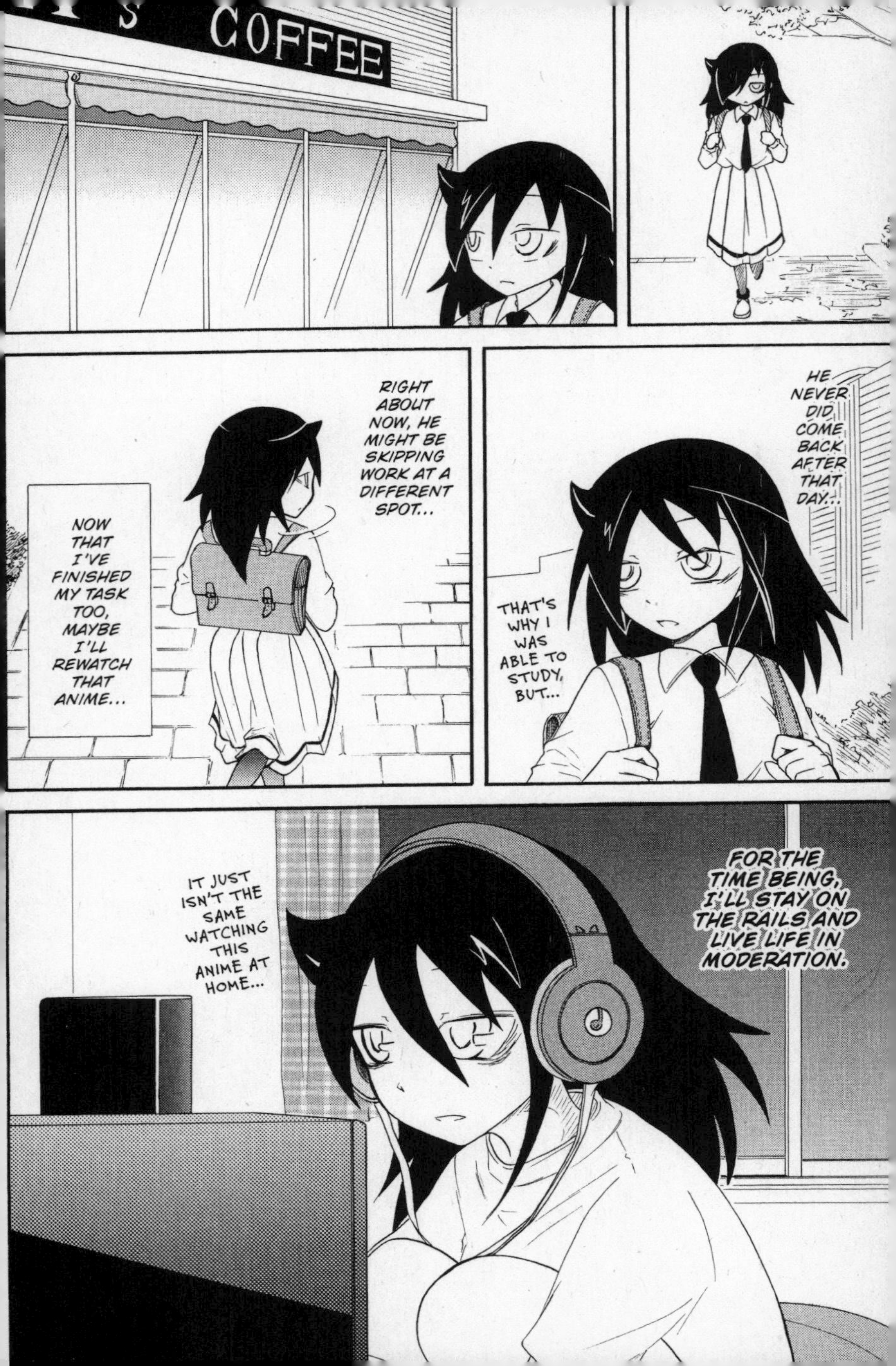
COFFEE
HE NEVER DID COME BACK AFTER THAT DAY...
THAT'S WHY I WAS ABLE TO STUDY, BUT...
RIGHT ABOUT NOW, HE MIGHT BE SKIPPING WORK AT A DIFFERENT SPOT...
NOW THAT I'VE FINISHED MY TASK TOO, MAYBE I'LL REWATCH THAT ANIME...
FOR THE TIME BEING, I'LL STAY ON THE RAILS AND LIVE LIFE IN MODERATION.
IT JUST ISN'T THE SAME WATCHING THIS ANIME AT HOME...

No Matter How I Look at It, It's You Guys' Fault I'm Not Popular!

FAIL 45: I'M NOT POPULAR, SO I'LL KILL TIME.

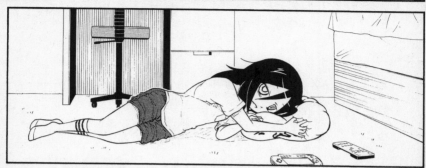

ALL RIGHT... LET'S SEE IF...

...I CAN FOOL LITTLE BRO.

OH, NOT IN A GAME. A REAL ONE.

YOU KNOW, I RECENTLY GOT A BOYFRIEND...

YA DON'T SAY.

SO, ANYWAY, THERE'S THIS SPACE BETWEEN THE NORTH AND SOUTH SCHOOL BUILDINGS. IT'S HARD TO NOTICE, BUT THERE'S A PATH THROUGH IT.

WE EAT LUNCH THERE TOGETHER A LOT.

......

SORRY ABOUT THAT...

OKAY.

YOU BETTER NOT COME BY THERE, FOR REAL, YOU HEAR ME!?

GOT IT.

WE'RE THERE ALMOST EVERY DAY, SO MAKE SURE YOU DON'T COME BY.

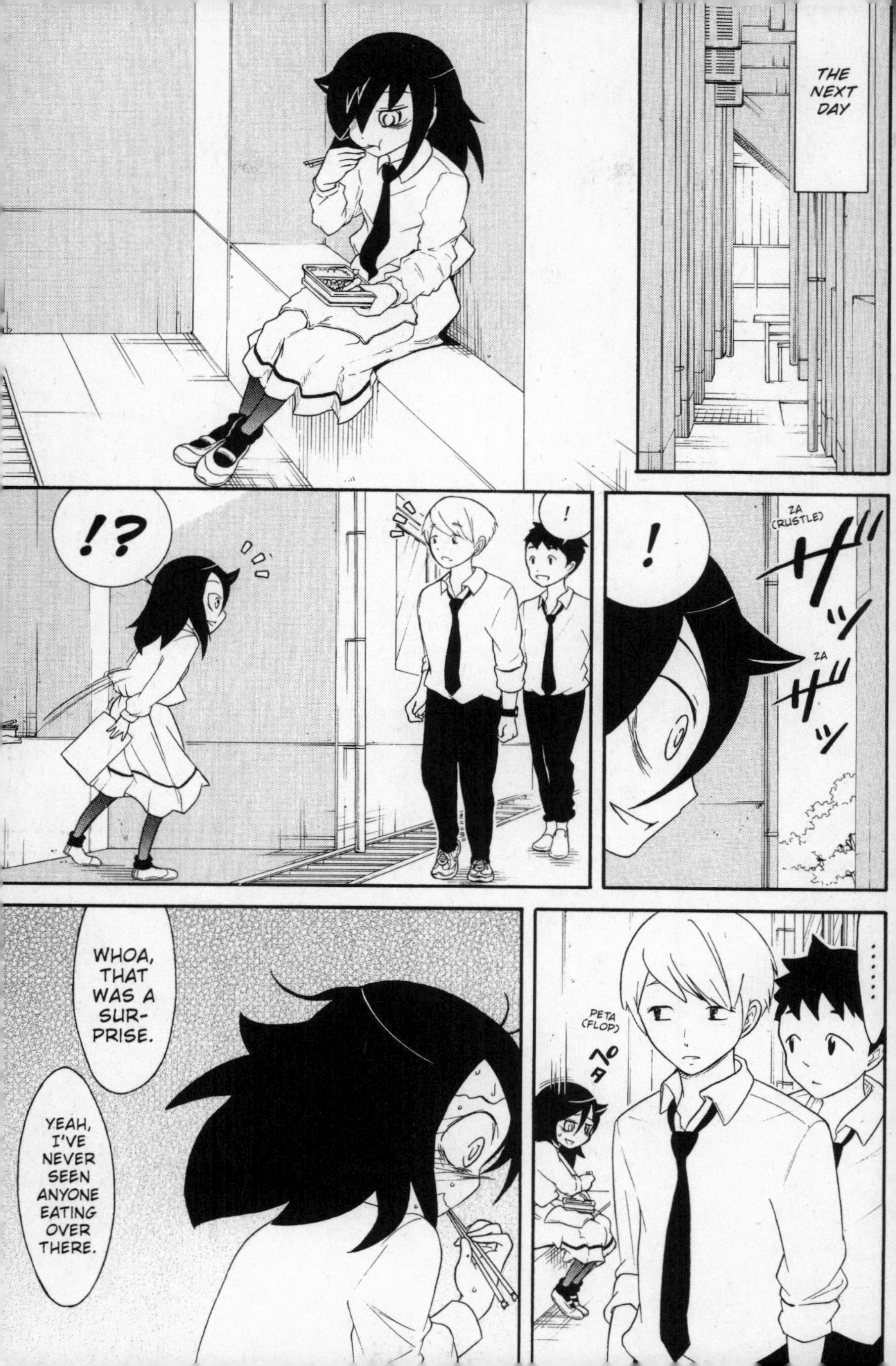
THE NEXT DAY
!
ZA (RUSTLE)
ザッ
ZA
ザッ
!
!?
......
PETA (FLOP)
ペタ
WHOA, THAT WAS A SUR-PRISE.
YEAH, I'VE NEVER SEEN ANYONE EATING OVER THERE.

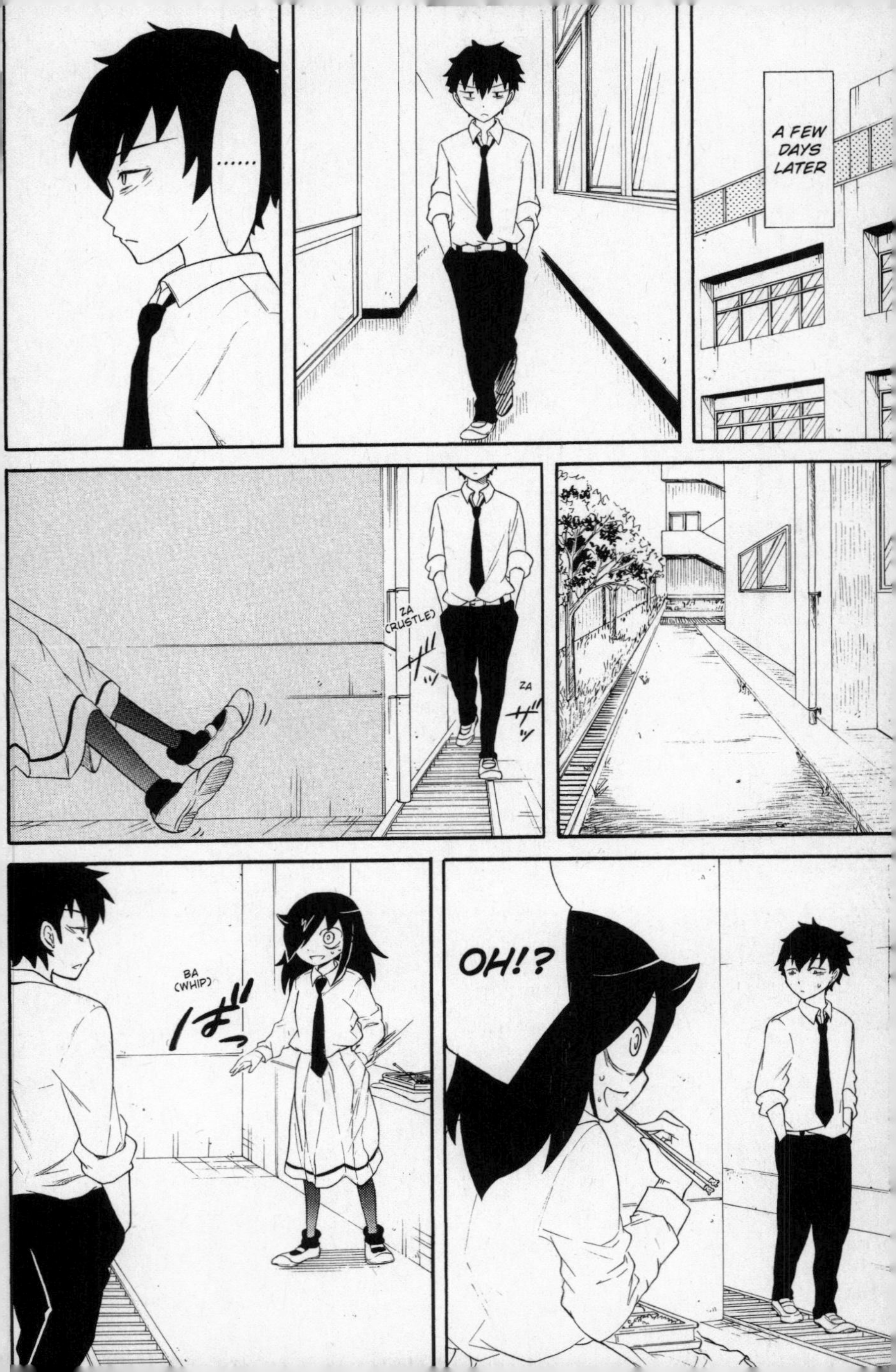

A FEW DAYS LATER
......
ZA (RUSTLE)
ザッ
ZA
ザッ
OH!?
BA (WHIP)
ばっ

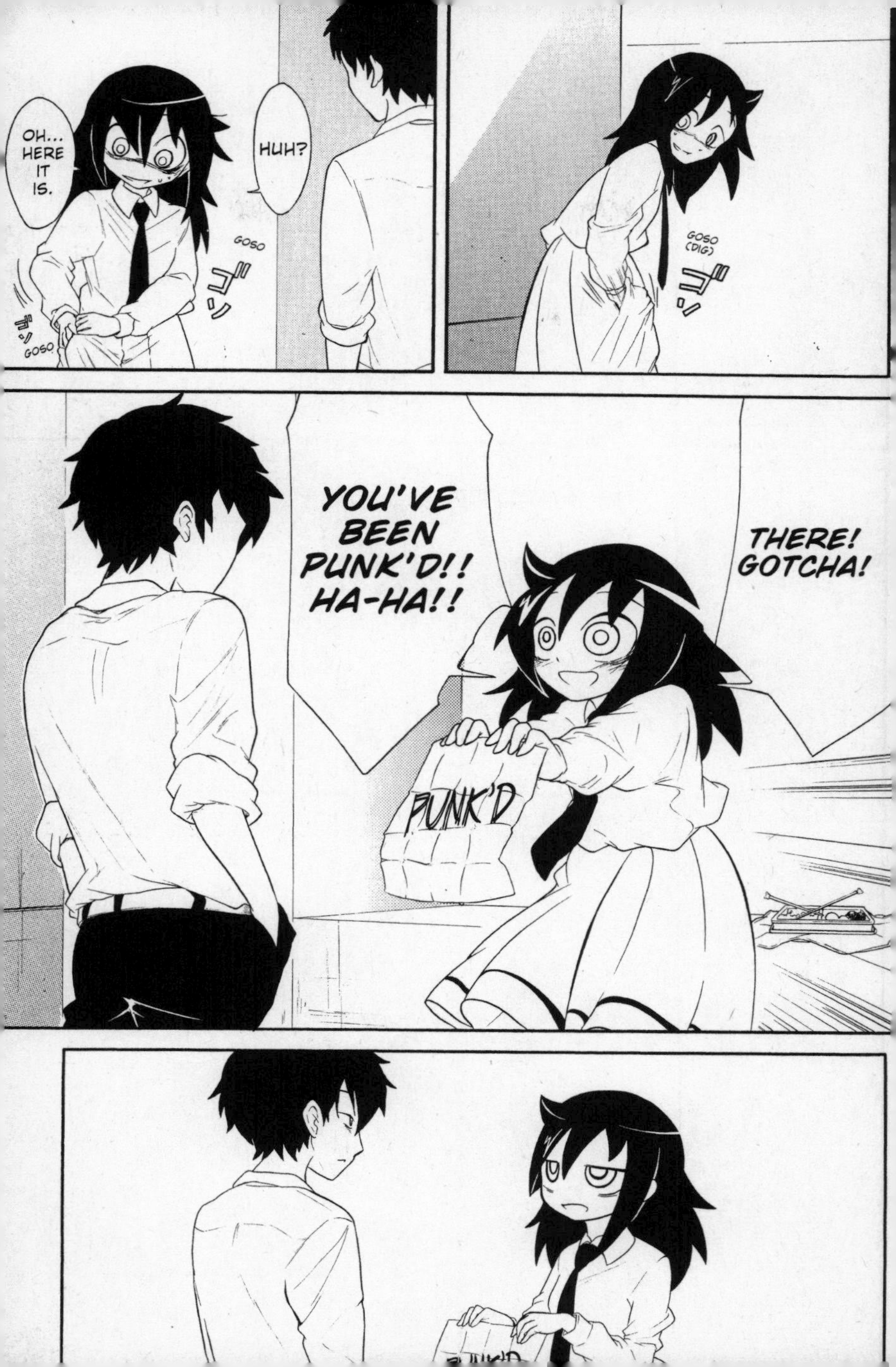
GOSO (DIG)
ゴソ
HUH?
OH... HERE IT IS.
GOSO
ゴソ
ゴソ
GOSO
THERE! GOTCHA!
YOU'VE BEEN PUNK'D!! HA-HA!!
PUNK'D

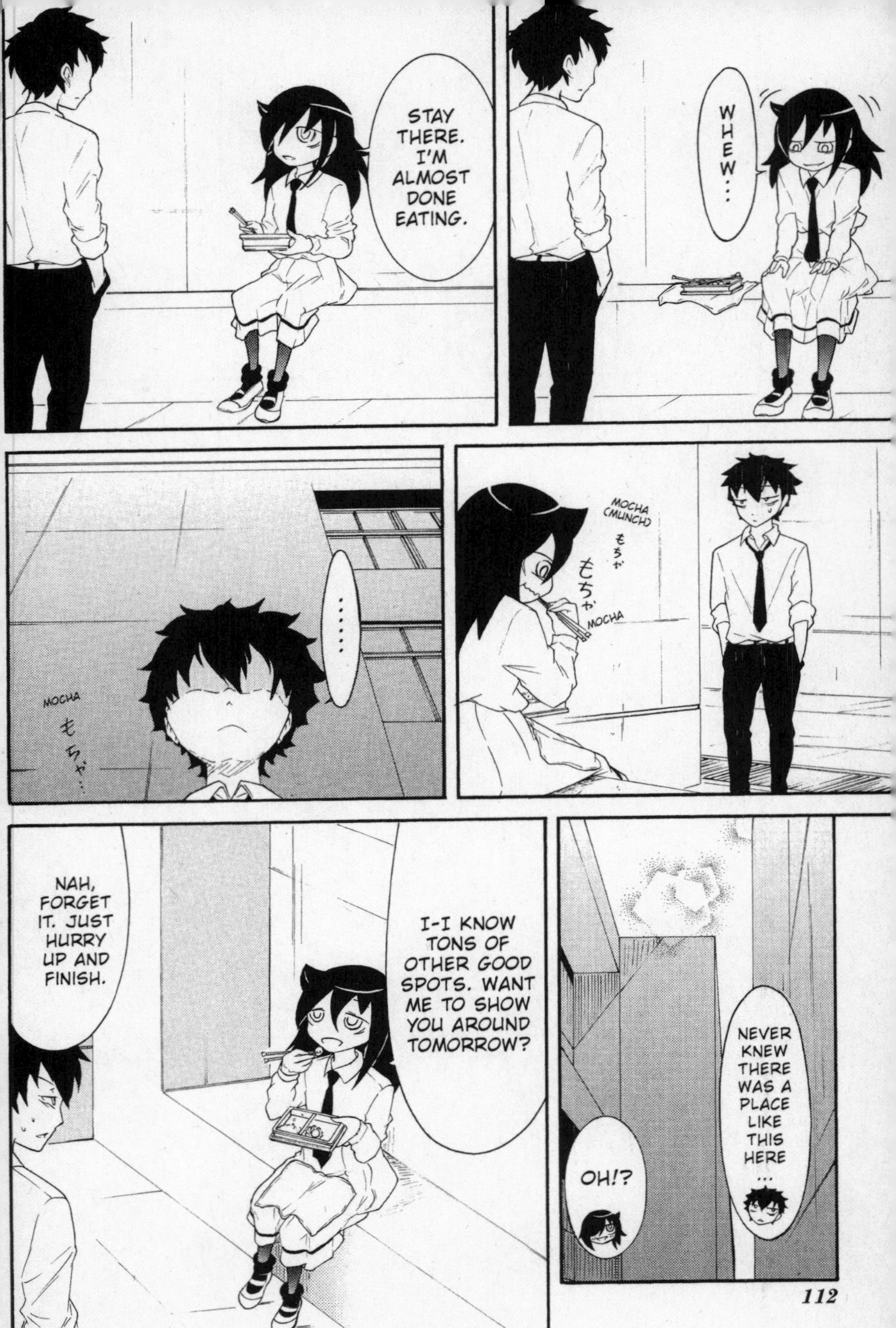
WHEW...
STAY THERE. I'M ALMOST DONE EATING.
MOCHA (MUNCH)
もちゃ
もちゃ
MOCHA
......
MOCHA
もちゃ...
NEVER KNEW THERE WAS A PLACE LIKE THIS HERE...
OH!?
I-I KNOW TONS OF OTHER GOOD SPOTS. WANT ME TO SHOW YOU AROUND TOMORROW?
NAH, FORGET IT. JUST HURRY UP AND FINISH.

No **M**atter **H**ow **I** **L**oo**k** at **I**t, **I**t's **Y**ou **G**uys' **F**au**l**t **I**'m **N**ot **P**op**u**lar!

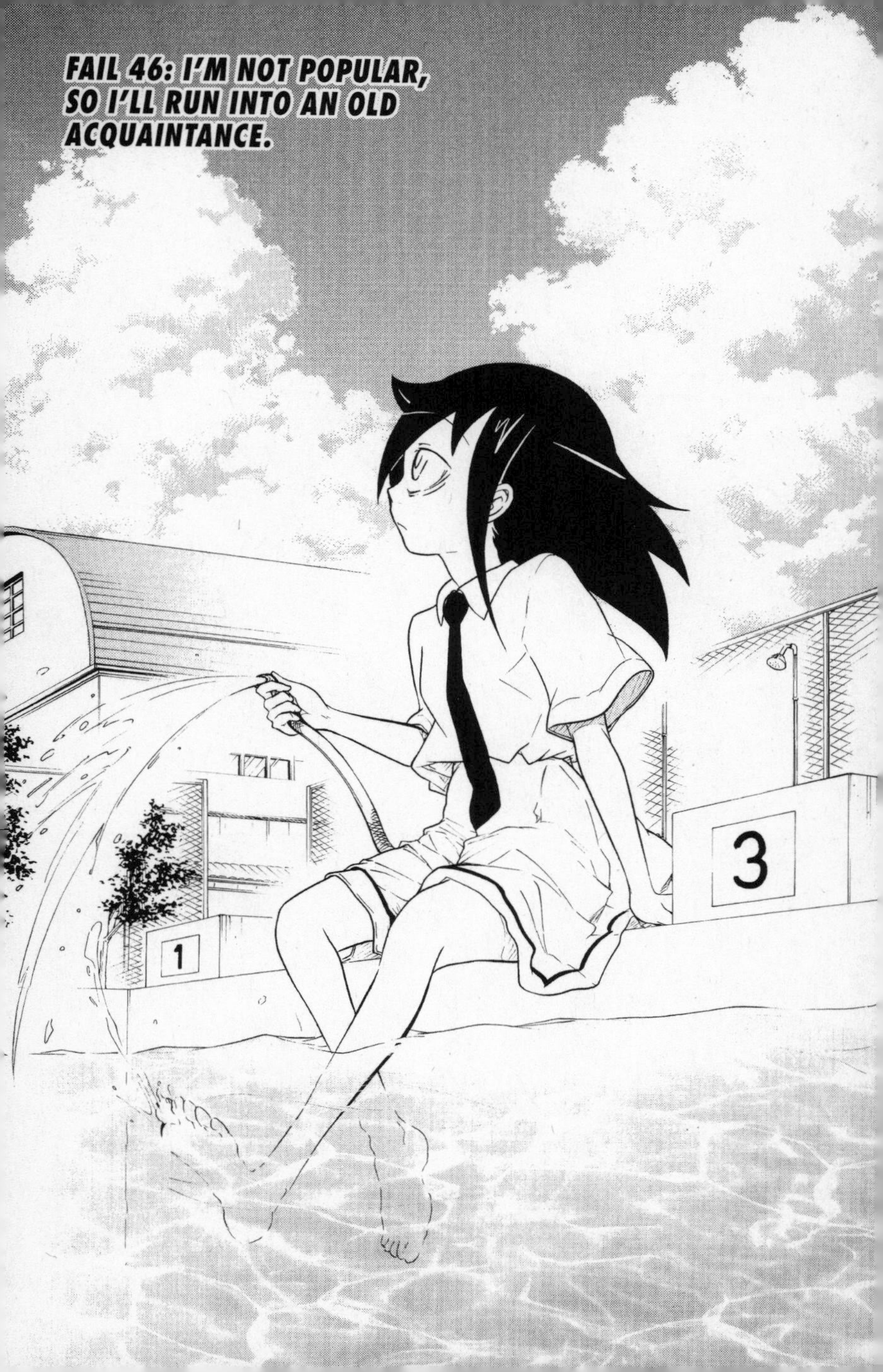
FAIL 46: I'M NOT POPULAR, SO I'LL RUN INTO AN OLD ACQUAINTANCE.
3
1

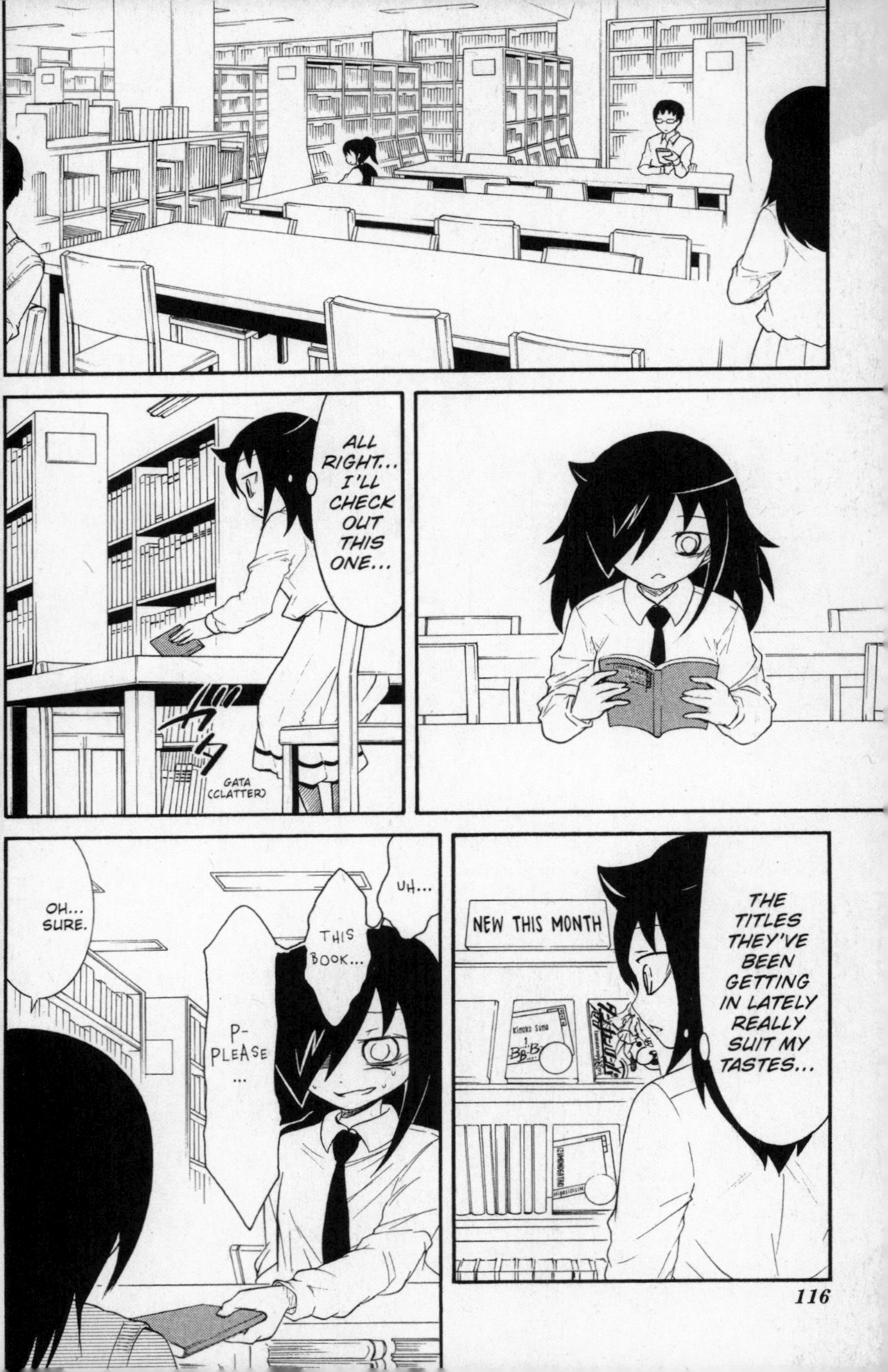
ALL RIGHT... I'LL CHECK OUT THIS ONE...
GATA (CLATTER)
NEW THIS MONTH
THE TITLES THEY'VE BEEN GETTING IN LATELY REALLY SUIT MY TASTES...
UH...
THIS BOOK...
P-PLEASE...
OH... SURE.

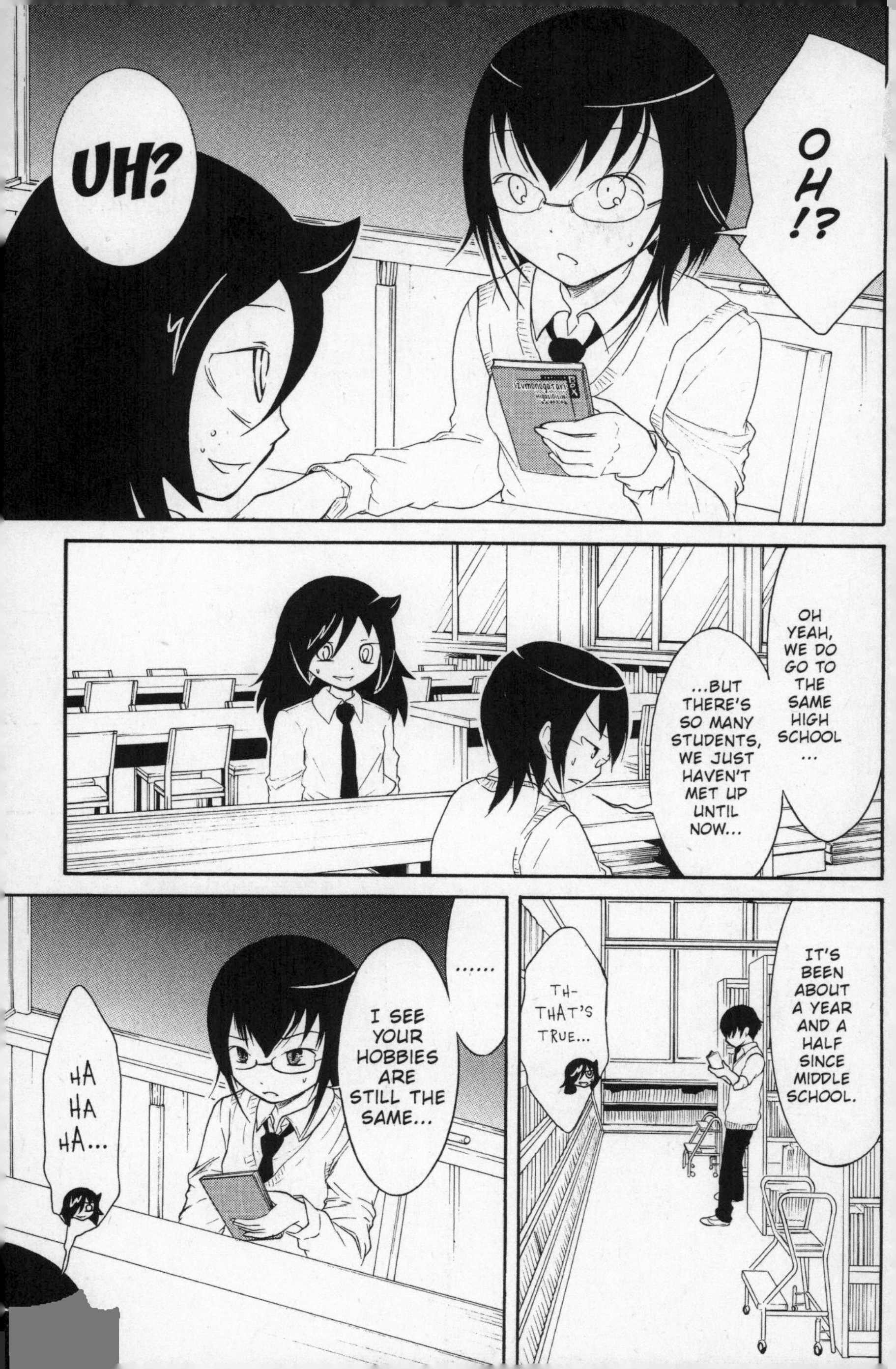
OH!?
UH?
OH YEAH, WE DO GO TO THE SAME HIGH SCHOOL...
...BUT THERE'S SO MANY STUDENTS, WE JUST HAVEN'T MET UP UNTIL NOW...
IT'S BEEN ABOUT A YEAR AND A HALF SINCE MIDDLE SCHOOL.
TH-THAT'S TRUE...
......
I SEE YOUR HOBBIES ARE STILL THE SAME...
HA HA HA...

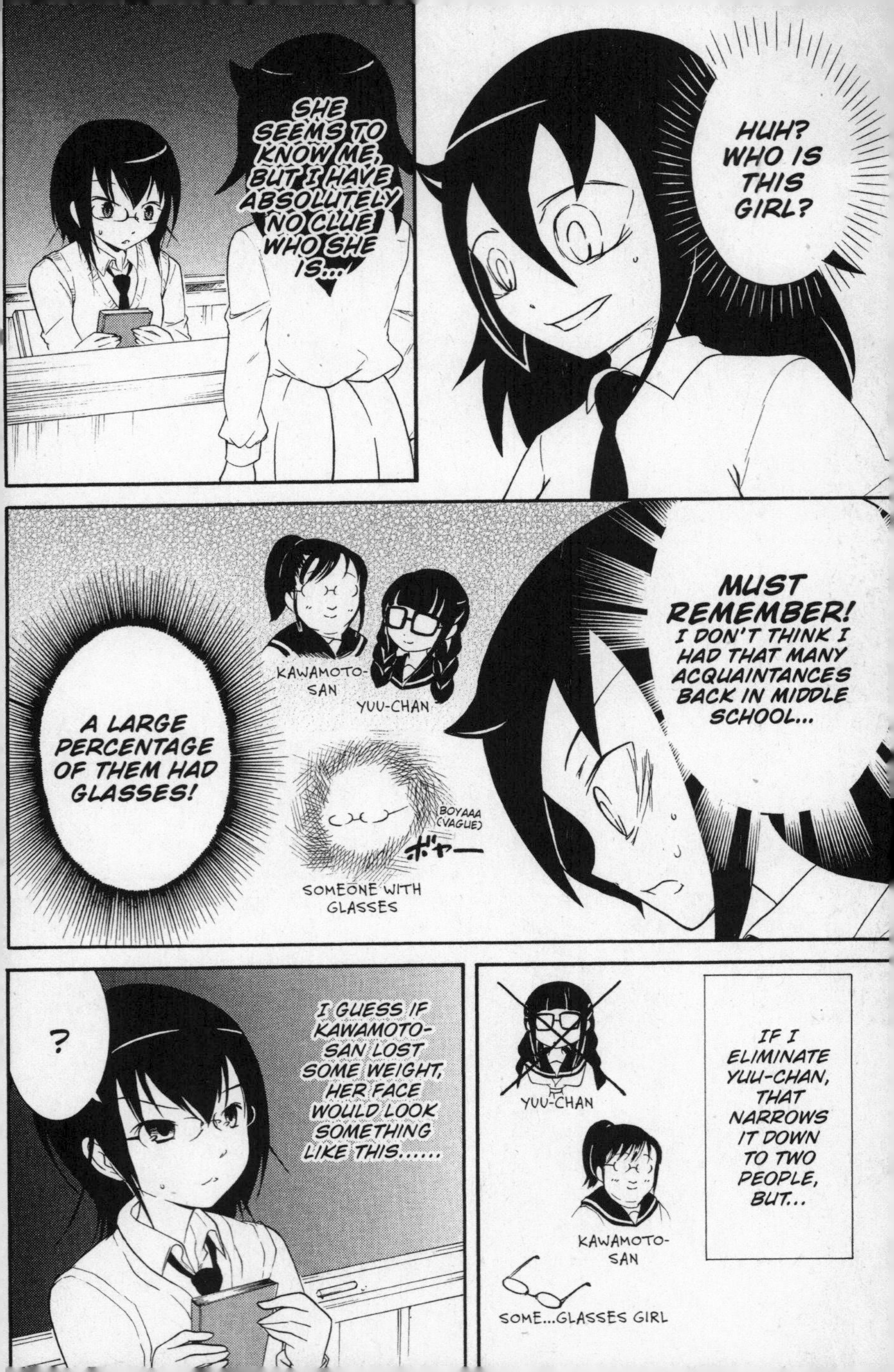
HUH? WHO IS THIS GIRL?
SHE SEEMS TO KNOW ME, BUT I HAVE ABSOLUTELY NO CLUE WHO SHE IS...
MUST REMEMBER! I DON'T THINK I HAD THAT MANY ACQUAINTANCES BACK IN MIDDLE SCHOOL...
KAWAMOTO-SAN
YUU-CHAN
BOYAAA (VAGUE)
ボヤー
SOMEONE WITH GLASSES
A LARGE PERCENTAGE OF THEM HAD GLASSES!
IF I ELIMINATE YUU-CHAN, THAT NARROWS IT DOWN TO TWO PEOPLE, BUT...
YUU-CHAN
KAWAMOTO-SAN
SOME...GLASSES GIRL
?
I GUESS IF KAWAMOTO-SAN LOST SOME WEIGHT, HER FACE WOULD LOOK SOMETHING LIKE THIS......

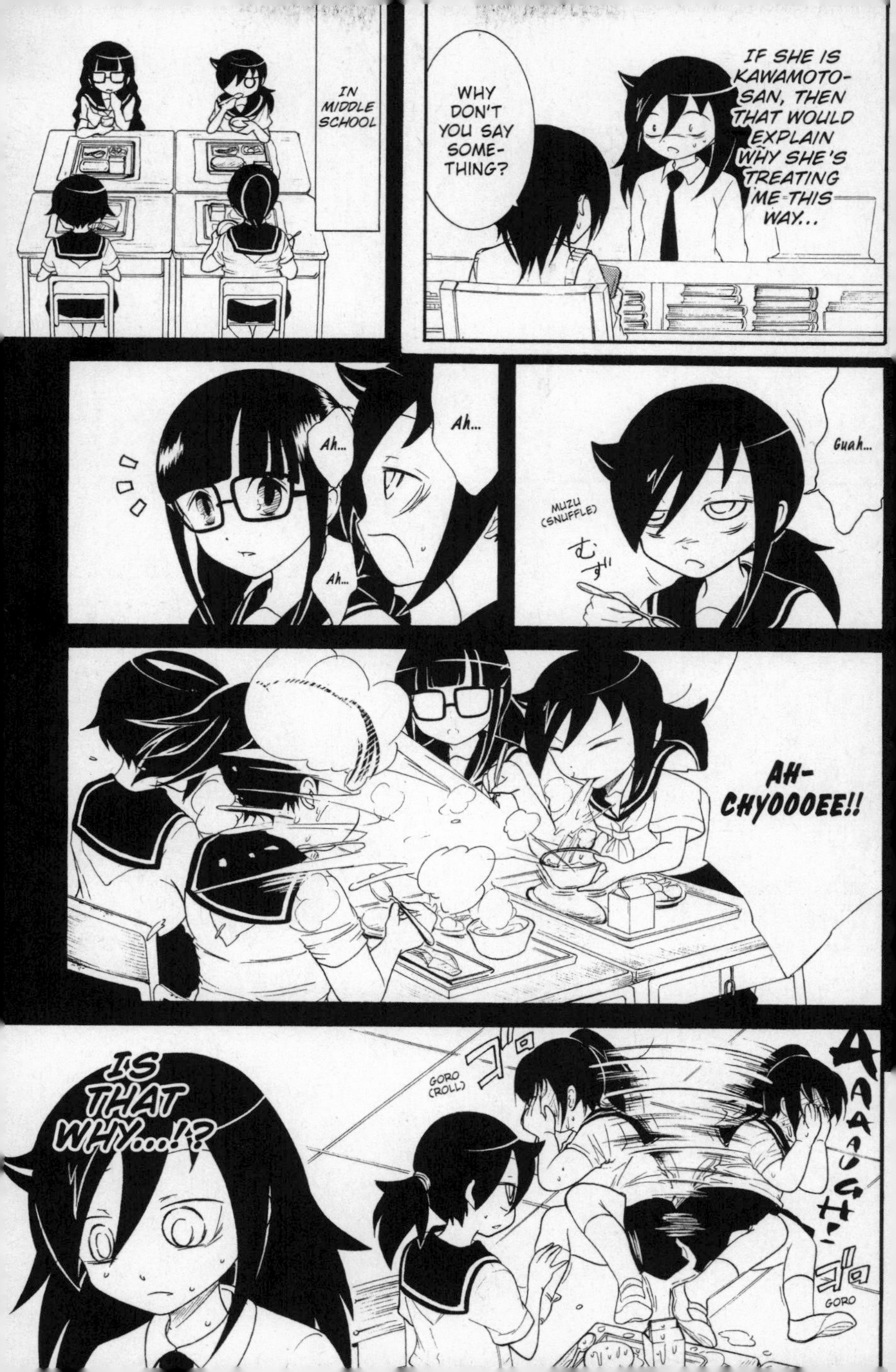

IF SHE IS KAWAMOTO-SAN, THEN THAT WOULD EXPLAIN WHY SHE'S TREATING ME THIS WAY...
WHY DON'T YOU SAY SOME-THING?
IN MIDDLE SCHOOL
Guah...
MUZU (SNUFFLE)
むず
Ah...
Ah...
Ah...
AH-CHYOOOEE!!
AAAAUGH!!
ゴロ
GORO
ゴロ
GORO (ROLL)
IS THAT WHY...!?

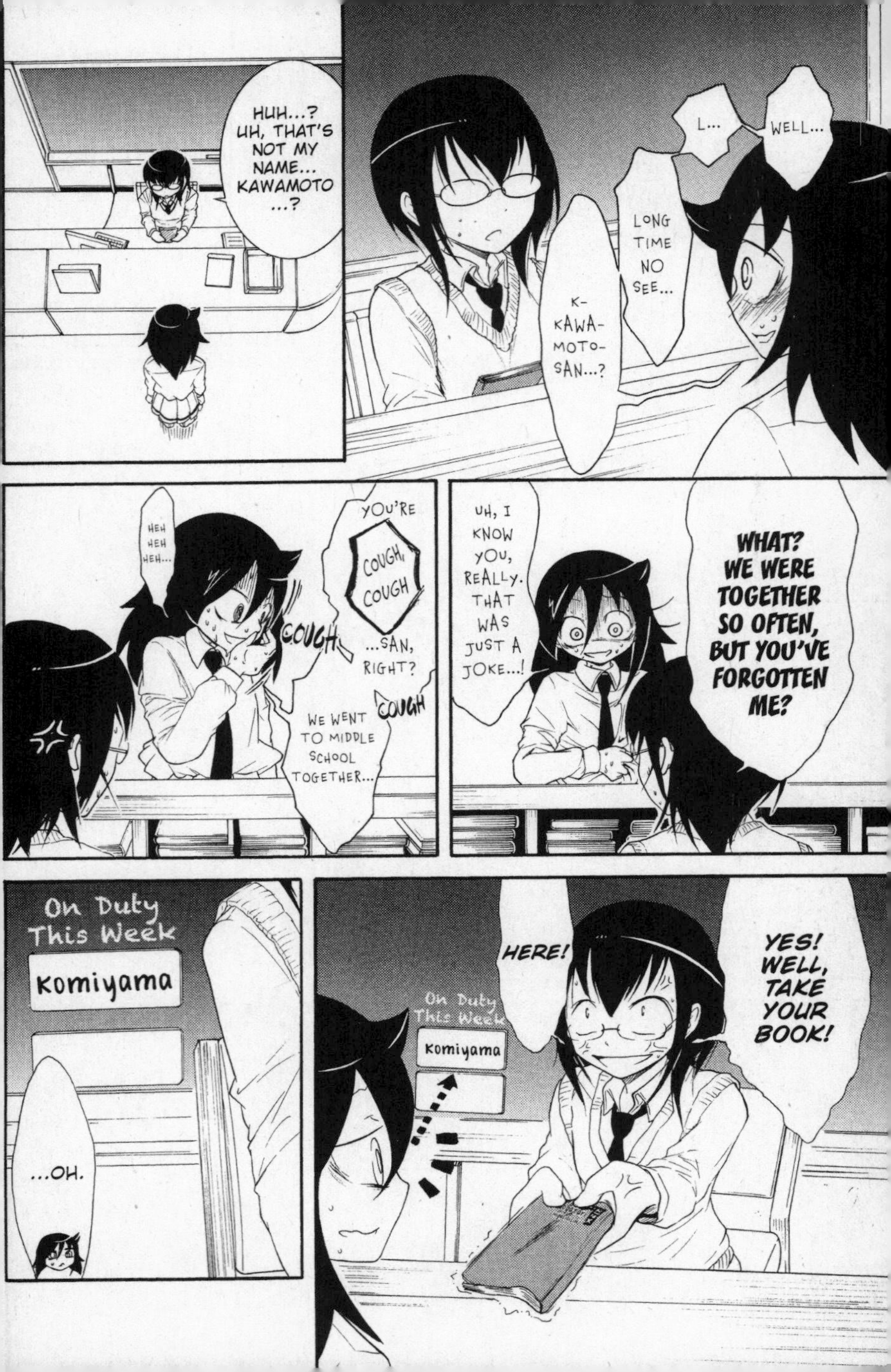
WELL...
L...
LONG TIME NO SEE...
K-KAWAMOTO-SAN...?
HUH...? UH, THAT'S NOT MY NAME... KAWAMOTO...?
WHAT? WE WERE TOGETHER SO OFTEN, BUT YOU'VE FORGOTTEN ME?
UH, I KNOW YOU, REALLY. THAT WAS JUST A JOKE...!
YOU'RE
COUGH, COUGH
...SAN, RIGHT?
COUGH
COUGH
WE WENT TO MIDDLE SCHOOL TOGETHER...
HEH HEH HEH...
YES! WELL, TAKE YOUR BOOK!
HERE!
On Duty This Week
Komiyama
On Duty This Week
Komiyama
...OH.

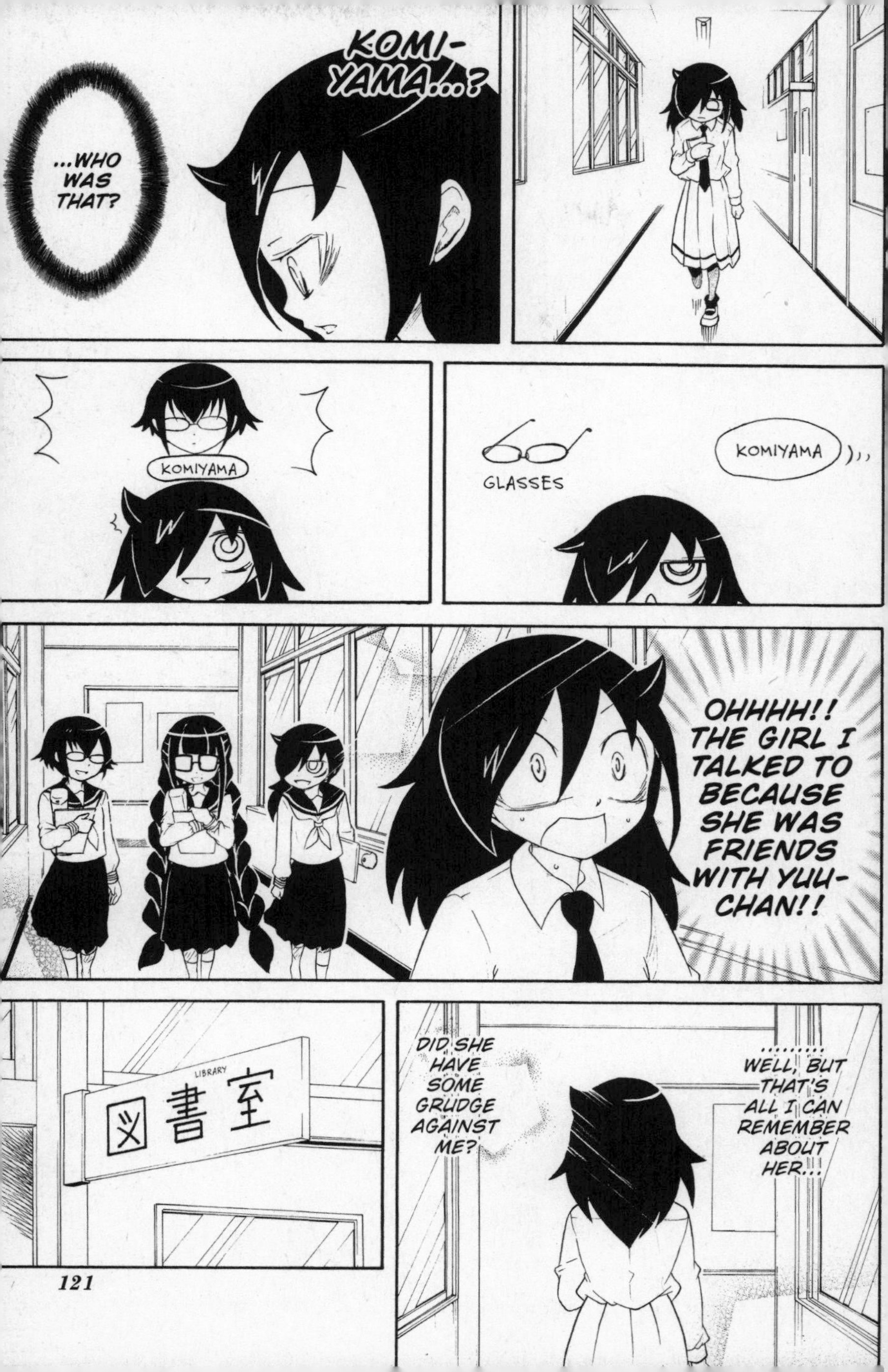
KOMI-YAMA...?
...WHO WAS THAT?
KOMIYAMA
GLASSES
KOMIYAMA
OHHHH!! THE GIRL I TALKED TO BECAUSE SHE WAS FRIENDS WITH YUU-CHAN!!
.... WELL, BUT THAT'S ALL I CAN REMEMBER ABOUT HER...
DID SHE HAVE SOME GRUDGE AGAINST ME?
LIBRARY
図書室

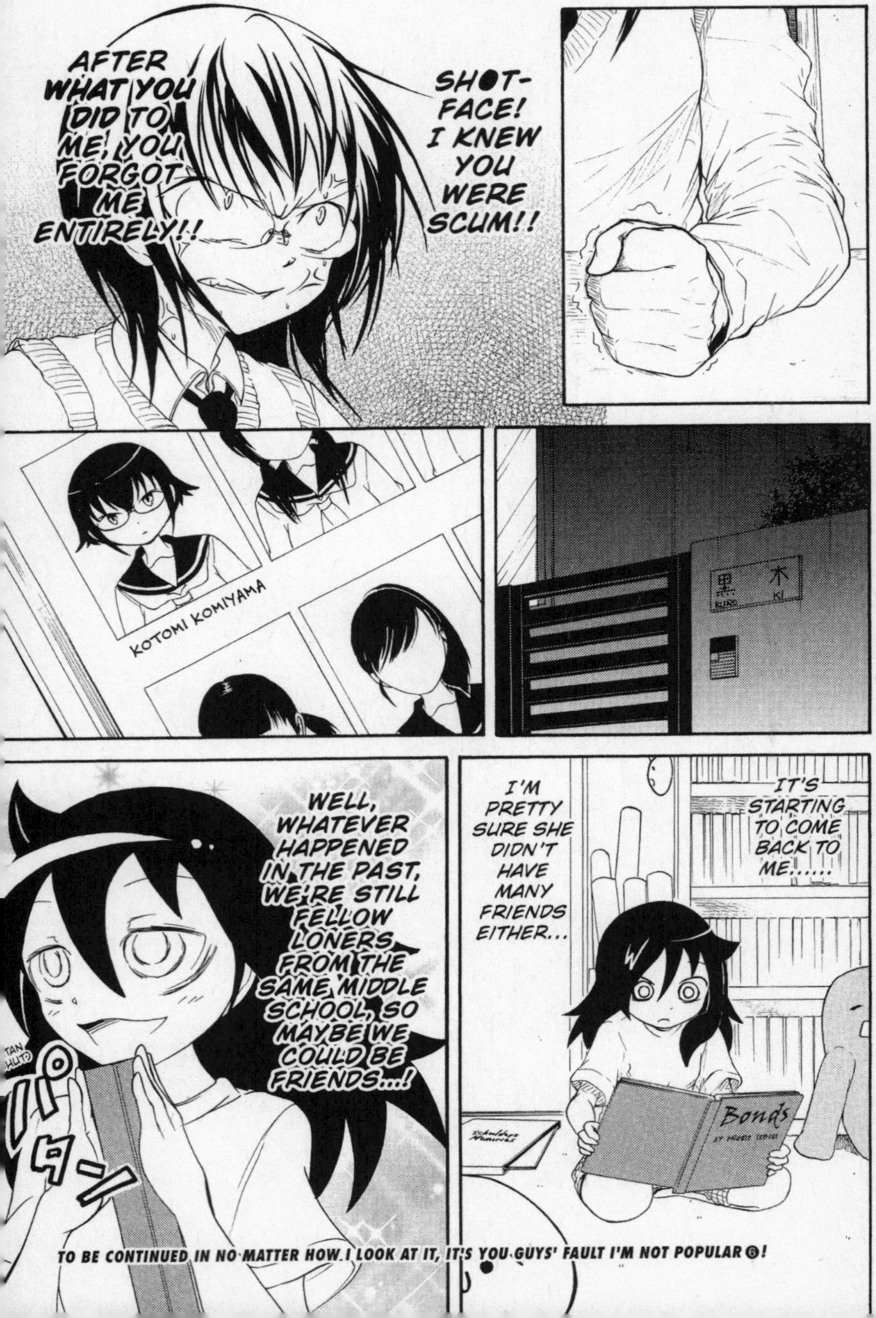
SHOT-FACE! I KNEW YOU WERE SCUM!!
AFTER WHAT YOU DID TO ME, YOU FORGOT ME ENTIRELY!!
黒 木
KOTOMI KOMIYAMA
IT'S STARTING TO COME BACK TO ME......
I'M PRETTY SURE SHE DIDN'T HAVE MANY FRIENDS EITHER...
Bonds
WELL, WHATEVER HAPPENED IN THE PAST, WE'RE STILL FELLOW LONERS FROM THE SAME MIDDLE SCHOOL, SO MAYBE WE COULD BE FRIENDS...!

TO BE CONTINUED IN NO MATTER HOW I LOOK AT IT, IT'S YOU GUYS' FAULT I'M NOT POPULAR ⑥!

No Matter How I Look at It, It's You Guys' Fault I'm Not Popular!

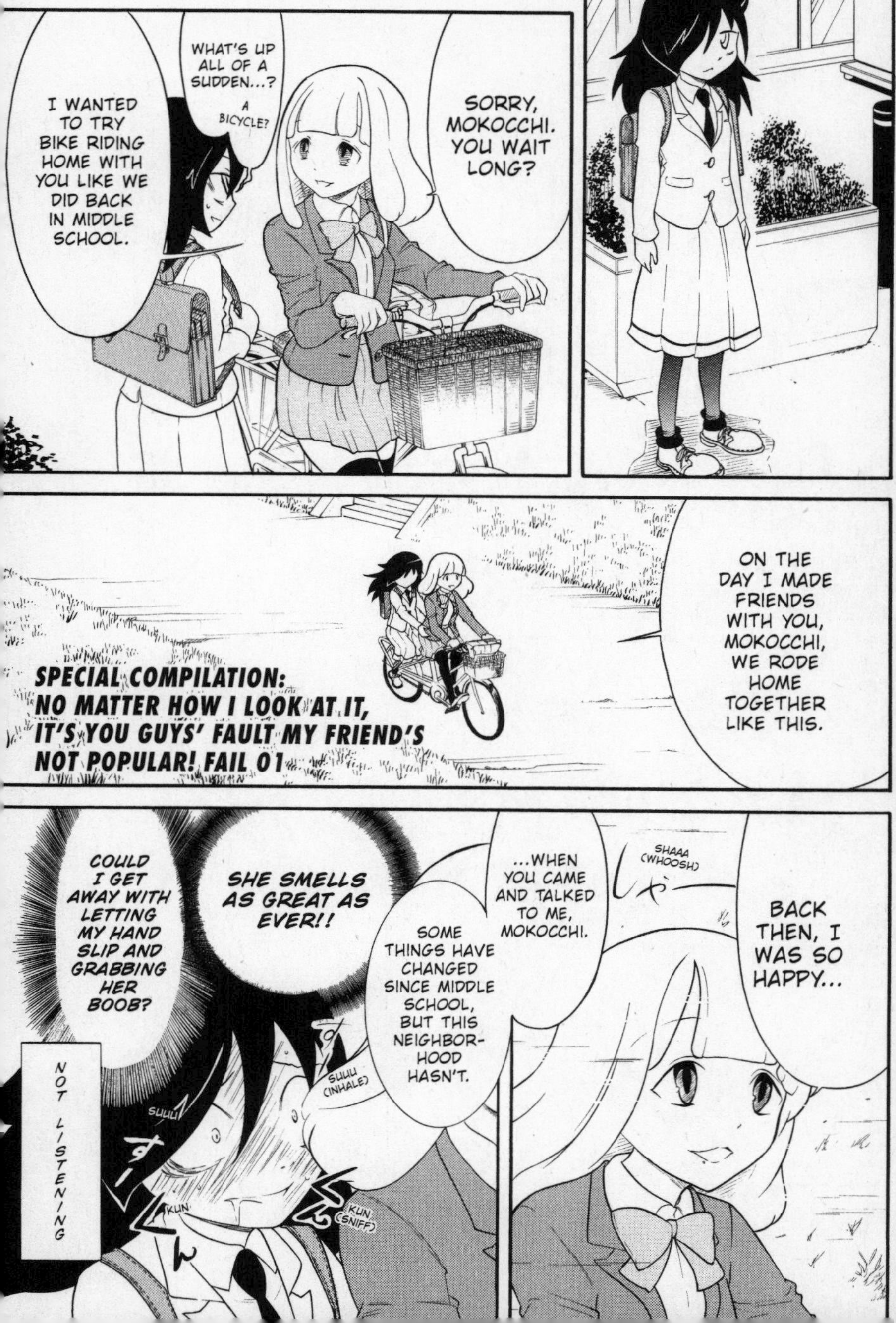
SORRY, MOKOCCHI. YOU WAIT LONG?
WHAT'S UP ALL OF A SUDDEN...?
A BICYCLE?
I WANTED TO TRY BIKE RIDING HOME WITH YOU LIKE WE DID BACK IN MIDDLE SCHOOL.
ON THE DAY I MADE FRIENDS WITH YOU, MOKOCCHI, WE RODE HOME TOGETHER LIKE THIS.
SPECIAL COMPILATION: NO MATTER HOW I LOOK AT IT, IT'S YOU GUYS' FAULT MY FRIEND'S NOT POPULAR! FAIL 01
SHAAA (WHOOSH)
BACK THEN, I WAS SO HAPPY...
...WHEN YOU CAME AND TALKED TO ME, MOKOCCHI.
SOME THINGS HAVE CHANGED SINCE MIDDLE SCHOOL, BUT THIS NEIGHBORHOOD HASN'T.
SUUU (INHALE)
KUN (SNIFF)
SHE SMELLS AS GREAT AS EVER!!
COULD I GET AWAY WITH LETTING MY HAND SLIP AND GRABBING HER BOOB?
SUUU
KUN
NOT LISTENING

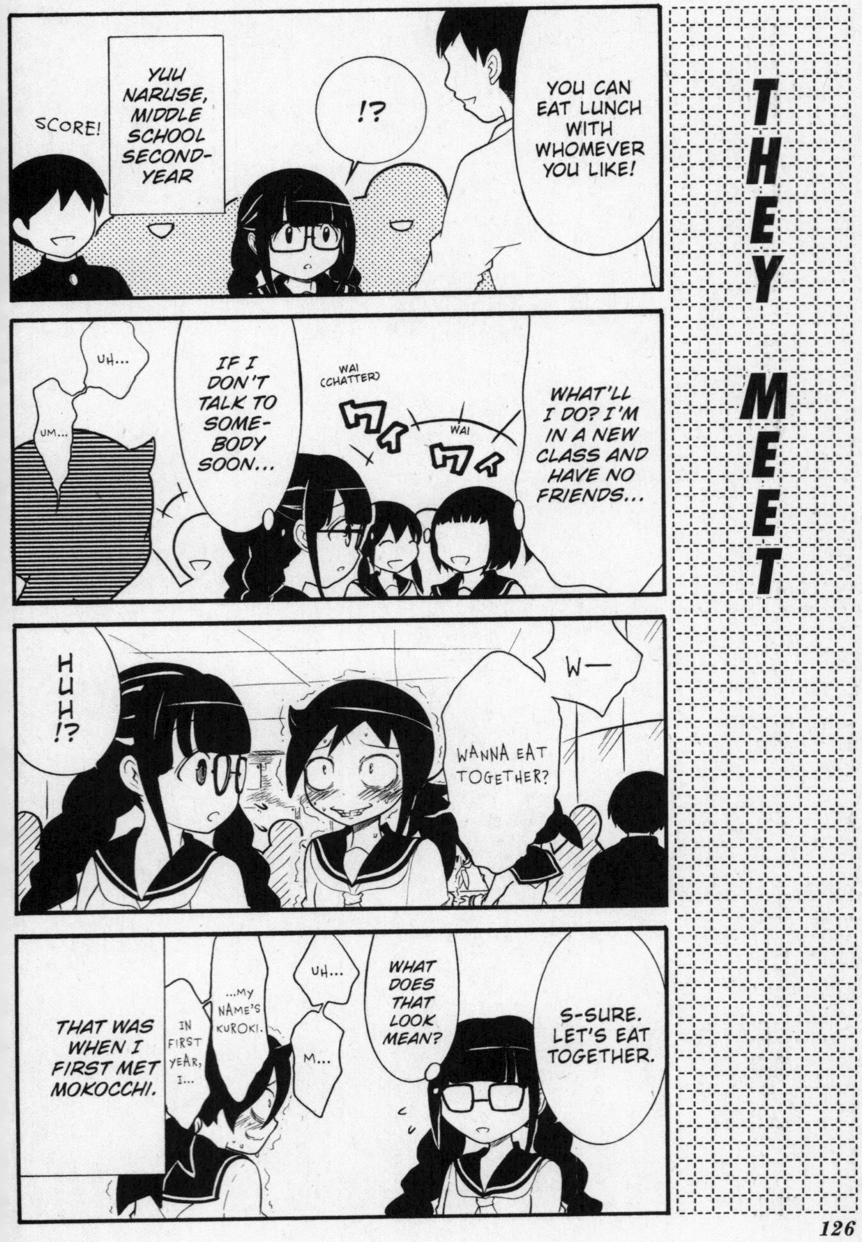
THEY MEET
YOU CAN EAT LUNCH WITH WHOMEVER YOU LIKE!
!?
YUU NARUSE, MIDDLE SCHOOL SECOND-YEAR
SCORE!
WHAT'LL I DO? I'M IN A NEW CLASS AND HAVE NO FRIENDS...
WAI
WAI (CHATTER)
IF I DON'T TALK TO SOMEBODY SOON...
UH...
UM...
W—
WANNA EAT TOGETHER?
HUH!?
S-SURE. LET'S EAT TOGETHER.
WHAT DOES THAT LOOK MEAN?
UH...
M...
...MY NAME'S KUROKI.
IN FIRST YEAR, I...
THAT WAS WHEN I FIRST MET MOKOCCHI.

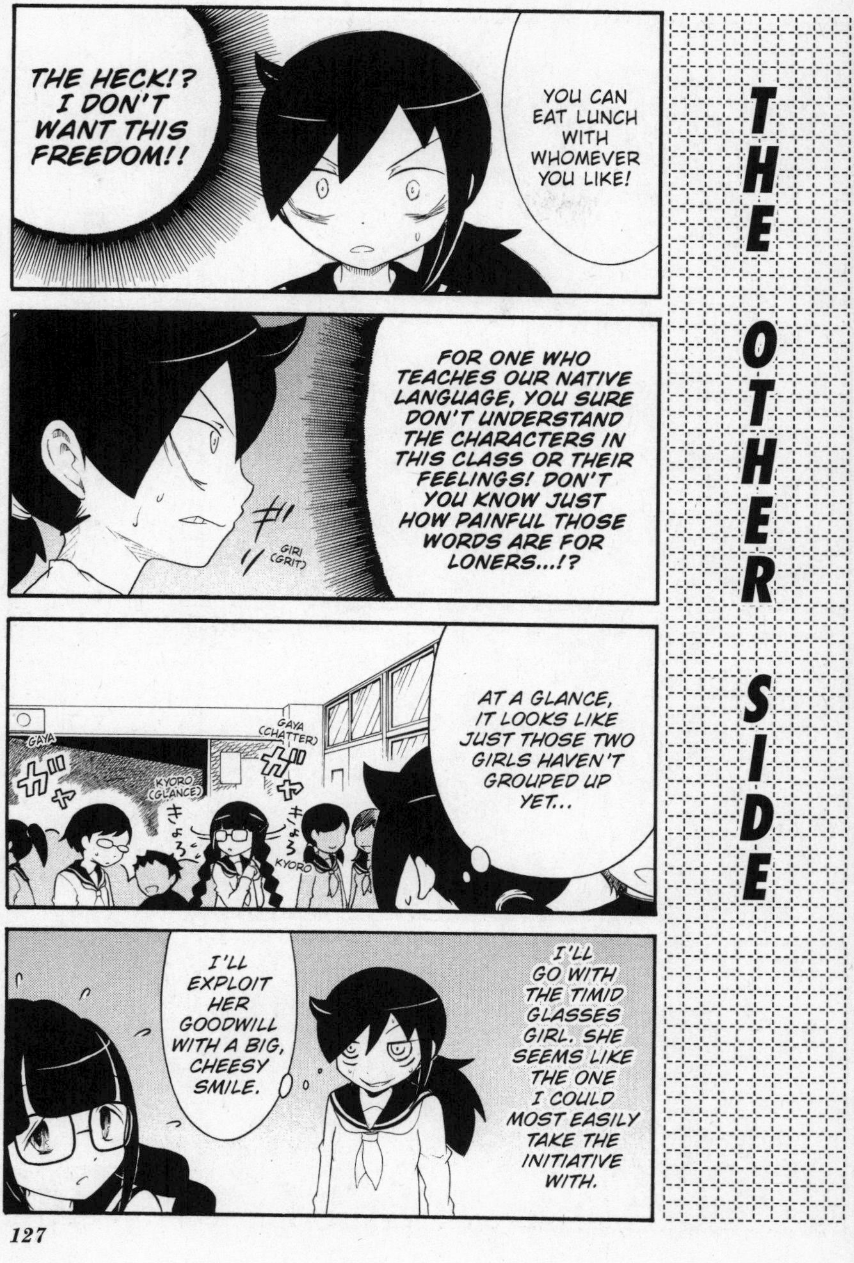
THE OTHER SIDE
YOU CAN EAT LUNCH WITH WHOMEVER YOU LIKE!
THE HECK!? I DON'T WANT THIS FREEDOM!!
FOR ONE WHO TEACHES OUR NATIVE LANGUAGE, YOU SURE DON'T UNDERSTAND THE CHARACTERS IN THIS CLASS OR THEIR FEELINGS! DON'T YOU KNOW JUST HOW PAINFUL THOSE WORDS ARE FOR LONERS...!?
GIRI (GRIT)
AT A GLANCE, IT LOOKS LIKE JUST THOSE TWO GIRLS HAVEN'T GROUPED UP YET...
GAYA (CHATTER)
KYORO
KYORO (GLANCE)
GAYA
I'LL GO WITH THE TIMID GLASSES GIRL. SHE SEEMS LIKE THE ONE I COULD MOST EASILY TAKE THE INITIATIVE WITH.
I'LL EXPLOIT HER GOODWILL WITH A BIG, CHEESY SMILE.

NICKNAME ①

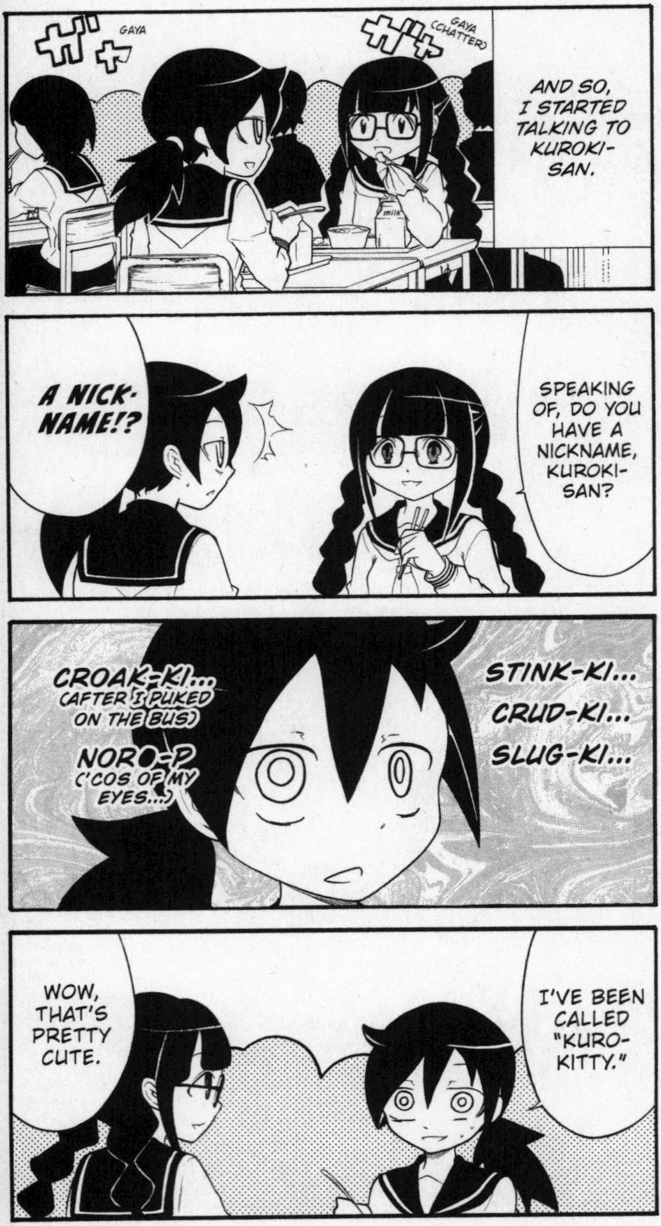
AND SO, I STARTED TALKING TO KUROKI-SAN.
ガヤ
GAYA (CHATTER)
ガヤ
GAYA
SPEAKING OF, DO YOU HAVE A NICKNAME, KUROKI-SAN?
A NICK-NAME!?
STINK-KI... CRUD-KI... SLUG-KI...
CROAK-KI... (AFTER I PUKED ON THE BUS)
NORO-P ('COS OF MY EYES...)
I'VE BEEN CALLED "KURO-KITTY."
WOW, THAT'S PRETTY CUTE.

OKAY ...?

SINCE YOU'RE TOMOKO-CHAN...

OKAY, CAN I CALL YOU "MOKOCCHI"?

"MOKOCCHI" SOUNDS LIKE A GUY WITH AN ERECTION.

"MOKOCCHI"... SHE'S GOT NO TASTE. FREAKING ME OUT...... BUT IT'D BE UNFRIENDLY TO JUST REFUSE IT...

OH, SHOOT... I WENT AND MADE A DIRTY JOKE...

ERECTION?

UH... IS THIS GIRL FOR REAL...?

"ERECTION"?

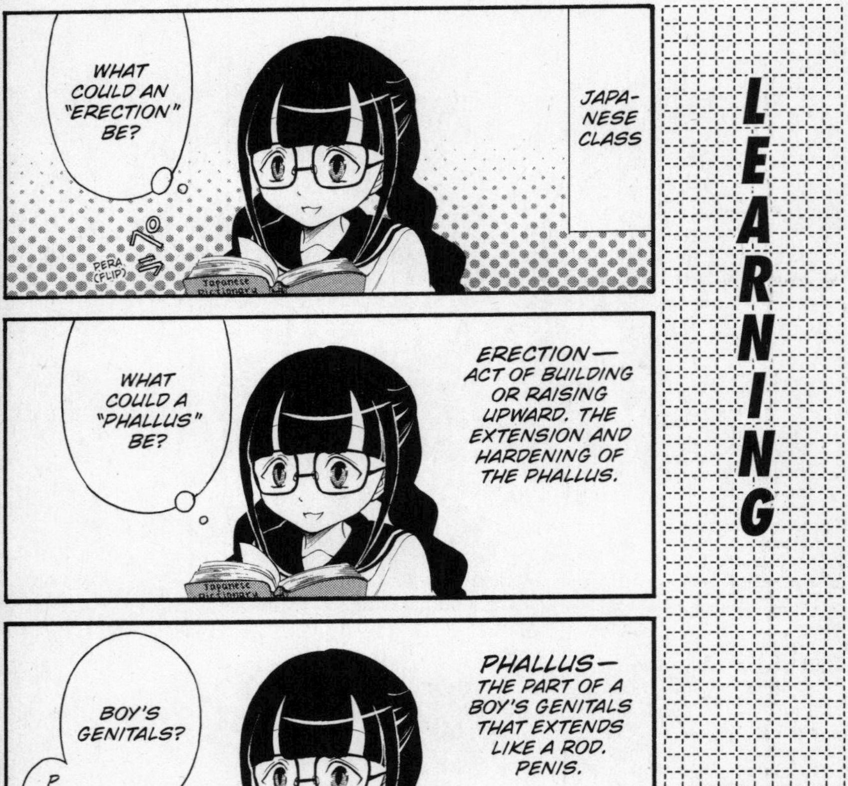
LEARNING
JAPANESE CLASS
WHAT COULD AN "ERECTION" BE?
PERA (FLIP)
ERECTION— ACT OF BUILDING OR RAISING UPWARD. THE EXTENSION AND HARDENING OF THE PHALLUS.
WHAT COULD A "PHALLUS" BE?
PHALLUS— THE PART OF A BOY'S GENITALS THAT EXTENDS LIKE A ROD. PENIS.
PERA
BOY'S GENITALS?
PENIS?
PERA
キーン
KIIIN (DIIING)
コーン
KOOON (DONNNG)
カーン
KAAAN (DAAANG)
OH! A WOLLY...
PERA
IT'S A WOLLY!

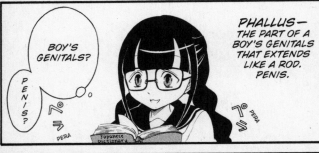

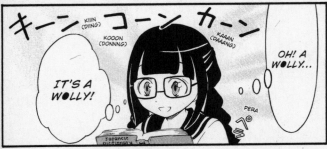

REASON FOR WALKING

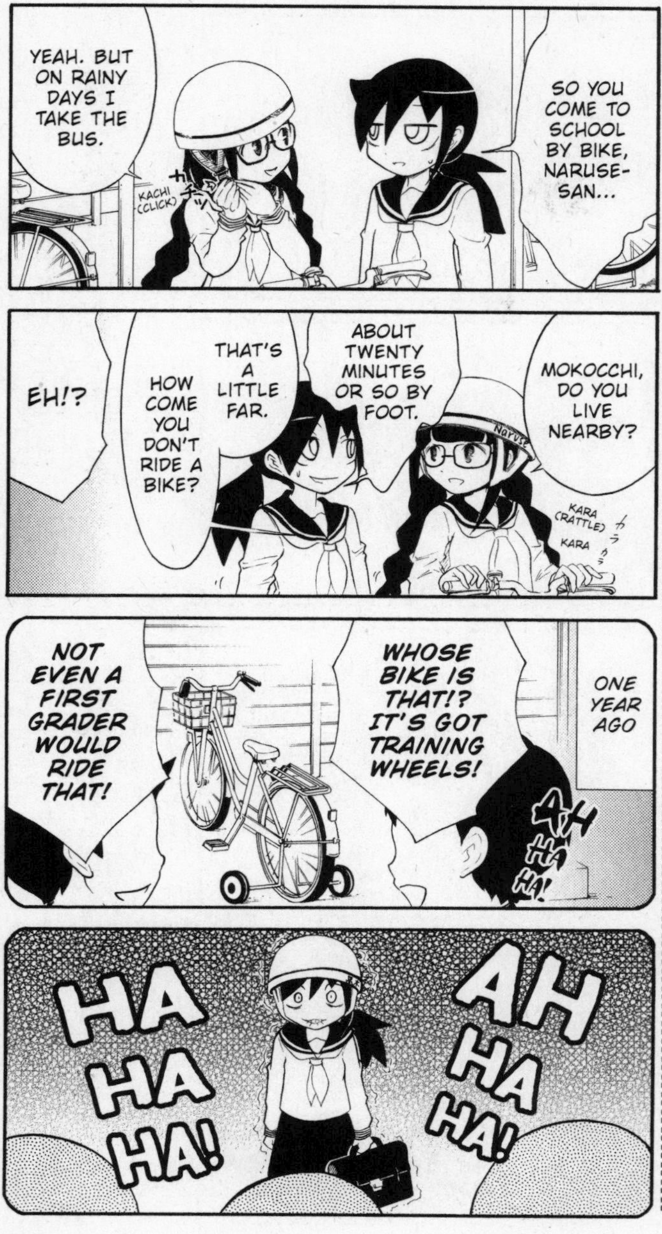
SO YOU COME TO SCHOOL BY BIKE, NARUSE-SAN...
YEAH. BUT ON RAINY DAYS I TAKE THE BUS.
KACHI (CLICK)
MOKOCCHI, DO YOU LIVE NEARBY?
ABOUT TWENTY MINUTES OR SO BY FOOT.
THAT'S A LITTLE FAR.
HOW COME YOU DON'T RIDE A BIKE?
EH!?
KARA (RATTLE) KARA
ONE YEAR AGO
WHOSE BIKE IS THAT!? IT'S GOT TRAINING WHEELS!
NOT EVEN A FIRST GRADER WOULD RIDE THAT!
AH HA HA HA!
AH HA HA HA!
HA HA HA!

IT'S LIKE NOTHING'S CHANGED

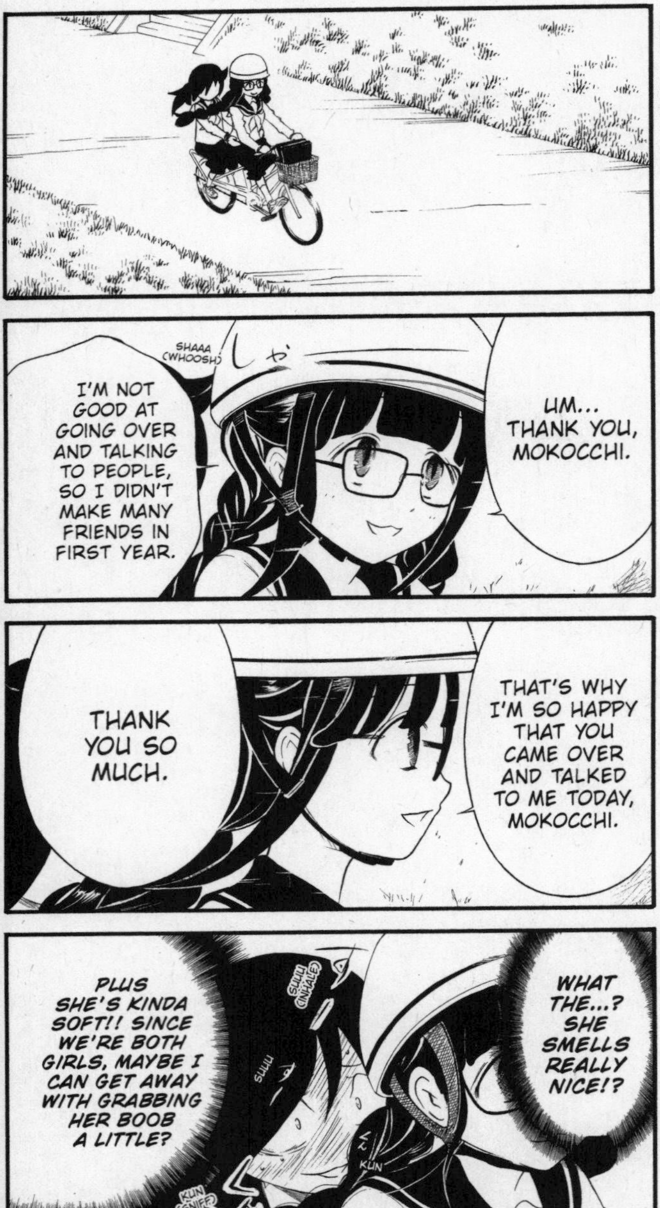
UM... THANK YOU, MOKOCCHI.
SHAAA (WHOOSH)
I'M NOT GOOD AT GOING OVER AND TALKING TO PEOPLE, SO I DIDN'T MAKE MANY FRIENDS IN FIRST YEAR.
THAT'S WHY I'M SO HAPPY THAT YOU CAME OVER AND TALKED TO ME TODAY, MOKOCCHI.
THANK YOU SO MUCH.
WHAT THE...? SHE SMELLS REALLY NICE!?
KUN
SUUU (INHALE)
SUUU
KUN (SNIFF)
PLUS SHE'S KINDA SOFT!! SINCE WE'RE BOTH GIRLS, MAYBE I CAN GET AWAY WITH GRABBING HER BOOB A LITTLE?

No Matter How I Look at It, It's You Guys' Fault I'm Not Popular!

BONUS: THE REASON THEY DRIFTED APART ①

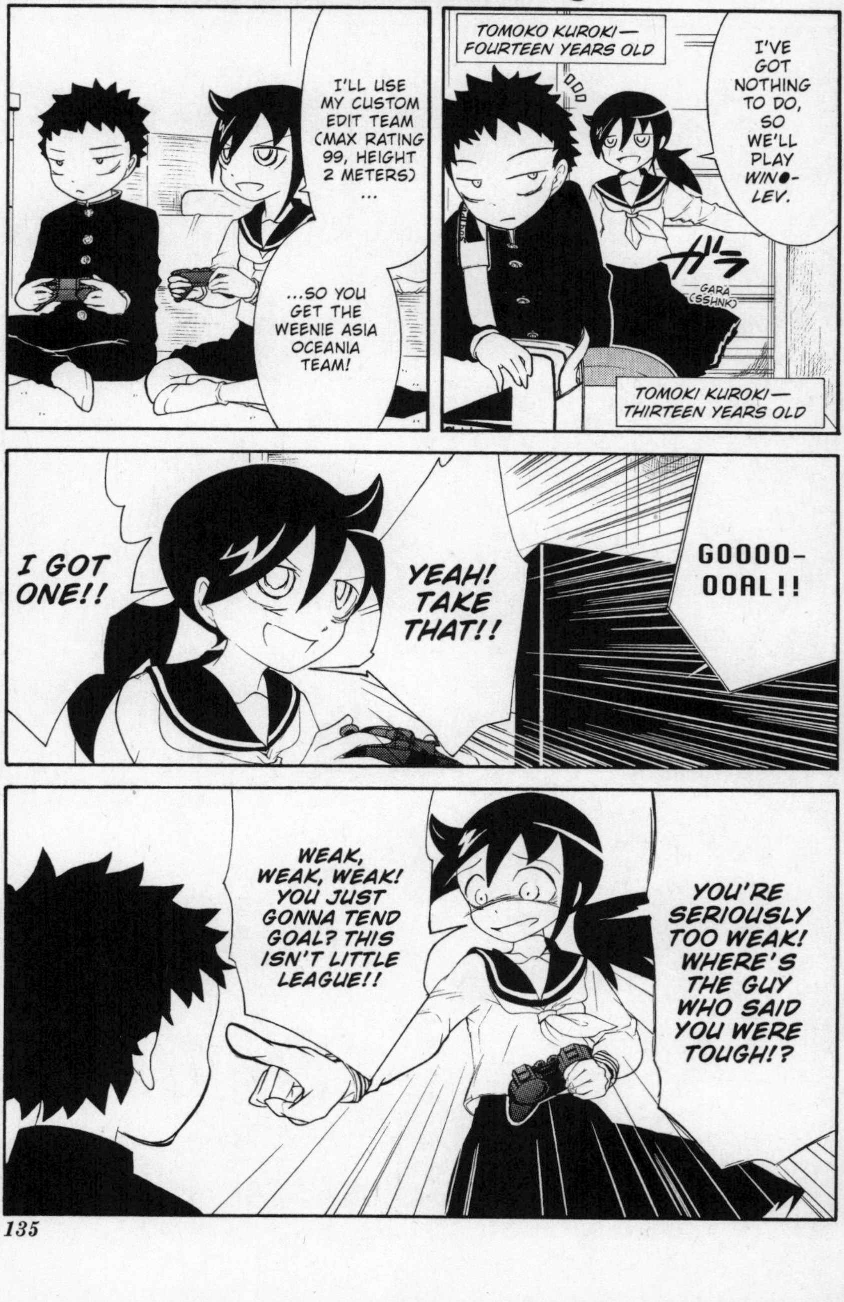
TOMOKO KUROKI—
FOURTEEN YEARS OLD
I'VE GOT NOTHING TO DO, SO WE'LL PLAY WIN●-LEV.
GARA (SSHNK)
TOMOKI KUROKI—
THIRTEEN YEARS OLD
I'LL USE MY CUSTOM EDIT TEAM (MAX RATING 99, HEIGHT 2 METERS) ...
...SO YOU GET THE WEENIE ASIA OCEANIA TEAM!
GOOOO-OOAL!!
YEAH! TAKE THAT!!
I GOT ONE!!
YOU'RE SERIOUSLY TOO WEAK! WHERE'S THE GUY WHO SAID YOU WERE TOUGH!?
WEAK, WEAK, WEAK! YOU JUST GONNA TEND GOAL? THIS ISN'T LITTLE LEAGUE!!

THE REASON THEY DRIFTED APART ②

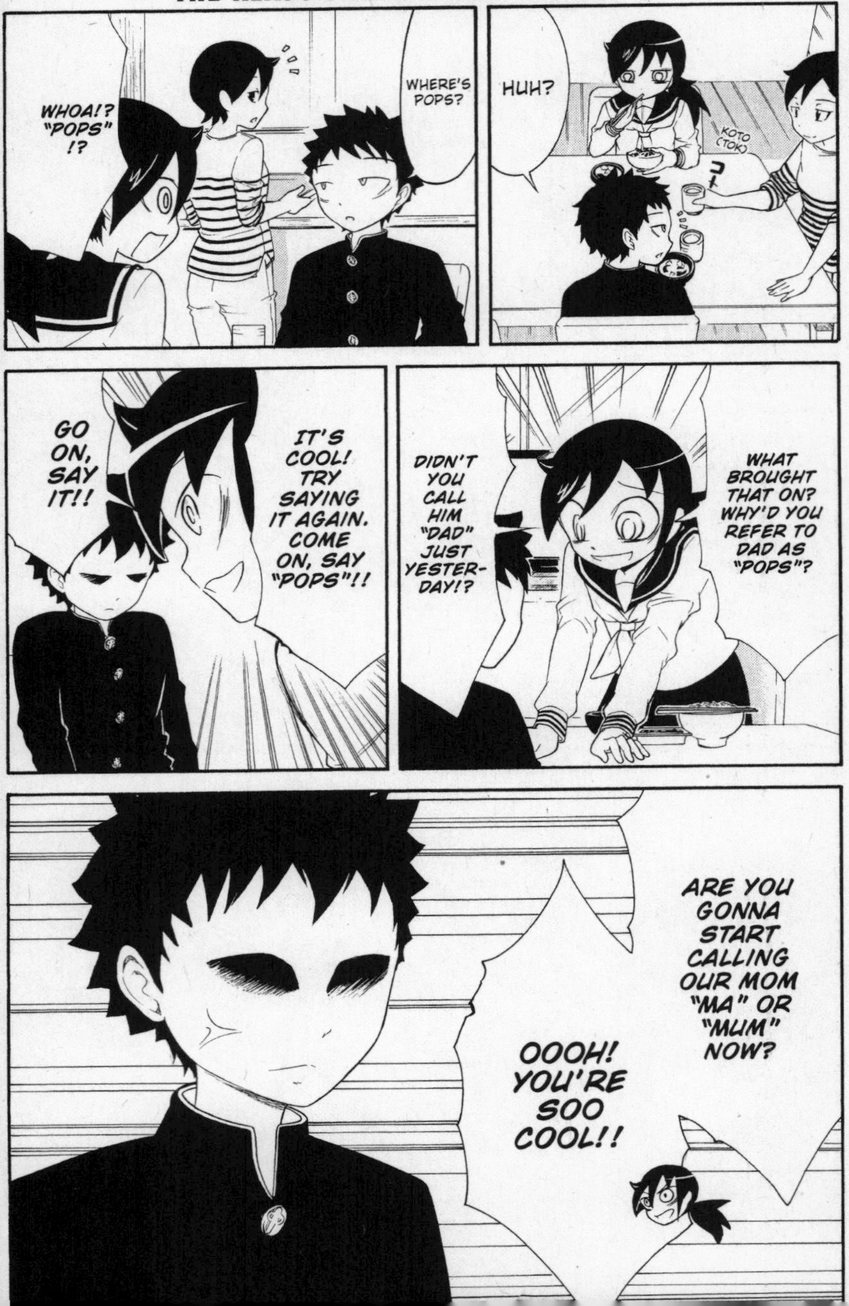
HUH?
KOTO (TOK)
WHERE'S POPS?
WHOA!? "POPS" !?
WHAT BROUGHT THAT ON? WHY'D YOU REFER TO DAD AS "POPS"?
DIDN'T YOU CALL HIM "DAD" JUST YESTER-DAY!?
IT'S COOL! TRY SAYING IT AGAIN. COME ON, SAY "POPS"!!
GO ON, SAY IT!!
ARE YOU GONNA START CALLING OUR MOM "MA" OR "MUM" NOW?
OOOH! YOU'RE SOO COOL!!

AFTERWORD

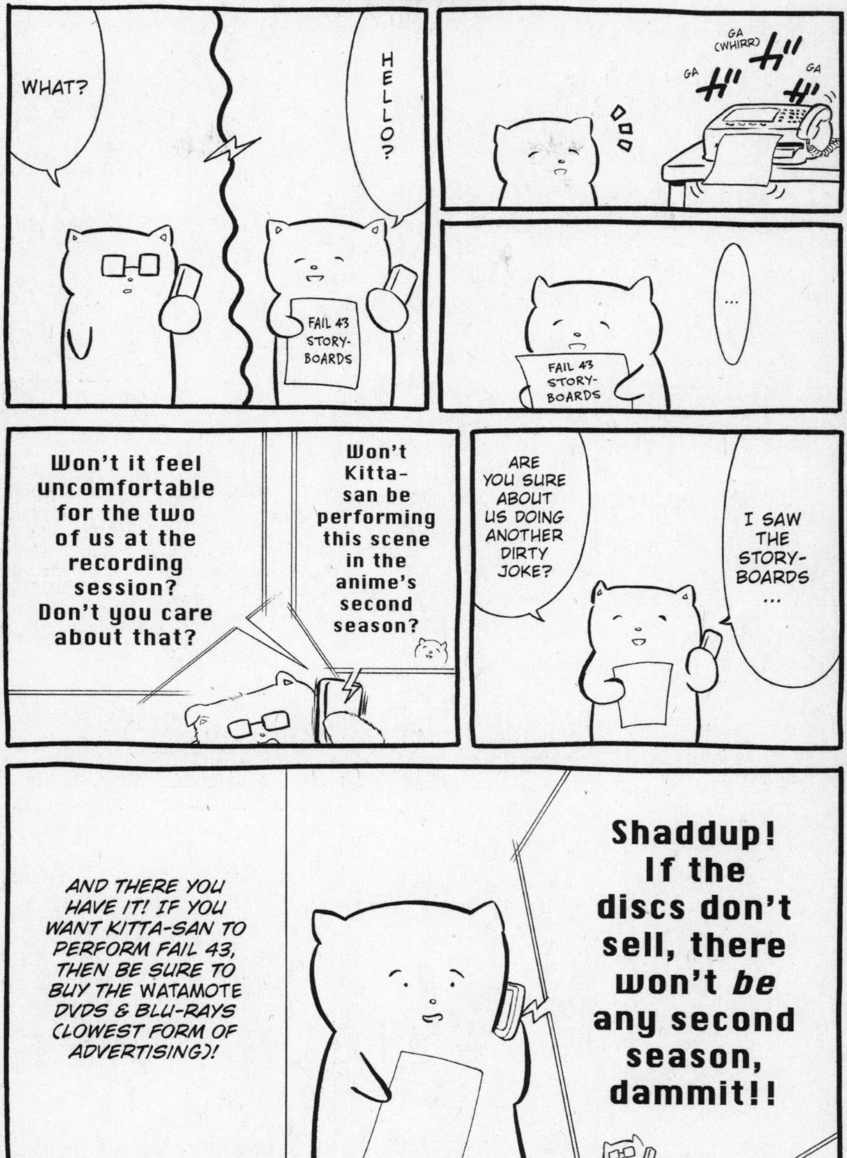
GA
(WHIRR)
GA
GA
...
FAIL 43 STORY-BOARDS
HELLO?
FAIL 43 STORY-BOARDS
WHAT?
I SAW THE STORY-BOARDS ...
ARE YOU SURE ABOUT US DOING ANOTHER DIRTY JOKE?
Won't Kitta-san be performing this scene in the anime's second season?
Won't it feel uncomfortable for the two of us at the recording session? Don't you care about that?
Shaddup! If the discs don't sell, there won't *be* any second season, dammit!!
AND THERE YOU HAVE IT! IF YOU WANT KITTA-SAN TO PERFORM FAIL 43, THEN BE SURE TO BUY THE WATAMOTE DVDS & BLU-RAYS (LOWEST FORM OF ADVERTISING)!

WITH HELP FROM ASSISTANT - YUUJI ASAKURA-SAN

No Matter How I Look at It, It's You Guys' Fault I'm Not Popular!

COVER BONUS

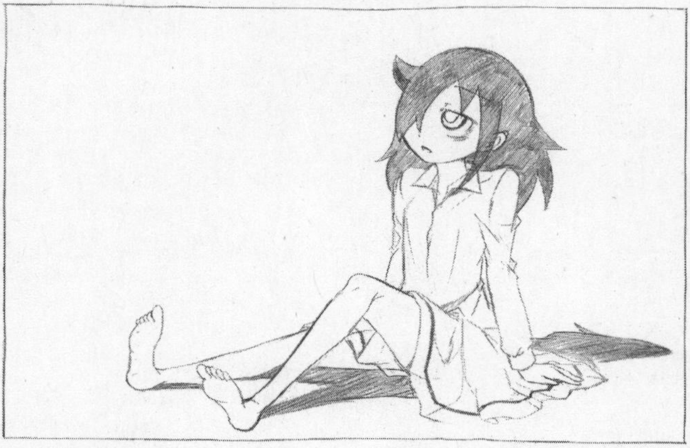

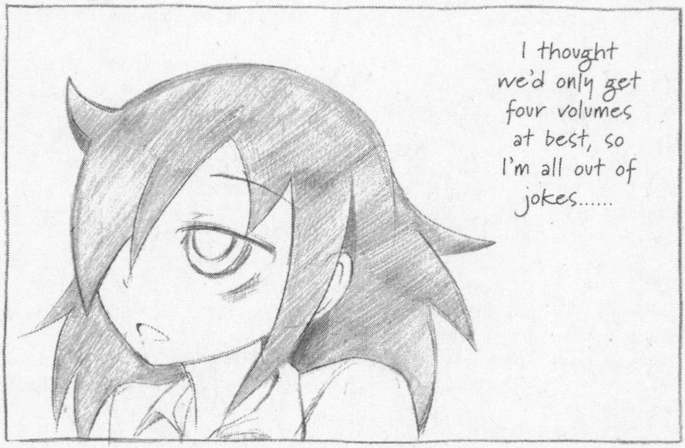
I thought we'd only get four volumes at best, so I'm all out of jokes......

PAGE 7

The **song** they are singing is "Aogeba Toutoshi," a song for Japanese graduation ceremonies that was first introduced in 1884. Though not all schools use it because the lyrics are archaic, it has great resonance for people and was chosen as one of the one hundred most known songs in Japan.

PAGE 21

Kill a vampire with a wooden stake is a reference to the manga *Higanjima*, which originally ran 2002–2010 in *Young Magazine* and came to thirty-three volumes, with a sequel series that is still ongoing. The character Atsushi wears round glasses and dresses in this way and often wears a face mask too.

PAGE 28

Ha⦿uhi is a reference to the main character of *The Melancholy of Haruhi Suzumiya* by Nagaru Tanigawa.

PAGE 30

The original gag for **Choriiizo!** was "Choriiisu," a nonsense word used as a greeting.

PAGE 34

Nemo is a mass-produced Gundam mobile suit that first appeared in the series *Zeta Gundam*.

PAGE 37

Ha⦿uhi-style intro is a joke version of Haruhi Suzumiya's infamous self-introduction from *The Melancholy of Haruhi Suzumiya*.

PAGE 37

S⦿men-sprayers (*shirudanyuu*) are male supporting actors who provide semen when required in adult videos.

PAGE 42-44

Tomoko is reading the various popular weekly boys' manga magazines that come out in large phonebook format. On Monday, Shueisha's *Weekly Shounen Jump* comes out; *Hunter x Hunter* is a popular adventure series that runs in it and is often on hiatus. On Wednesday she's reading Kodansha's *Weekly Shounen Magazine* (usually just called *Magazine*), which includes the long-running boxing series *Hajime no Ippo*. On Thursday, she's reading *Young Jump*, which is sold that day. The following Monday she's buying *Shounen Jump* again.

PAGE 44

Oh! Oh! Oh! is a reference to an actual seafood-shaped snack called Ottotto to match an emoticon/saying popular on the message board 2channel: (^ω^)おっおっおっ ("Oh! Oh! Oh!").

PAGE 56

The anime Tomoko references is *Denpa Onna to Seishun Otoko*, where the male lead used "Seishun Points" to get his shut-in female cousin to interact more normally.

PAGE 60

Fruits Au Lait is a brand of fruit-flavored milk drink. The actual name doesn't seem to be changed, although there's normally a dash or dot between the *Au* and *Lait*.

PAGE 68

Greeting exercises (*aisatsu undou*) is a real term for higher-ups greeting students/employees at the start of the school/workday as shown here, but it's also a description of what Tomoko ends up having to do.

PAGE 73

Ingredients are for cooking class in Japanese schools, where all students are usually required to bring at least one specific food item that will be used in the recipe, such as an egg or a slice of bacon.

PAGE 78

"Guilty" & "Throwing the entire lot into chaos" are terms specific to the cult-favorite restaurant chain Ramen Jiro, which serves big bowls of very fatty ramen that can be hard for novices to finish eating without getting sick. A "lot" is their term for a batch of ramen, which usually comprises five portions.

PAGE 87

"I-it exists..." is an adaptation of a line by younger sister Kirino from the series *Oreimo: My Little Sister Can't Be This Cute*.

PAGE 89

Y⦿suke Yamada is a reference to Yusuke Yamada, whose horror novel *Riaru Onigokko* (*Real Hide-and-Seek*) sounds similar to "rearu ochinchin" to Tomoko.

PAGE 94

The **abuse CD** Tomoko is listening to is the *Ai Áru Batou!!* ("*Loving Abuse*") drama CD 1.

PAGE 94

Toush⦿n High School is a reference to Toushin High School, which is a national chain of cram schools that is famous for commercials featuring its teachers, some of whom Tomoko is picturing: physics lecturer Naoyuki Sonoda, English lecturer Hiroshi Imai, classical lit lecturer Keisuke Yoshino, and English lecturer Katsuhiko Watanabe.

PAGE 108
The **book** Tomi is reading has the same title in Japan, but the author is really international Japanese soccer player Shunsuke Nakamura.

PAGE 111
The Japanese word Tomoko uses instead of **punk'd** is *dokkiri* ("shocked, startled"). *Dokkiri Camera* was a hidden-camera series that ran on Japanese TV from the 1970s to the 1990s, following a similar concept to the series *Candid Camera* or *Punk'd* on U.S. TV.

PAGE 116
The **new titles** Tomoko is looking at are all game or *otaku*-related light novels from the Kodansha BOX line. *BBB* by Suna Kinoko is a reference to *DDD* by Nasu Kinoko, the writer for Type-Moon visual novels like *Fate/stay night* and *Tsukihime*. *Tankanropa: zero* is a reference to *Danganronpa: zero*, a novel set in the world of the murder mystery game *Danganronpa*. *Izumonogatari* is a reference to *Kizumonogatari*, the prequel to *Bakemonogatari* by NisiOisiN, both of which have received a popular animated film/series adaptation. This is the book that Tomoko is checking out.

PAGE 122
"Sh●tface!" ("Kusomushi ga!") is a quoted insult by Sawa Nakamura, a character in the manga series *Flowers of Evil* by Shuzo Oshimi.

PAGE 128
Nor●-P (Nori-P) was the nickname for Noriko Sakai, a pop singer and actress who was convicted of amphetamine possession in 2009.

PAGE 135
Win●Lev; Custom Edit Team is the hugely popular soccer game *Winning Eleven* (*Pro Evolution Soccer* outside Asia) that allows people to make patches to alter names and stats.

PAGE 135
"You're seriously too weak..." is an adaptation of the Japanese trash-talk lines by the player-character Dudley in *Street Fighter III: 3rd Strike*.

PAGE 136
"Pops" in the original is the Japanese word *oyaji*, a slightly rougher term some males use for their fathers. Tomoko mentions *fukuro* and *okan*, equivalent terms for one's mother.

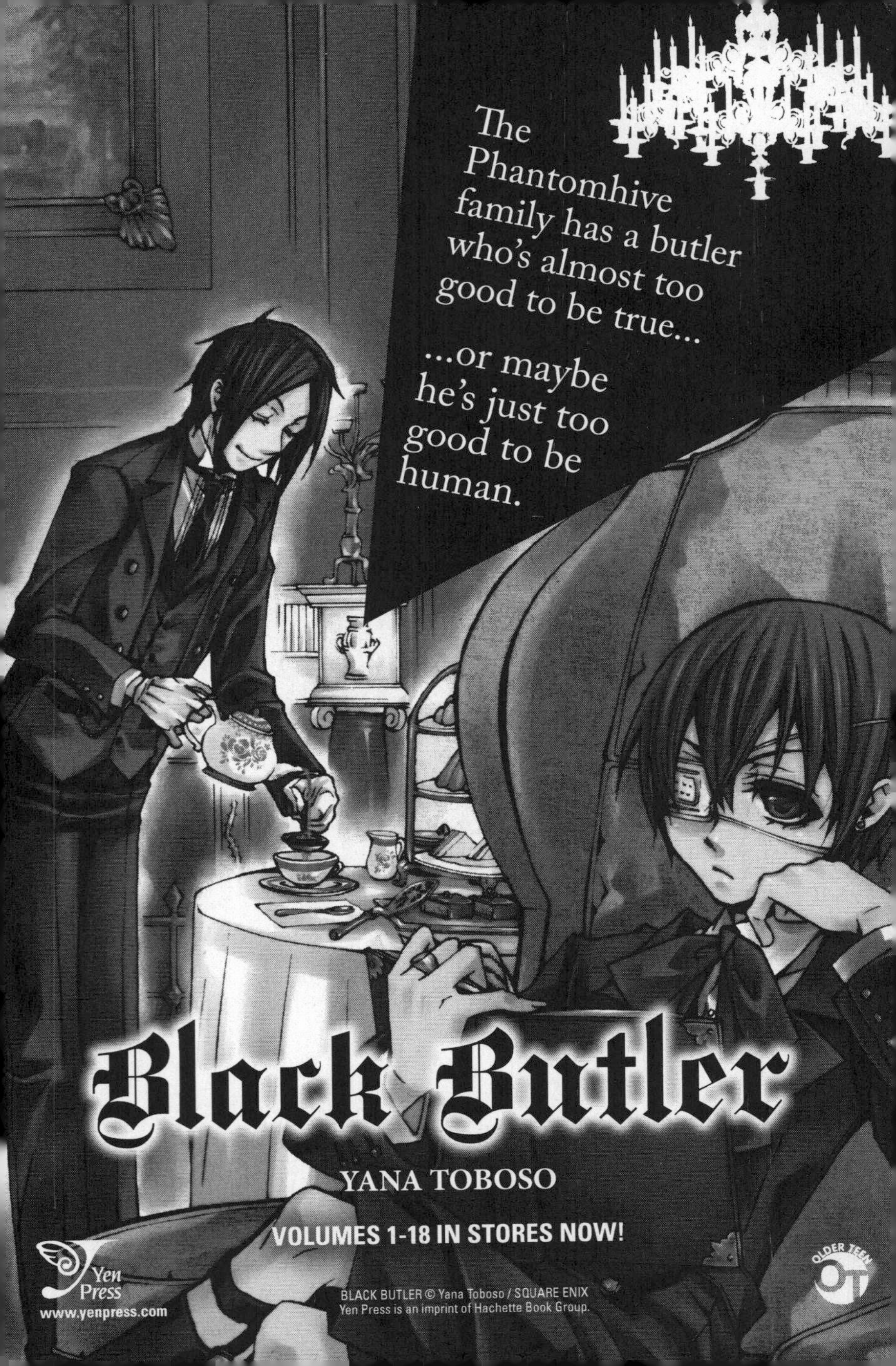
The Phantomhive family has a butler who's almost too good to be true...
...or maybe he's just too good to be human.
Black Butler
YANA TOBOSO
VOLUMES 1-18 IN STORES NOW!
Yen Press
www.yenpress.com
BLACK BUTLER © Yana Toboso / SQUARE ENIX
Yen Press is an imprint of Hachette Book Group.
OLDER TEEN
OT

WELCOME TO IKEBUKURO, WHERE TOKYO'S WILDEST CHARACTERS GATHER!!

baya

NO MATTER HOW I LOOK AT IT, IT'S YOU GUYS' FAULT I'M NOT POPULAR! ❺

NICO TANIGAWA

Translation/Adaptation: Krista Shipley, Karie Shipley
Lettering: Lys Blakeslee

WATASHI GA MOTENAI NOWA DOU KANGAETEMO OMAERA GA WARUI! Volume 5 © 2013 Nico Tanigawa / SQUARE ENIX CO., LTD. First published in Japan in 2013 by SQUARE ENIX CO., LTD. English translation rights arranged with SQUARE ENIX CO., LTD. and Yen Press, LLC through Tuttle-Mori Agency, Inc.

English translation © 2014 by SQUARE ENIX CO., LTD.

Yen Press
1290 Avenue of the Americas
New York, NY 10104

Visit us at yenpress.com
facebook.com/yenpress
twitter.com/yenpress
yenpress.tumblr.com

First Yen Press Edition: October 2014

Yen Press is an imprint of Yen Press, LLC.
The Yen Press name and logo are trademarks of Yen Press, LLC.

ISBNs: 978-0-316-33609-3 (paperback)
       9780316384308 (ebook)
       978-0-316-38431-5 (app)

10 9 8 7 6 5 4

OPM

Printed in the United States of America